IMAGES
of America

YADKIN COUNTY

THE FIRST ONE HUNDRED YEARS

IMAGES of America

YADKIN COUNTY

THE FIRST ONE HUNDRED YEARS

The Yadkin County Historical & Genealogical Society, Inc.
Frances H. Casstevens, President and Editor-in-Chief

ARCADIA PUBLISHING

ISBN 978-0-7385-6874-4

Published by Arcadia Publishing
Charleston, South Carolina

Printed in the United States of America

Library of Congress Catalog Card Number: Applied for

For all general information contact Arcadia Publishing at:
Telephone 843-853-2070
Fax 843-853-0044
E-mail sales@arcadiapublishing.com
For customer service and orders:
Toll-Free 1-888-313-2665

Visit us on the Internet at www.arcadiapublishing.com

CONTENTS

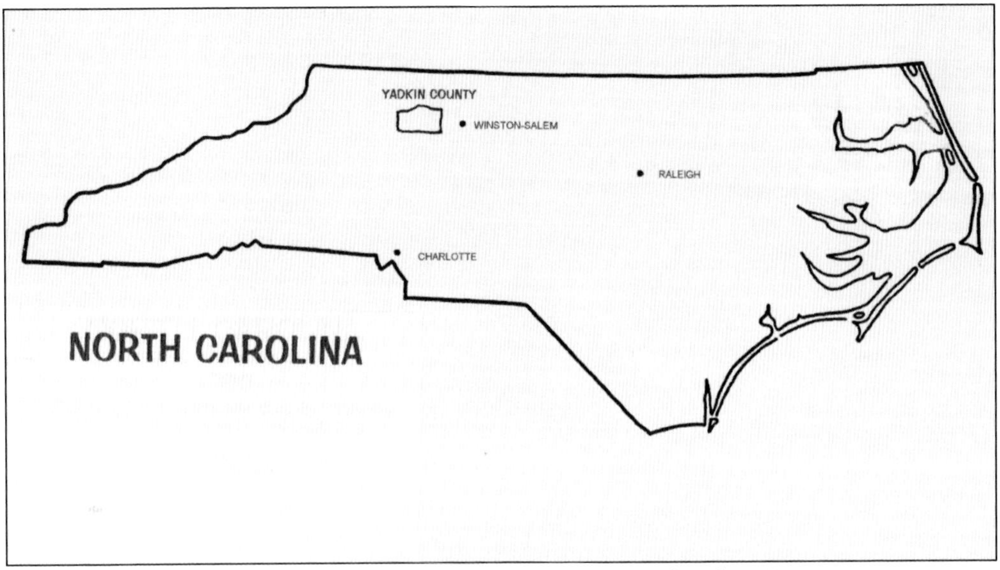

A map of North Carolina showing the location of Yadkin County.

ACKNOWLEDGMENTS

The pictures in this volume are presented as a result of the joint efforts of: members of the Yadkin County Historical & Genealogical Society, Inc.; the Yadkin County Public Library; a number of private collectors; J.E. Brown, Photographer; Jim Drum, Photography Unlimited; and the staff of Studio One.

INTRODUCTION

Yadkin County, North Carolina, is situated in the rolling hills of the Piedmont section of North Carolina. The land was originally settled around 1748, when what is now Yadkin County was part of Anson County, and later of Rowan County. Formed from the part of Surry County that lay south of the Yadkin River, Yadkin County was formally established in 1850.

The purpose of this book is to present a pictorial view of Yadkin County as it was during its first one hundred years, from 1850 to 1950. It has been compiled in an effort to preserve our history and heritage by making the reader aware of the history of the region through the medium of vintage photographs. The photographs, most of which have never before been published, have been selected specifically to show a variety of people, places, events, and activities. We have tried to represent all of the county's communities, but as both East Bend and Boonville have recently published town histories, we have included fewer old photographs of those communities.

The book is divided into eleven chapters, each portraying an aspect of life in Yadkin County before 1950. While the county was (and still is) a rural, agricultural area, we have covered a variety of themes in an attempt to present a full and well-balanced picture of the people and their activities.

Most of the photographs were taken before 1950; however, we used a few recent photographs to show certain important structures of which there were no old photographs available or for which the old photographs were of poor quality. Due to the limitations of time and space, we could not use all of the photographs available to us, but we hope that the photographs that could not be included here will become material for a second volume.

As each day passes, the simpler way of life that was prevalent in Yadkin County becomes more remote, and less familiar to those of us living in the last quarter of the twentieth century. Many young readers will be unfamiliar with some of the objects and activities portrayed here. The photograph captions are designed to overcome that obstacle, and to describe the scene, place it in a time frame, and identify the people, whenever possible. Credits for the use of pictures are given at the end of the captions. (See the Key to Photo Credits on p. 8 for the complete list of photograph donors.)

The pace and quality of life in Yadkin County is changing almost daily, as new structures are built and old ones destroyed. In the process, the landscape is unavoidably modified. Life here will never again be as it is depicted in these pictures. We hope that we have accurately presented a portrait of the life and times of the people of Yadkin County in that bygone era. We, the members of the Yadkin County Historical & Genealogical Society, Inc., feel honored for the privilege of sharing that view.

Frances H. Casstevens
President

KEY TO PHOTO CREDITS

AB—Alice Brumfield
AS—Arvil Speer collection, courtesy of Ann Speer Riley
AB—Alfred "Teen" Blackburn collection, courtesy of Ann Blackburn
BHM—Bertha Hinshaw Mackie collection, courtesy of Andrew Mackie
BJM—Betsy Johnson Middleton
BW—Betty Warren
CDC—Carl D. Casstevens
DAB—Diane Allred Reece Burns
DMcL—Dorothy Shugart McLeod
EBR—Edna Bray Reece
EG—Ernest Groce
EM—Eli Mosteller
EGS—Edith Garner Sharpless
FHC—Frances Harding Casstevens
HHM—H.H. Mackie collection
IMR—Irma Matthews Robertson collection, courtesy of Mattie Harris
JA—Jason Allgood
JC—Judy Cleary
JD—Julia Dalton
JEB—Courtesy of J.E. Brown
JGM—James Gray Mackie collection, courtesy of Andrew Mackie
JL—Jasper Long collection
JMD—Julia Mackie Draughon collection, courtesy of Andrew Mackie
JN—John and Barbara K. Norman
KC—Kenneth and Shirley Campbell
KMcE—Kim McEwen
LBH—Lucy Brendle Hinshaw
LMW—Lora Mackie Warden collection
LW—Lupton Wood
MC—Marler collection, courtesy of the Yadkin County Public Library
MDL—Martha Doub Logan
MLH—Mozelle L. Hinshaw collection, courtesy of Andrew Mackie
MM—Mildred Mackie
MMS—Martha Moxley Shore
MSP—Morene Shermer Phillips collection, courtesy of Andrew Mackie
NMD—Nancy Mills Davis
NH—Nancy Holt
NLG—Nina Ruth Long Groce
PW—Paul Williams and Ruth W. Holcomb
RH—Roger Hardy
RW—Ruth Wishon and Larry Wishon
RY—Robert York
SO—Studio One
VS—Victor and Wanda Hauser Seiders
WC—Wanda Craaybeek

One

Beyond the Yadkin
Beautiful Land, Beautiful People

Yadkin County is situated in the Piedmont section of North Carolina. It is bordered on two sides by the Yadkin River. A land of gently rolling hills, it is criss-crossed by winding creeks and streams that merge gently with the river. The northwestern part of the county is graced by the Brushy Mountains, which rise gently from tree-covered slopes. It is a beautiful land, undefiled by the noise of trains and planes, by industrial pollution or city slums.

The land was fertile, game was plentiful, and the climate was mild. The area had been used for centuries as a hunting ground by various Indian tribes. The people who settled in Yadkin County came from many counties, states, and countries. Their ancestors were English, German, French, Swedish, Scots-Irish, African, and American Indian. These settlers carved out homes in the wilderness and established towns and communities. Some of those pioneers lived out their lives here, and their descendants remain. Others moved on in search of new lands.

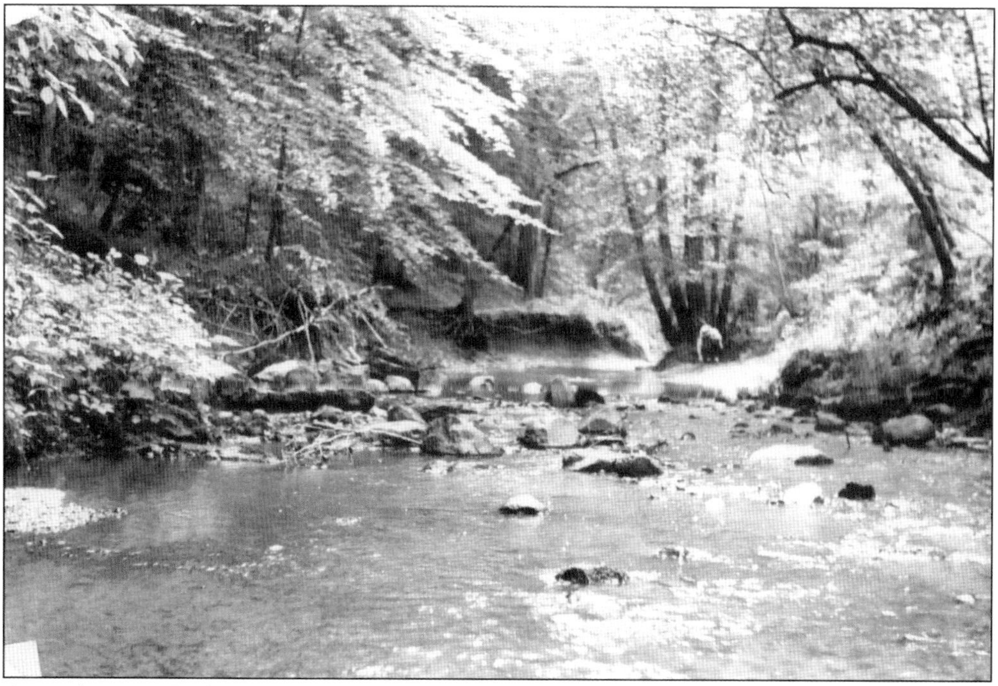

Around 1843 Abraham Groce built a dam on Harmon Creek to run a sawmill. Abraham and his wife, Ann Lee, lived in a primitive shelter on the creek bank until a cabin was completed in 1844. (EG)

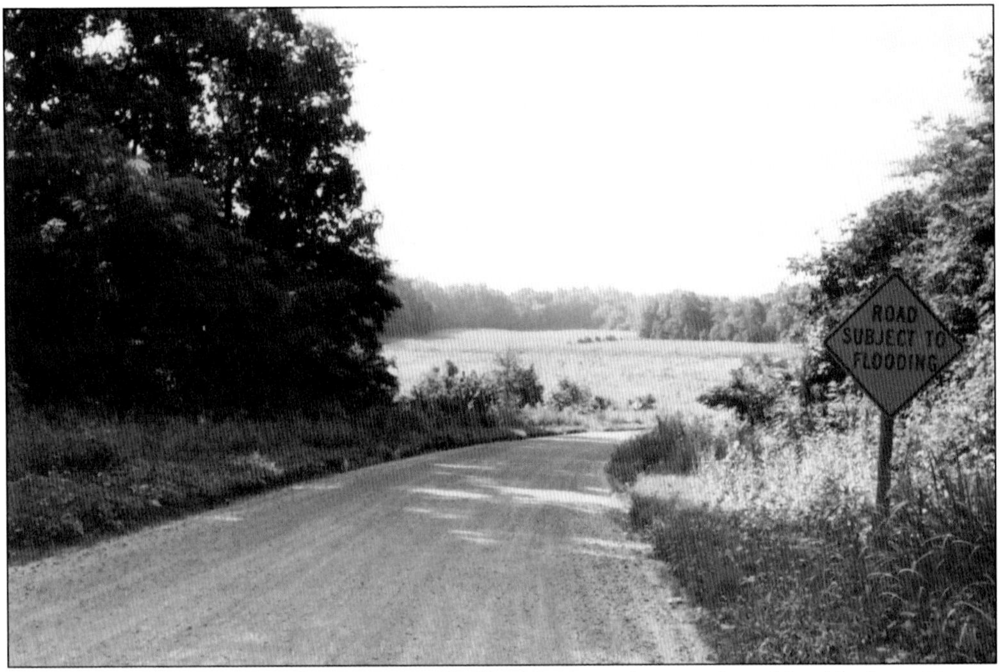

The fertile land of the river bottom near Shallow Ford was first purchased by Abraham Creson in the 1750s, and is still owned by his descendants. (FHC)

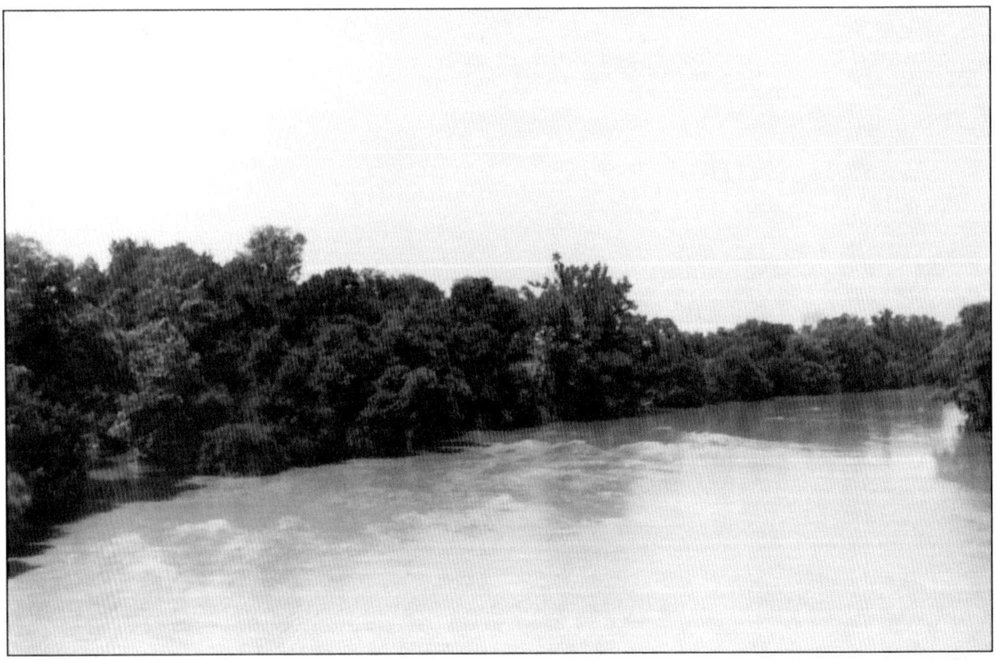

The left-hand part of this photograph shows the point at which Deep Creek enters the Yadkin River. (FHC)

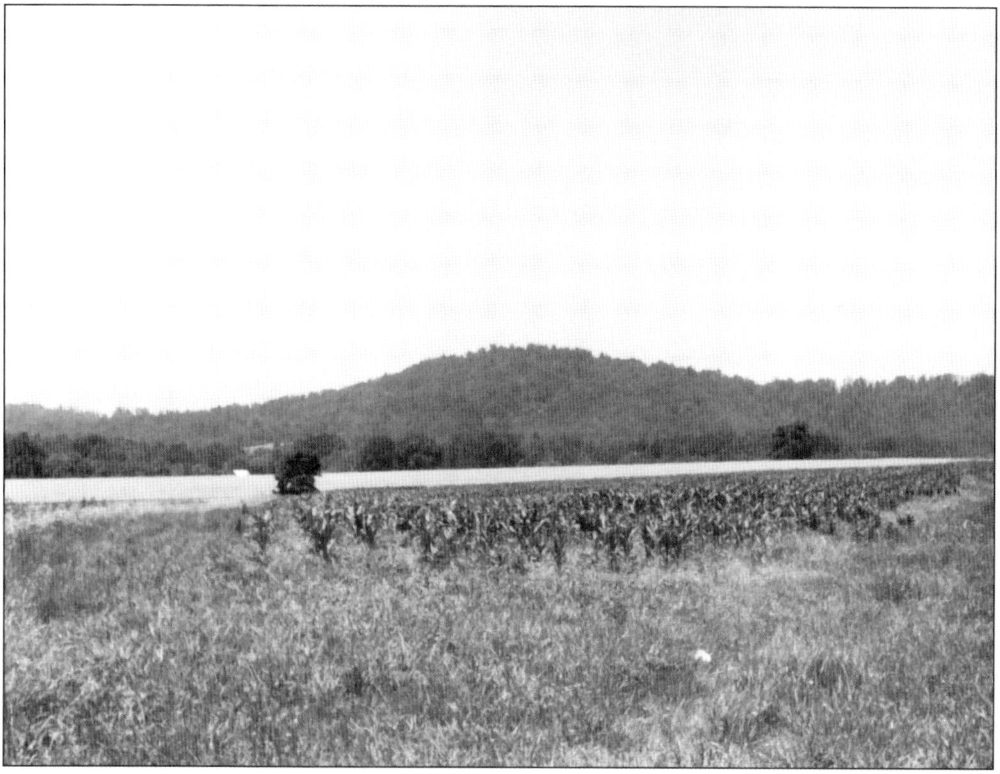

Wheat and corn grow in the shadow of the Brushy Mountains off Center Road. (FHC)

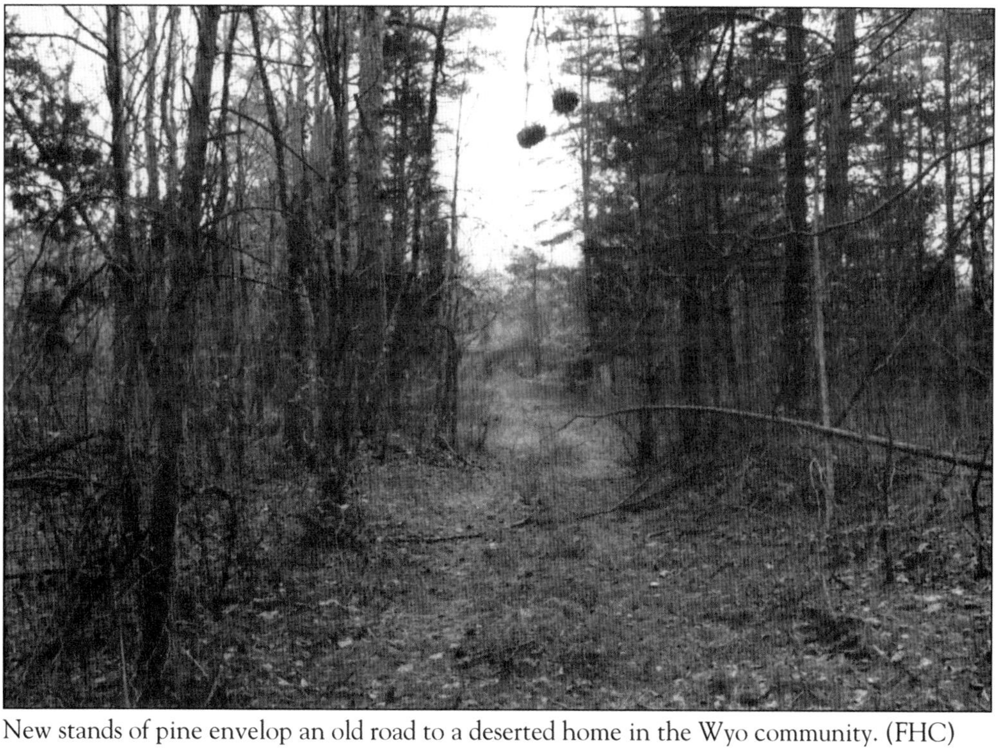

New stands of pine envelop an old road to a deserted home in the Wyo community. (FHC)

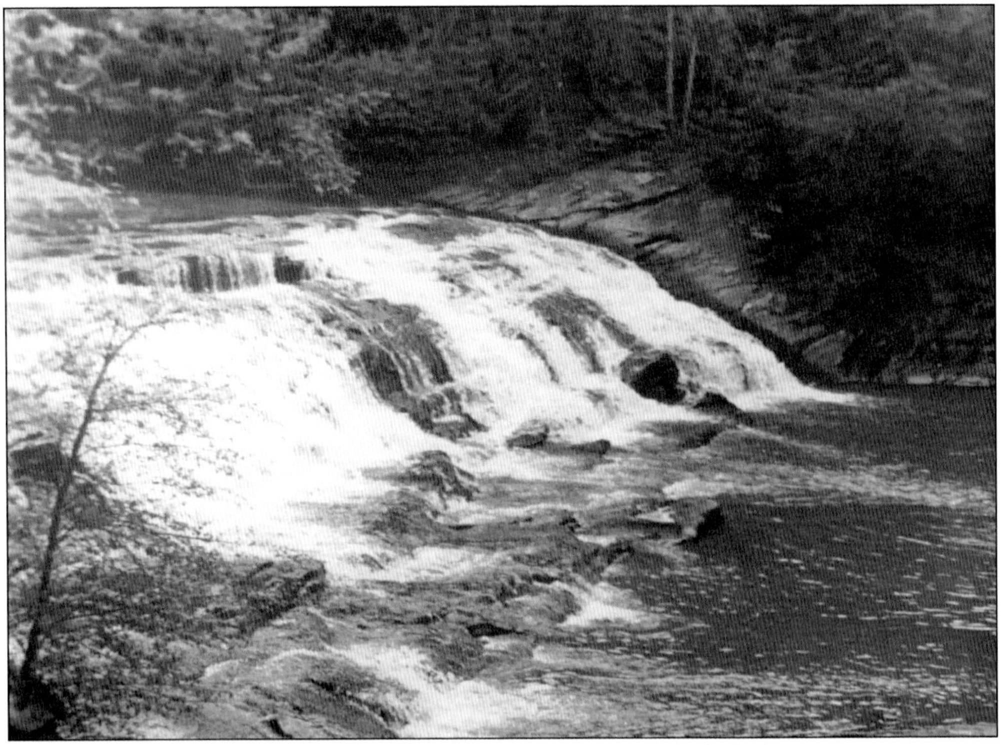

The waterfall below the former Shore-Styers Mill on Deep Creek. (DRB)

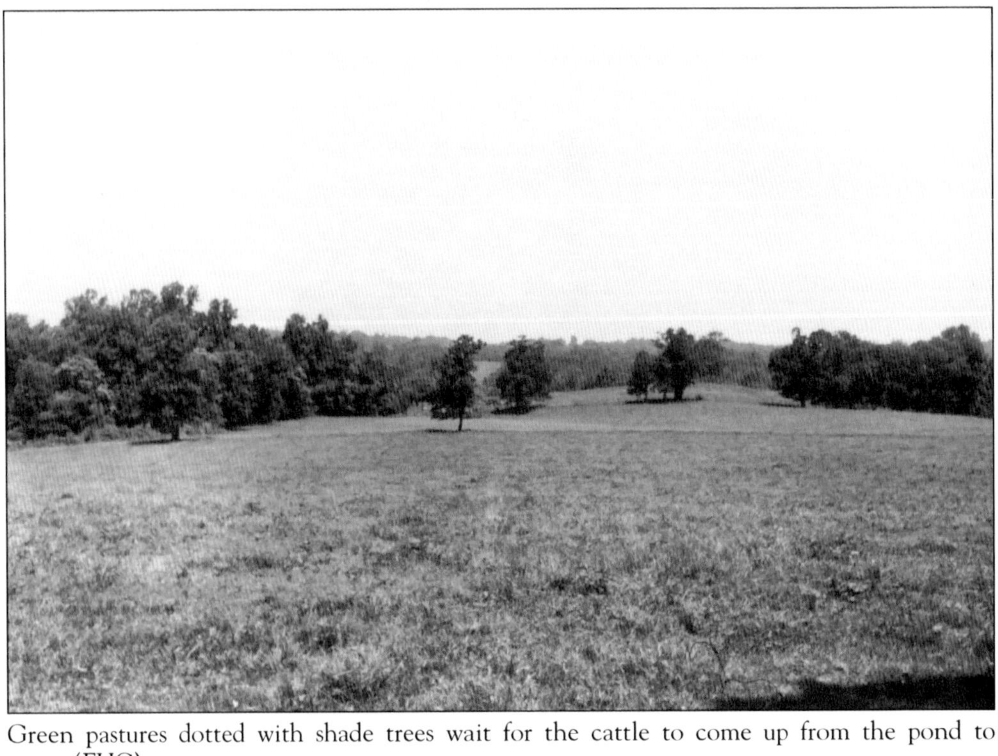

Green pastures dotted with shade trees wait for the cattle to come up from the pond to graze. (FHC)

This picture was taken when Annie Laurie (Wade) Morse (1861–1940) was a young woman: she would later become the wife of T.E. Morse and the mother of Rosebud (Morse) Garriott, the well-known East Bend dentist. (JN)

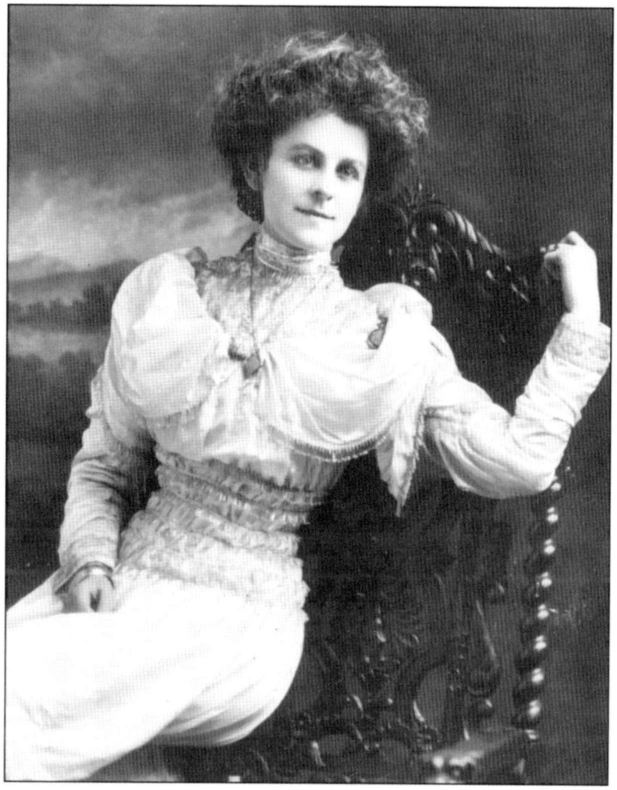

Below Left: Annie Conrad, a native of Enon, taught school at Boonville and Lewisville. This photograph was taken c. 1891. (FHC)

Below Right: An unknown woman in a daguerreotype dating from the 1860s. (FHC)

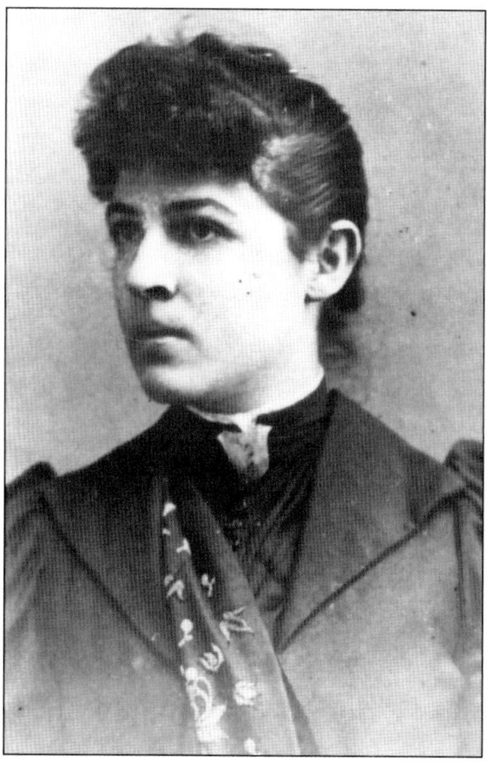

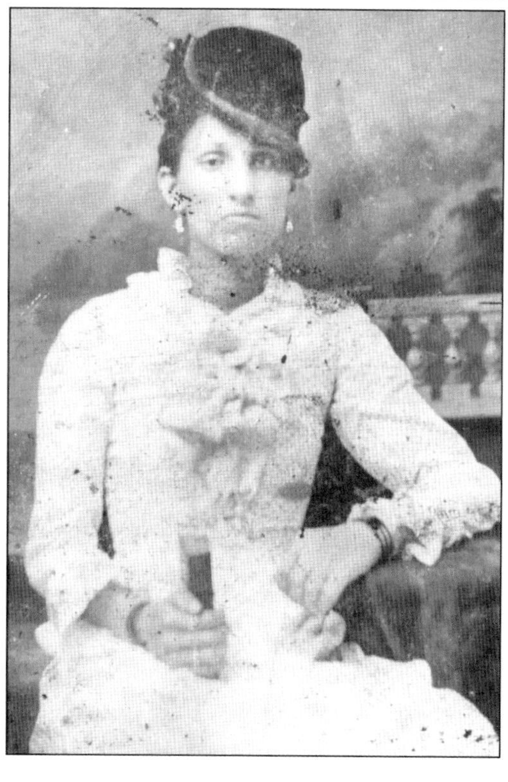

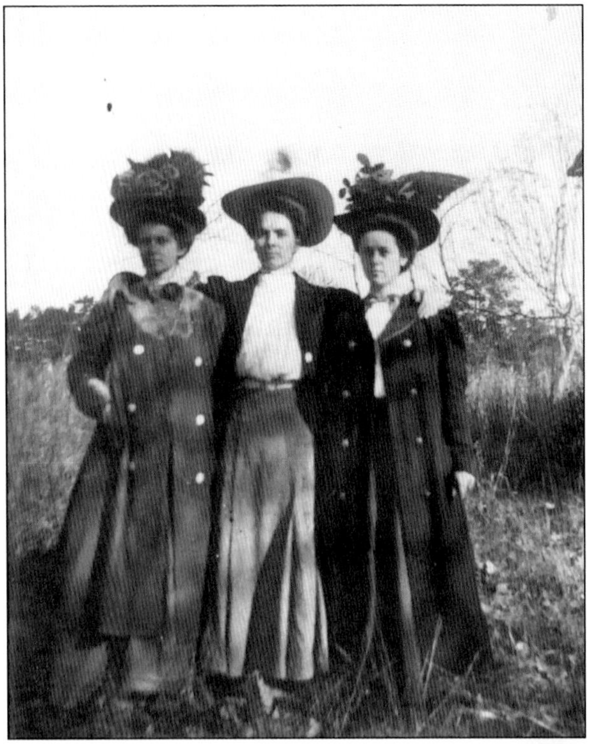

The three Warden sisters, Percy, Fannie, and Effie, c. 1912. Fannie, born in 1888, married William Ed Wishon. (RW)

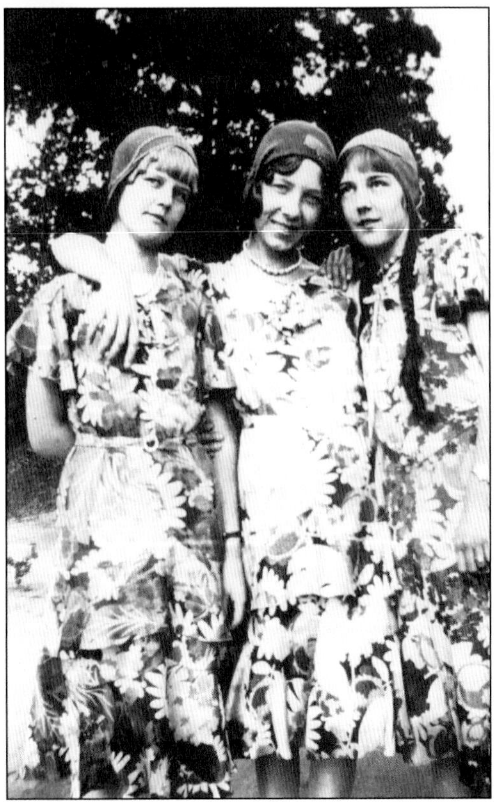

Three "flappers"—Valena (Jolly) Mosteller, Helen (Nance) Church, and Rita (Jolly) Misenheimer. (EM)

Nettie (Reavis) Hauser, *c*. 1907, the wife of John Henry Hauser Jr. (VS)

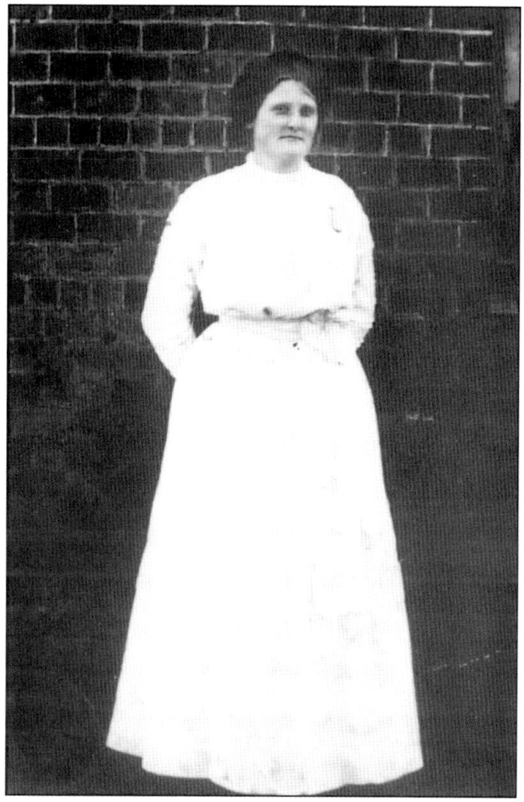

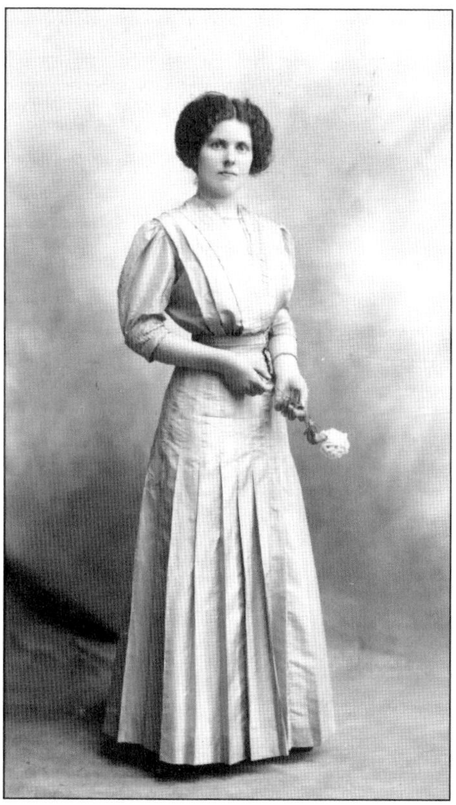

Minnie (Shugart) Mackie, the wife of H. Edward Mackie. (HHM)

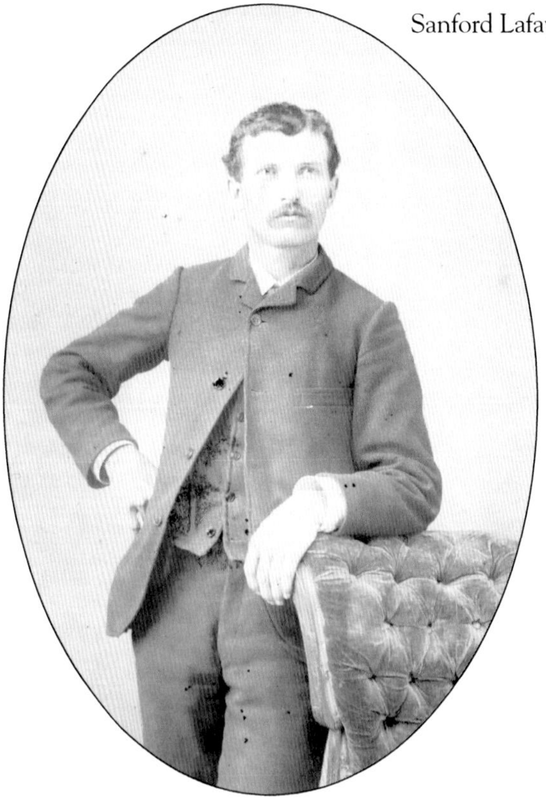

Sanford Lafayette Doub (1860–1924). (MDL)

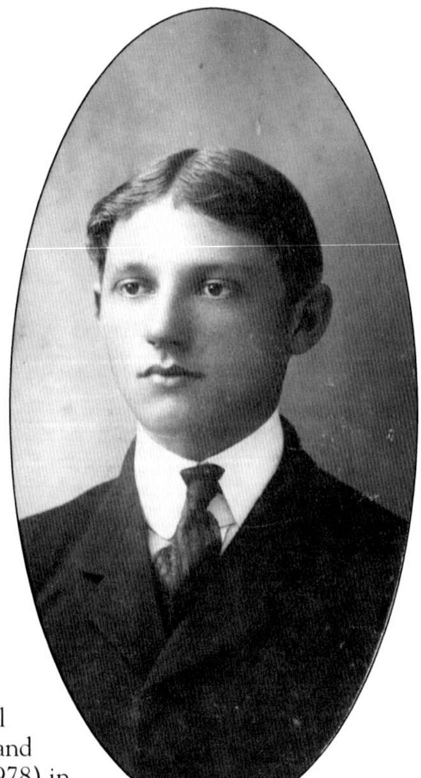

The son of Eli Thomas and Nannie Marion Davis, Paul Price Davis (1886–1952) was a religious, educational, and civic leader. He married Elma Leigh Farabow (1897–1978) in 1925. (NMD)

Gerald ("Jerry") Royce Casstevens (1933–1990) as a school boy about 1947. "Jerry" later became a famous bluegrass banjo picker. (FHC)

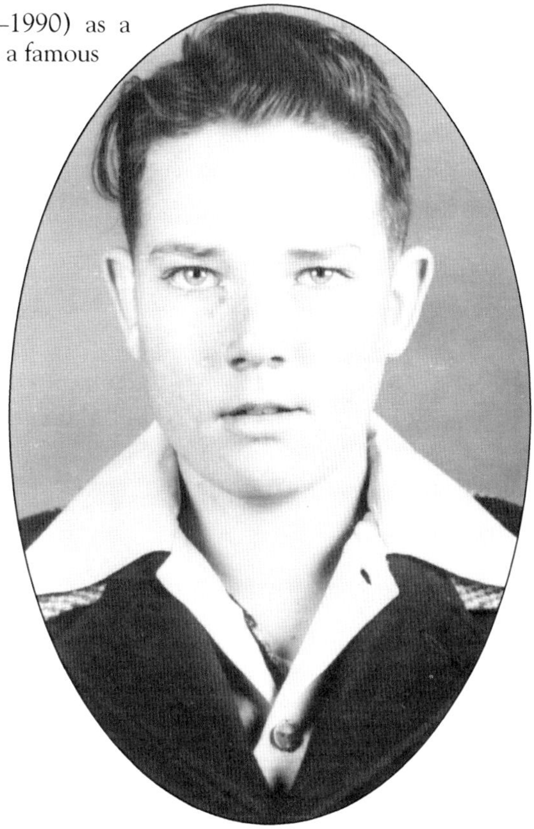

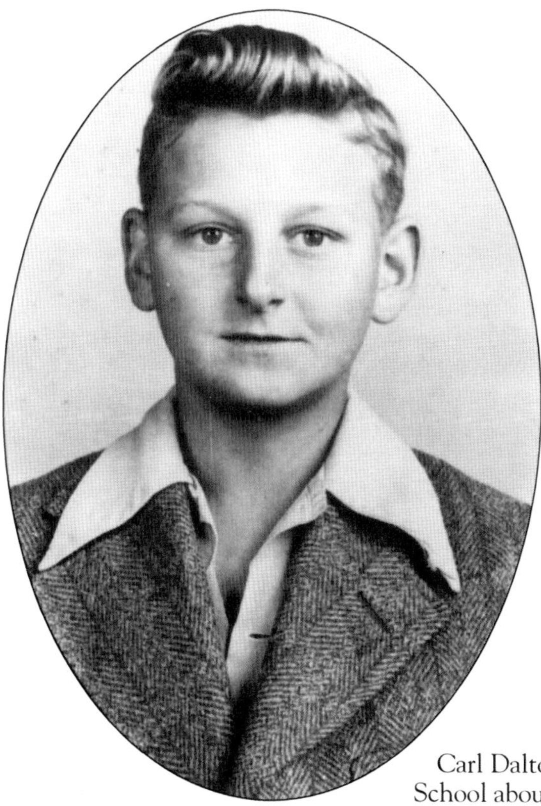

Carl Dalton Casstevens while a student at Boonville School about 1948. (CDC)

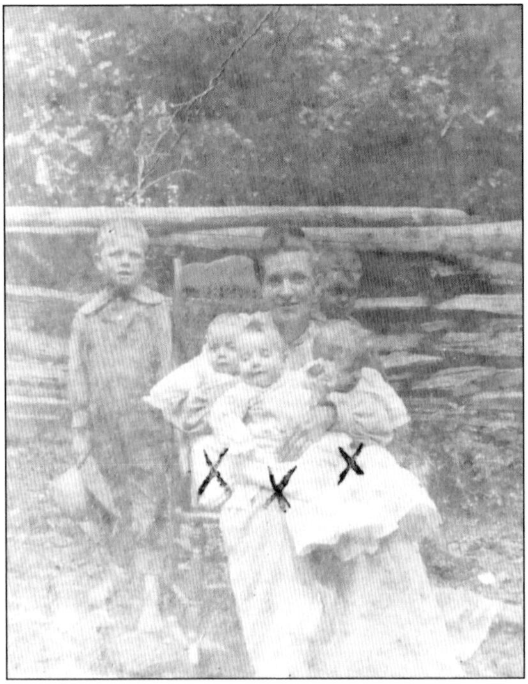

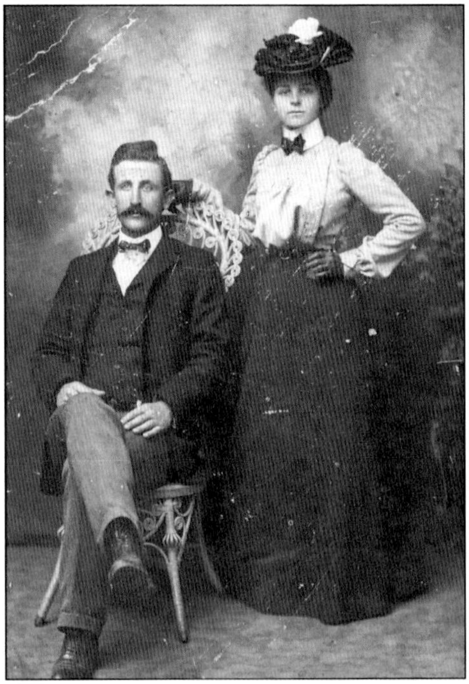

Left: Martha (Hutchens) Royal with her children, who appear to be triplets. Note the rail fence in the background. Martha was later murdered by an unknown assailant. (AS)
Right: This photograph of a lovely couple, Henry B. and Lula G. Lawton James, was probably taken about the time of their marriage in 1899. Henry, who was born to John H. James (a Yadkinville merchant) and Mahaly Jane Douglas James in 1874, ran a livery stable in Yadkinville. (FHC)

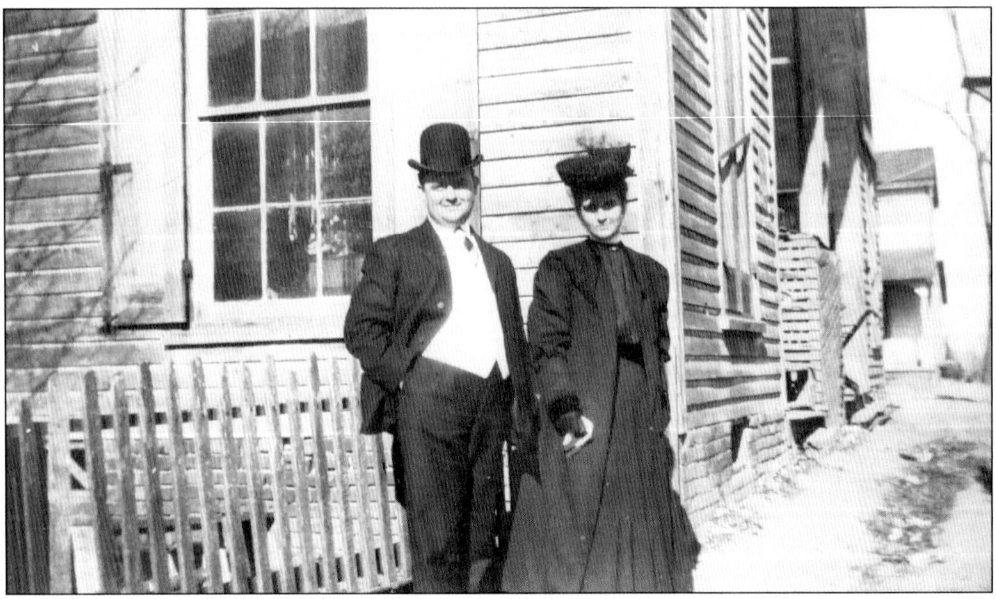

John D. Holcomb, Sr. and wife Nora Hamlin Holcomb stand near T.C. Hauser's store. The store, which later became J.A. Logan's, stood on the west side of the courthouse at the intersection of old Highway 421 and Highway 601. Note the picket fence. (HHM)

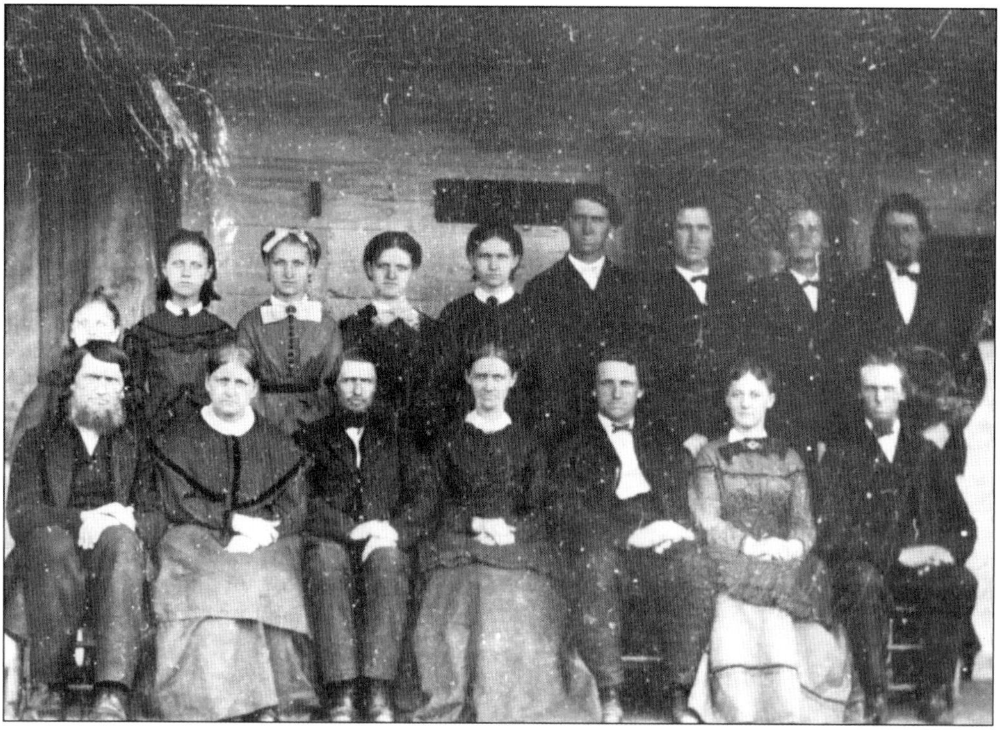

Thomas Locke Davis (1820–1898) and his wife, Anna Malinda Speas (1820–1900), with some of their children and their spouses. Thomas and two of his sons were Confederate soldiers during the Civil War. (MDL)

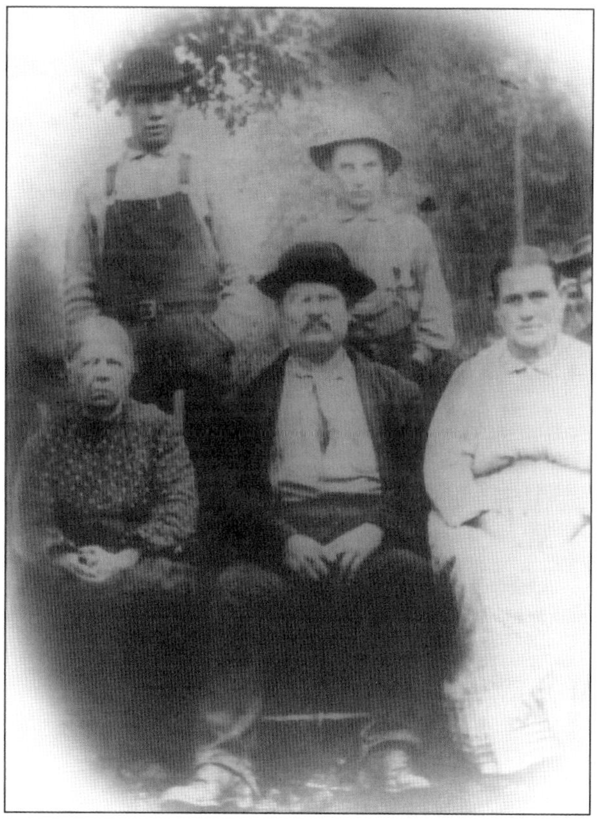

Three generations of the Hutchens family in 1909. In the front row are, from left to right: Nancy Shermer Hutchens (1839–1916), the widow of John Ellis Hutchens Sr.; her son, John Ellis Hutchens Jr., (b. 1862); and his wife, Mary Algood Hutchens (b. 1866). In the back row are, from left to right: Harrison, Dewey, and John "Tant" Hutchens. (JA)

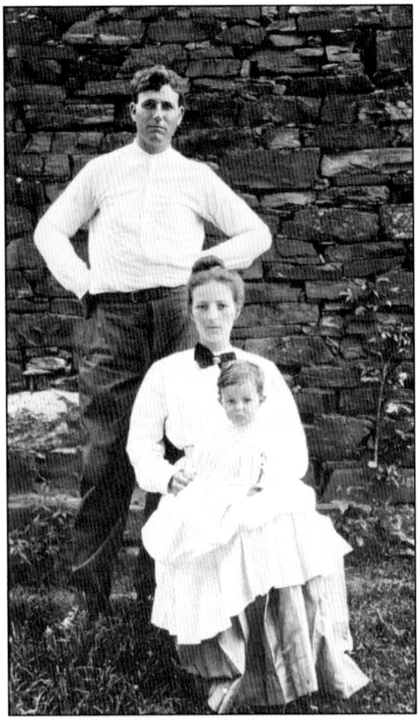

Sidney E. Shermer (1888–1974) with his wife, Cora (Mackie) Shermer (1887–1974), and their daughter Blanche, about 1914. (MSP)

Isaac Lee Holcomb (1857–1939) with his wife, Maggie Elen (Holcomb) Holcomb, and their daughters, Vallie (Mrs. L.V. Weatherman), Stella (Mrs. D.E. Whitaker), and Ola Ennis Holcomb. Isaac was a justice of the peace and a member of the board of the Center Methodist Church, located near his home. (RH)

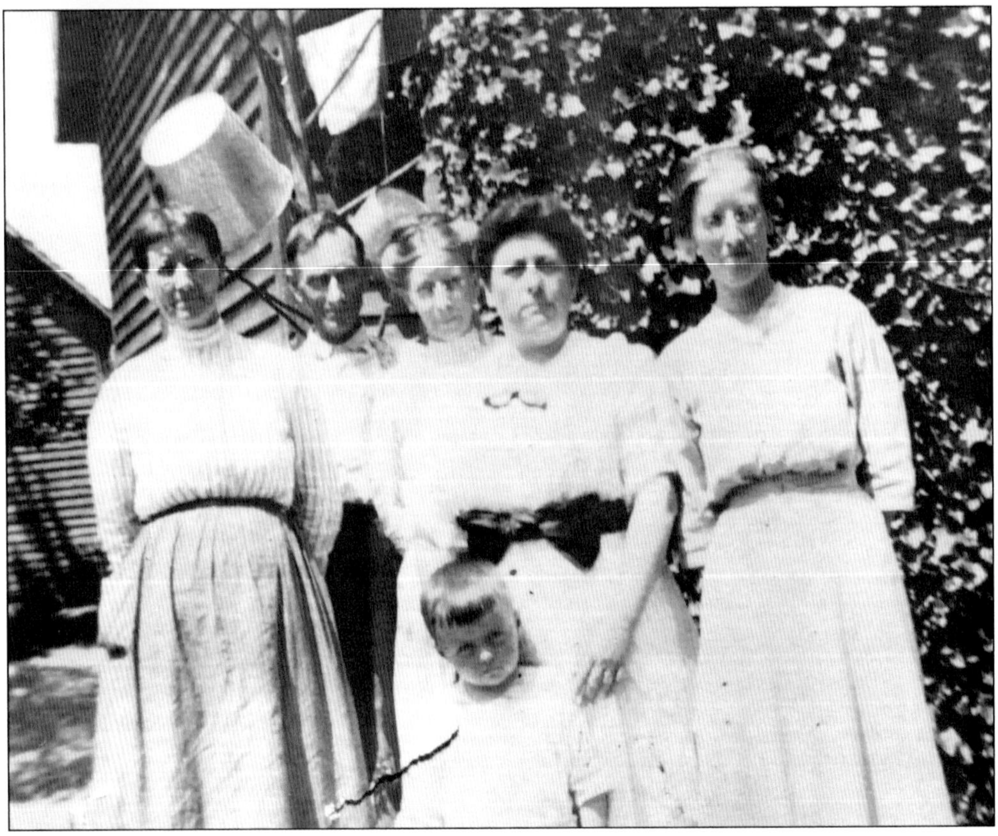

John Madison Haire (1857–1935), the son of First Lieutenant Risdon Odell Haire and Sarah Gross Haire, was three years old when this photograph was taken in 1860. Risdon Odell Haire was killed at Chancellorsville, VA, on May 2, 1863, when John was only six years old. (DMcL)

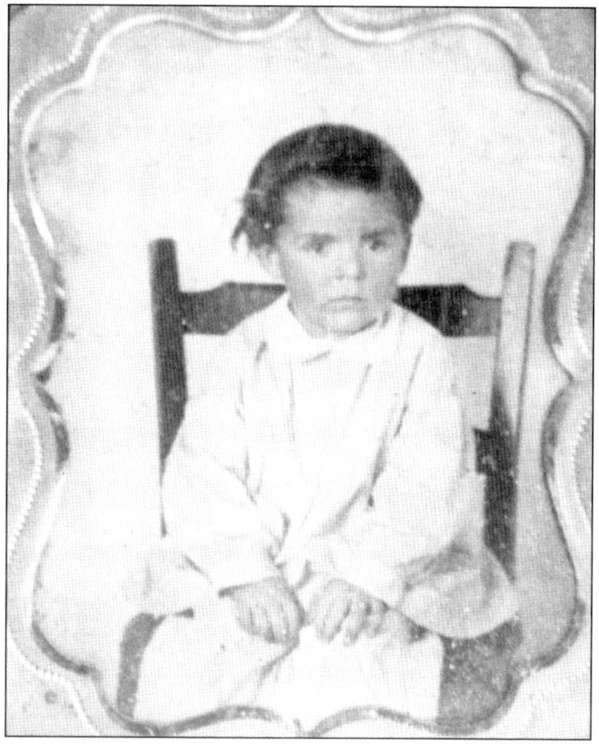

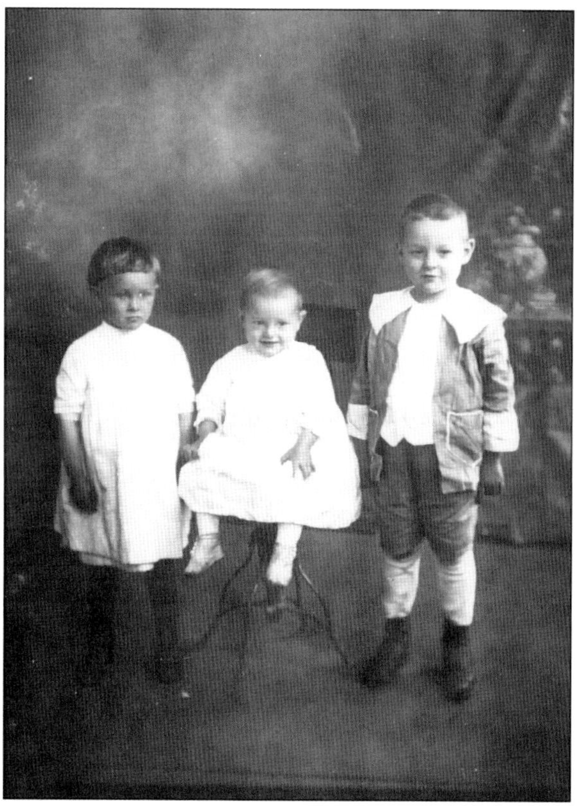

Maude, Ethel, and Eli Mosteller of the Shady Grove community, c. 1916. (EM)

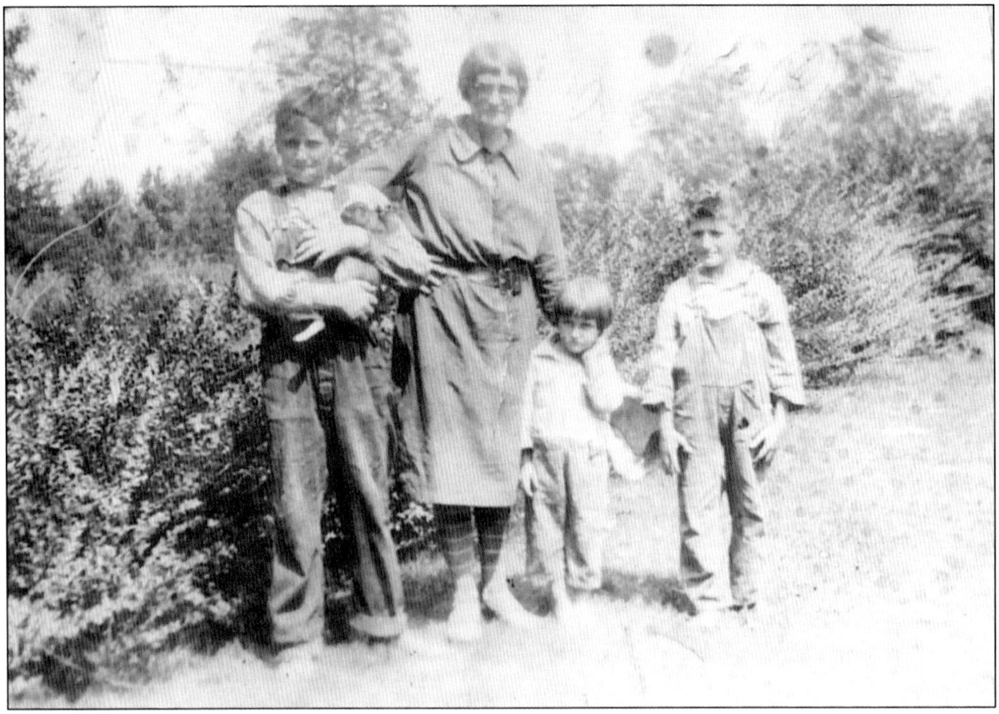

Nettie (Reavis) Hauser with her children, Labon, Jessie, and Tom, *c.* 1927. (VS)

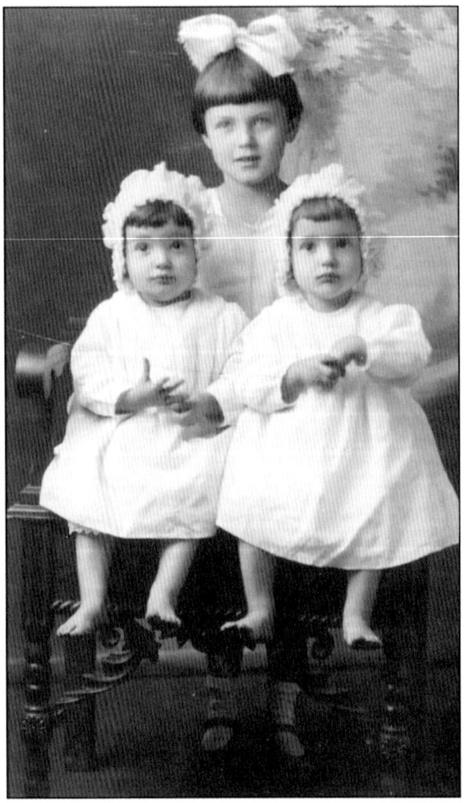

These pretty girls with their bonnets and bows are Emily, Martha, and Mildred Myers, the daughters of Lula (Fleming) Myers. (MMS)

Nannie (Marion) Davis watches her grandchild in the bassinet. (NMD)

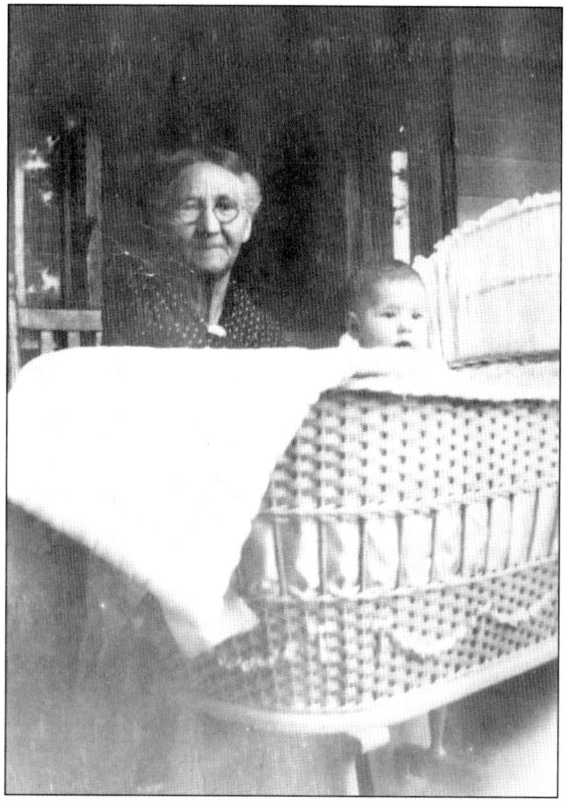

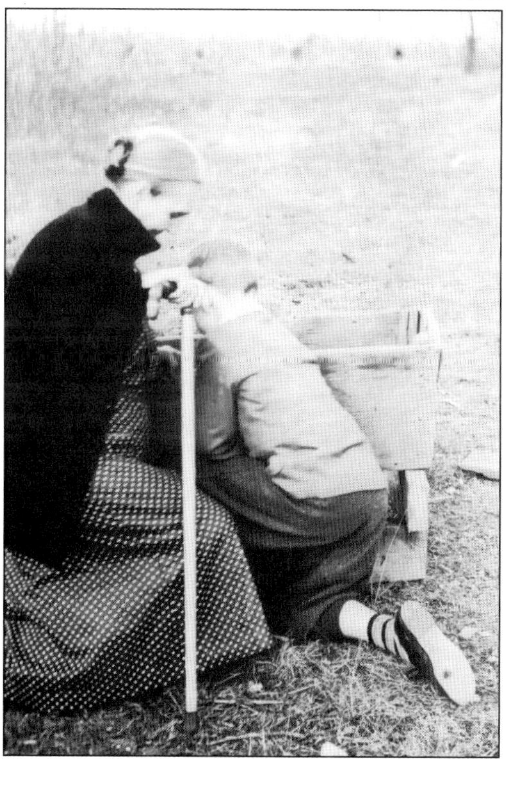

Mina (Smith) Speer (1877–1969) and her grandson look at a cradle that rocked three generations as babies. (AS)

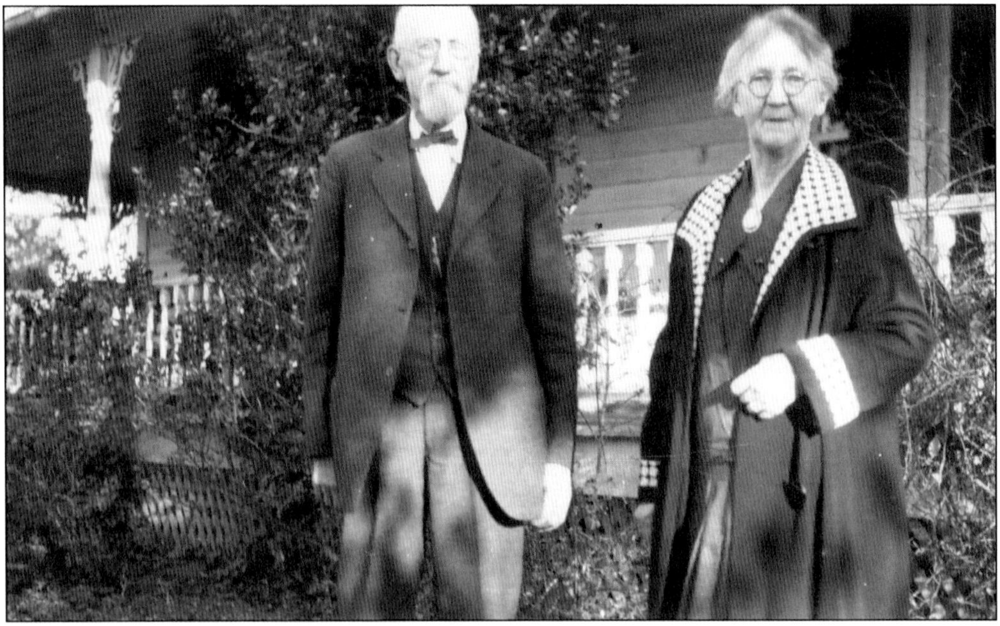

Eli Thomas and Nannie (Marion) Davis in front of their home. (NMD)

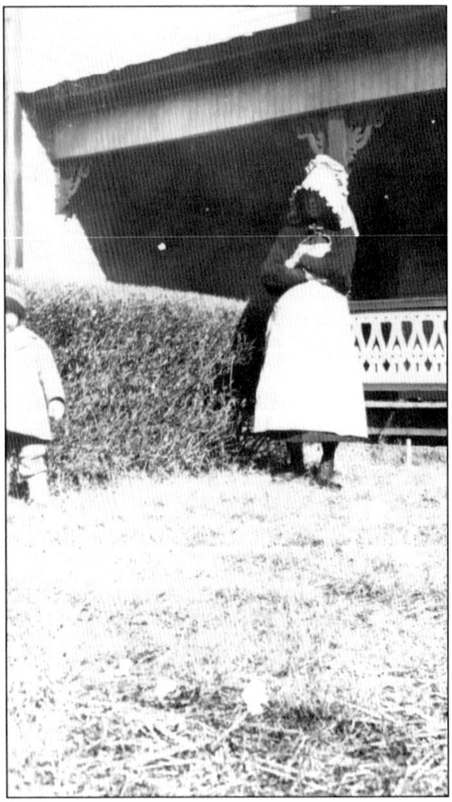

Emma (Shugart) Mackie (1861–1949) in the yard of her home in Yadkinville. Note the bonnet that she is wearing. (HHM)

Two

Wagon Wheels Rolling

Transportation

Before the turn of the twentieth century, travel was difficult, and many country people would live out their lives without venturing farther than the nearest town. Roads were few and almost impassable during the winter months. They were used by horseback riders and wagons, buggies, or other conveyances pulled by oxen, mules, ponies, donkeys, and horses. There were no bridges across the river until 1872, when a covered bridge was built at Jonesville. The river was crossed at fords such as Island Ford (Jonesville), White Rock Ford (Rockford), Yellowbank Ford (Donnaha), and Shallow Ford (Huntsville), or on ferries, which were operated at several sites. A trip to Winston-Salem was a three-day journey and required camping overnight at the river.

Transportation improved greatly in the 1920s with the construction of paved highways. The era of the automobile brought tremendous changes to the county, and gave the citizens easy access to the world outside Yadkin County.

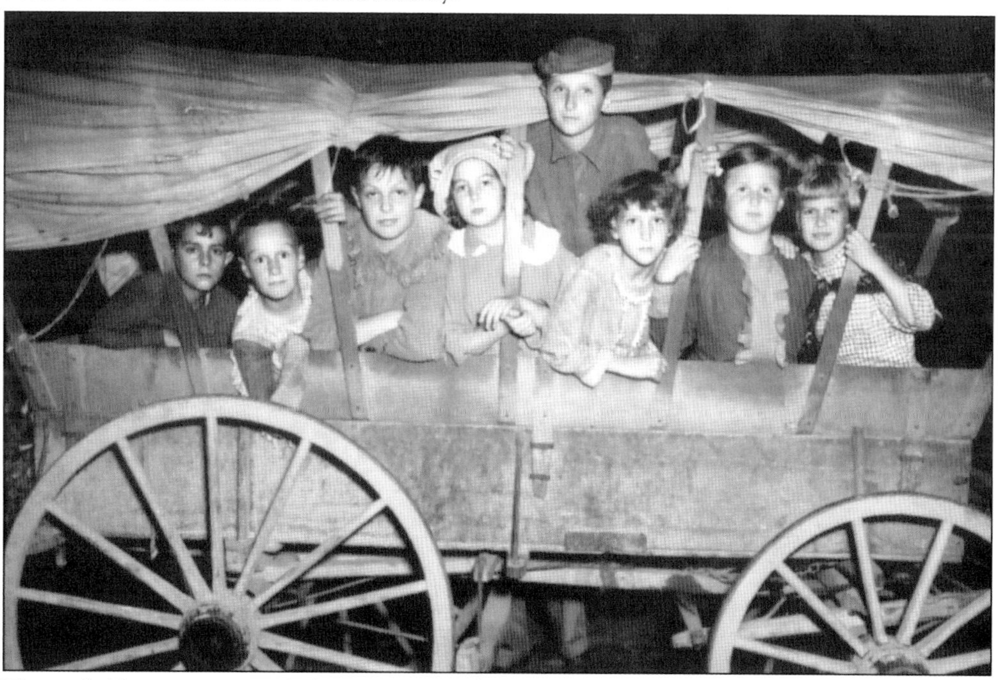

These children were crowded into a covered wagon for an event that took place during the 1950 Yadkin County Centennial Celebration. Shown, from left to right, are Glenn Carroll Oakes, Billy Henric, Johnny Mock, Nancy Gentry, Tommy Fletcher, Claira Mendenhall, Ann Reece, and Nancy Steelman. (SO)

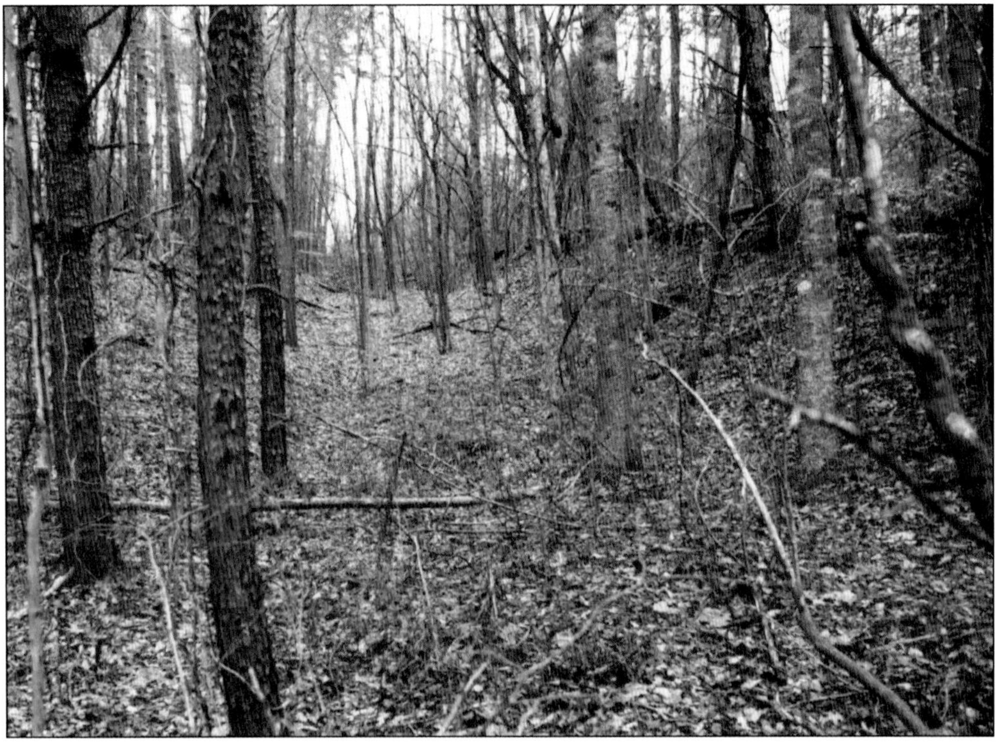

A portion of the old Georgia Road near Wyo, once a main route from Shallow Ford on the Yadkin River to Augusta, GA, is now overgrow with trees. Early roads had deep ruts made by the heavy wagons that traveled them. (FHC)

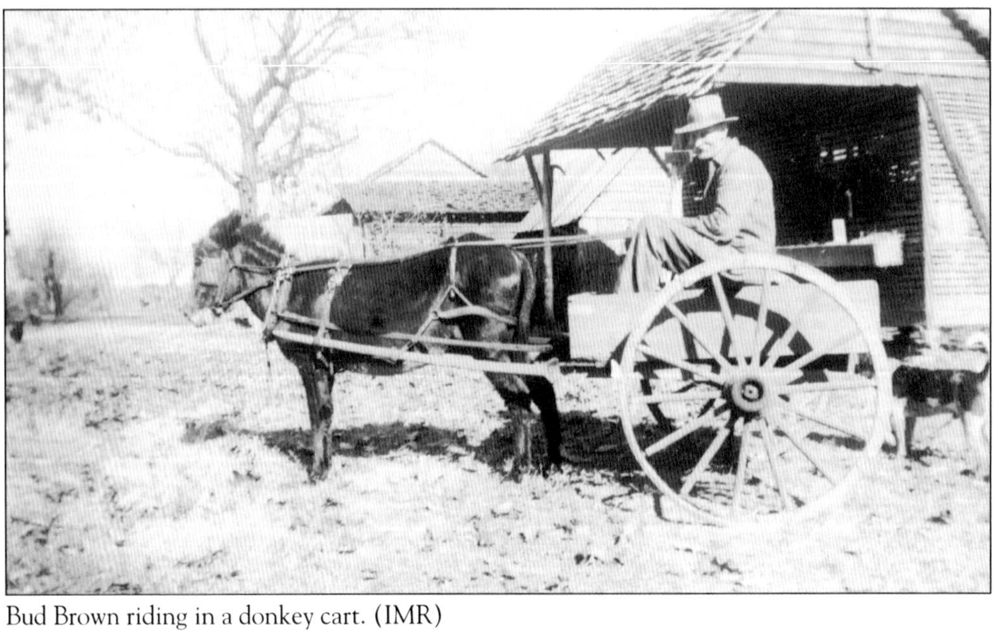

Bud Brown riding in a donkey cart. (IMR)

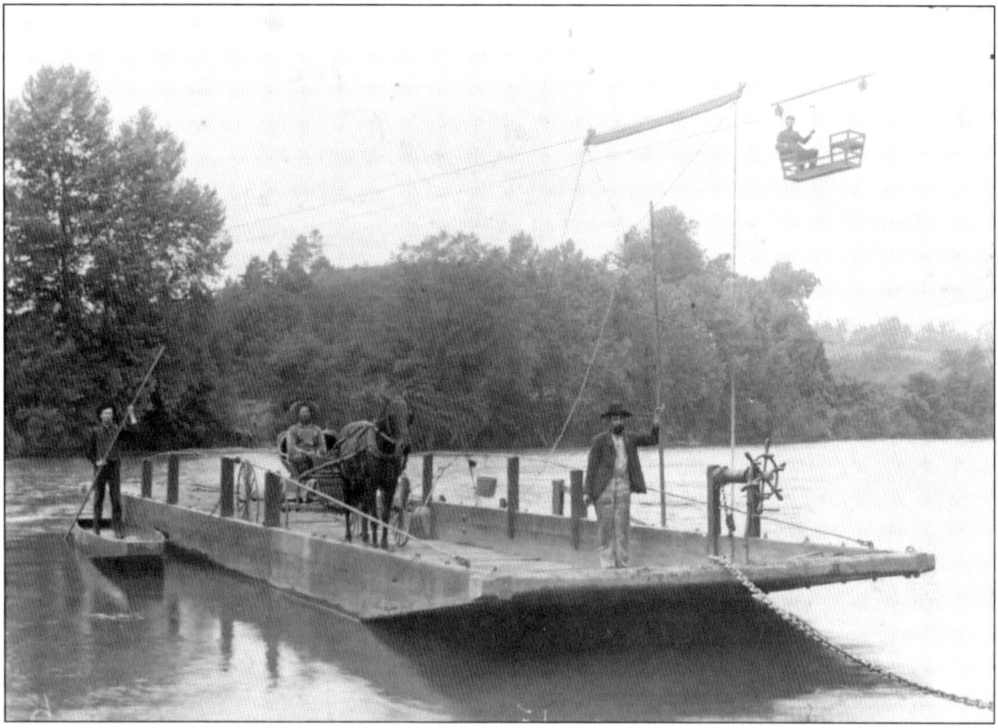

Hall's ferry took passengers across the Yadkin River at Siloam. (LW)

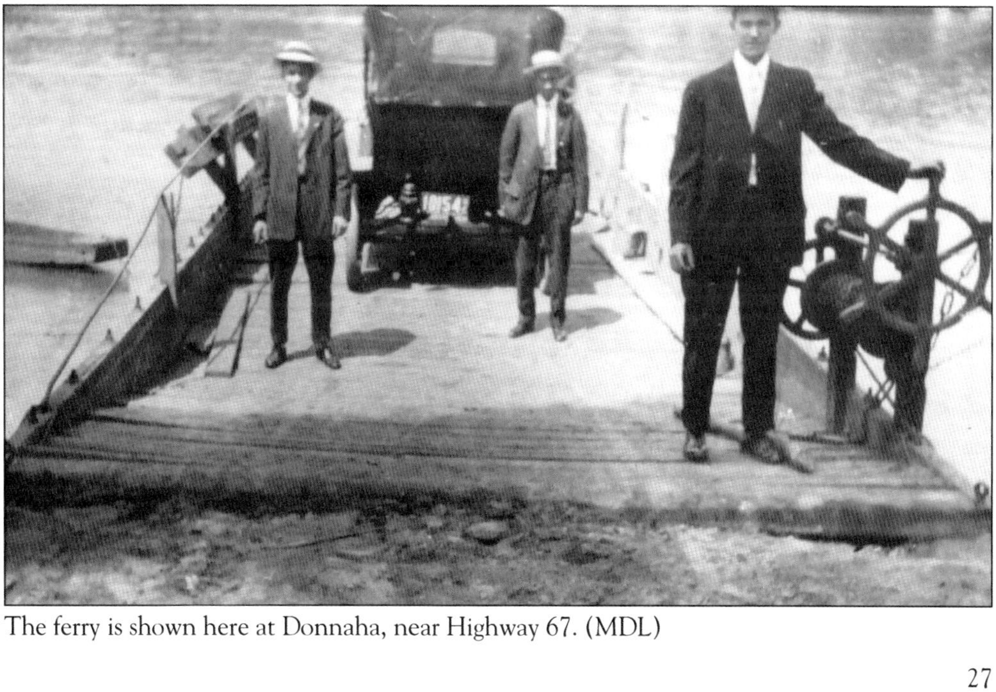

The ferry is shown here at Donnaha, near Highway 67. (MDL)

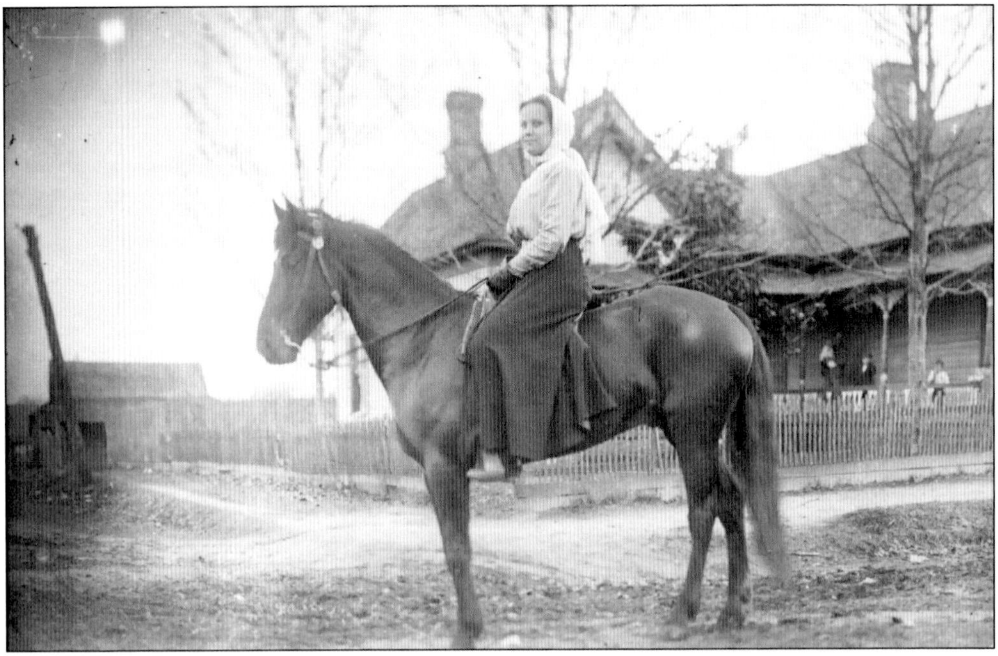

Stella Reece is shown here on a horse in front of the Harding-Hauser-Holcomb house in Yadkinville, *c.* 1910. The house stands at the corner of Elm and Jackson Streets. (JEB)

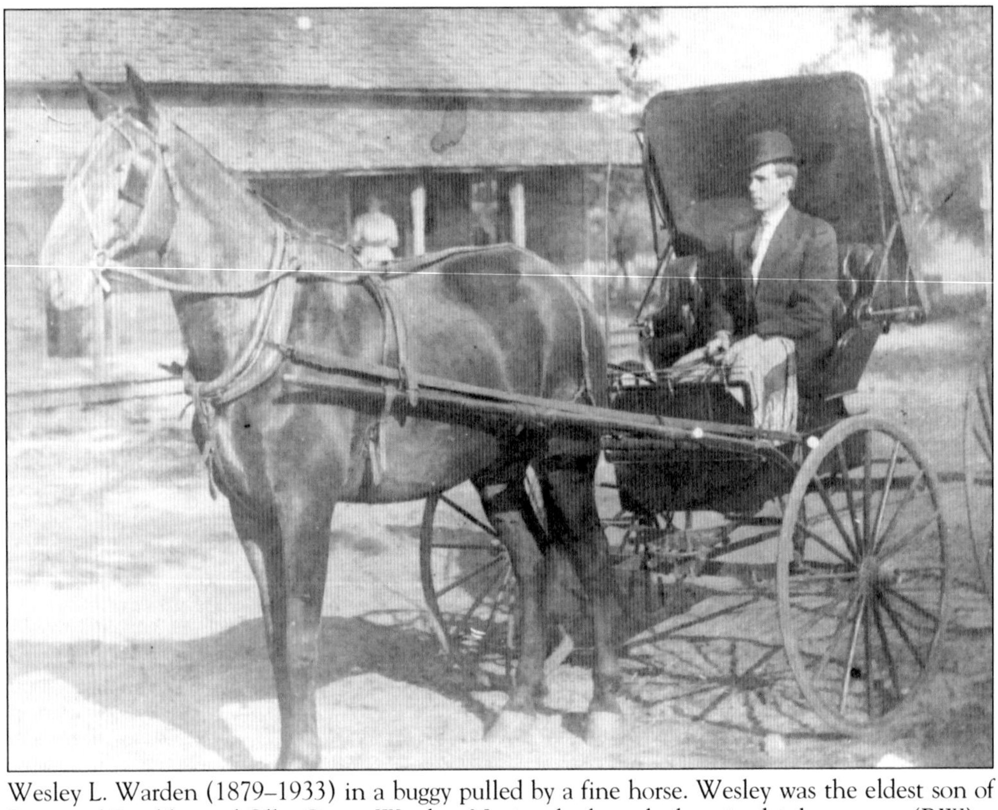

Wesley L. Warden (1879–1933) in a buggy pulled by a fine horse. Wesley was the eldest son of Reverend Franklin and Ollie Carter Warden. Notice the lap robe keeping his legs warm. (RW)

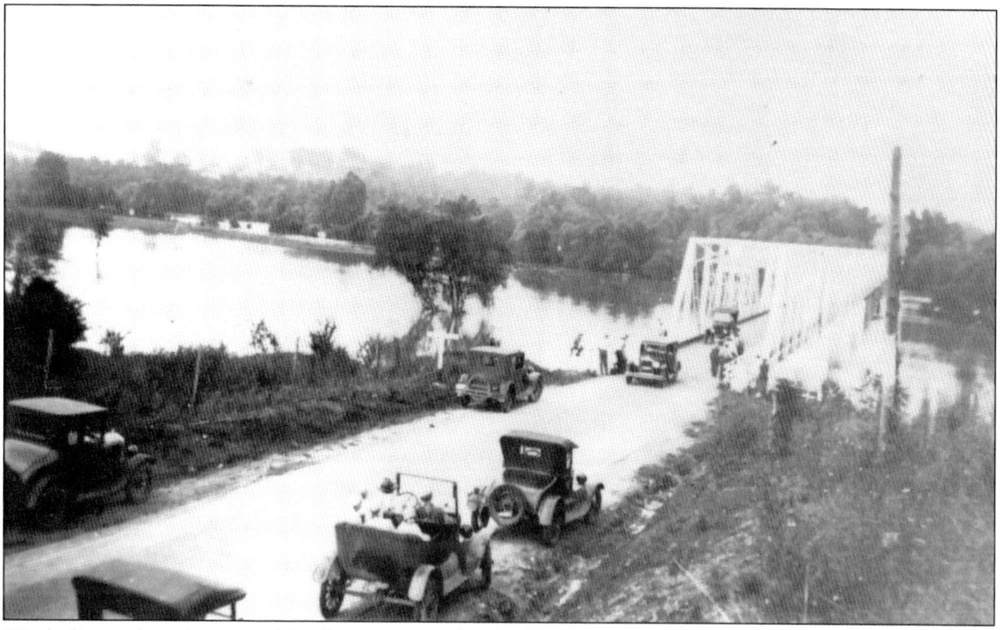

We believe that this metal bridge spanned the Yadkin River between Jonesville and Elkin. The automobiles indicate that the picture was probably taken in the 1920s. (AS)

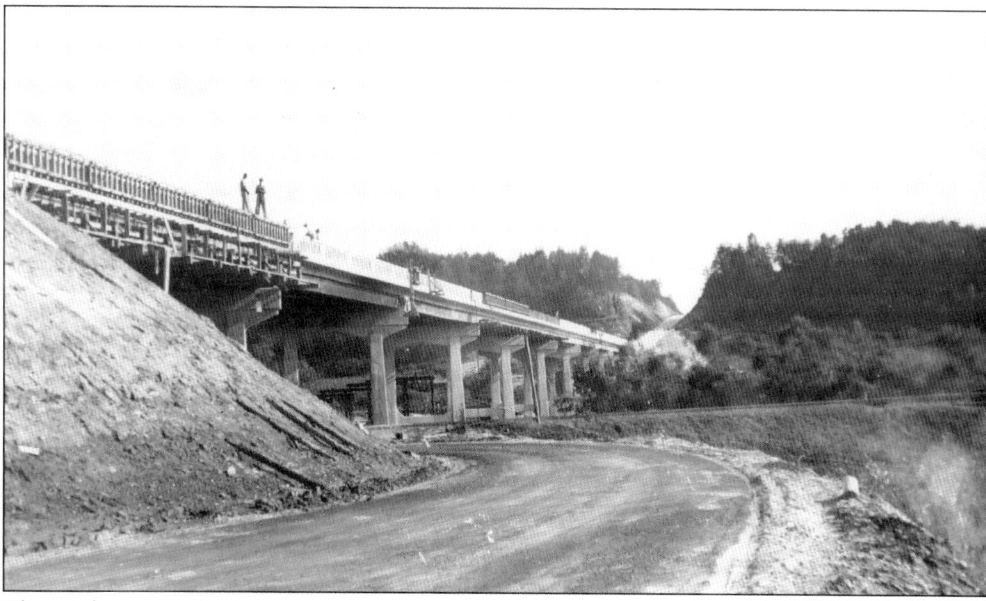

The Highway 601 bridge at Crutchfield during construction in 1939–40. (AS)

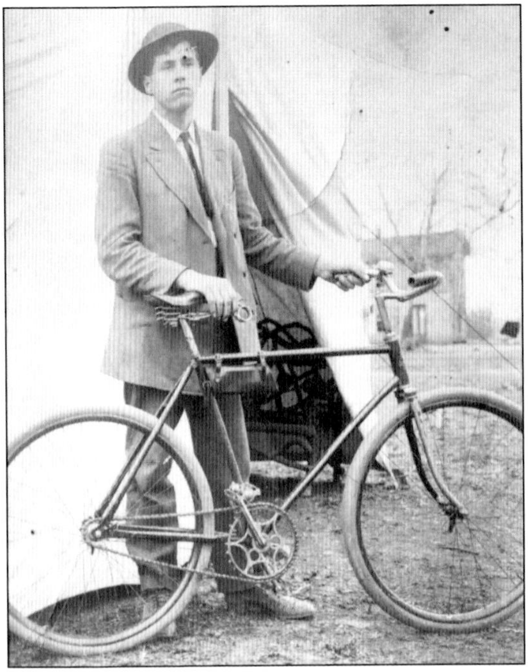

Charlie Pardue as a young man. Charlie later became a Yadkinville merchant. (RW)

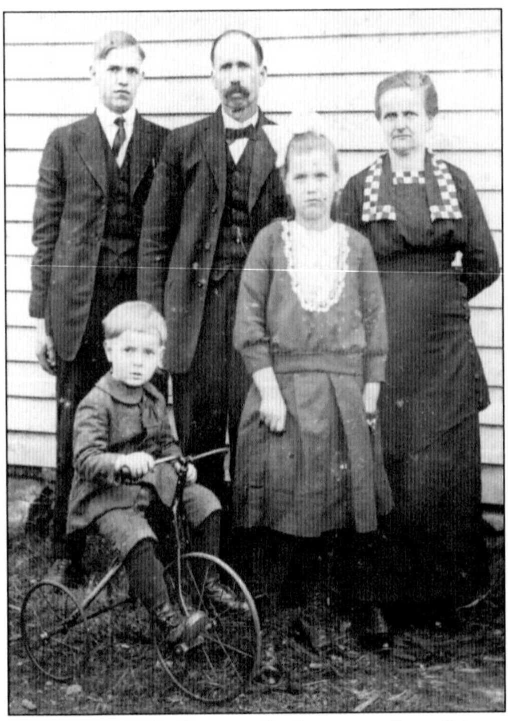

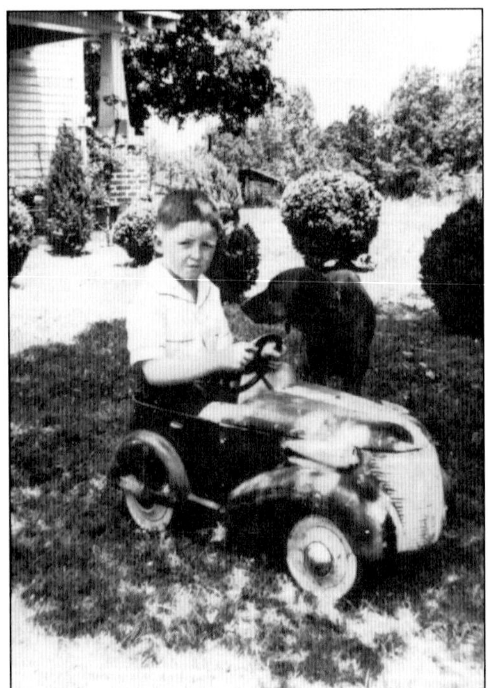

Left: Folger Matthews rides his tricycle as his parents, Bob and Annie, his brother Joe, and his sister Irma look on. Irma (Matthews) Robertson went on to become a teacher, local historian, and author. (IMR)
Right: Jack Fleming Shore in a pedal car about 1938. (MMS)

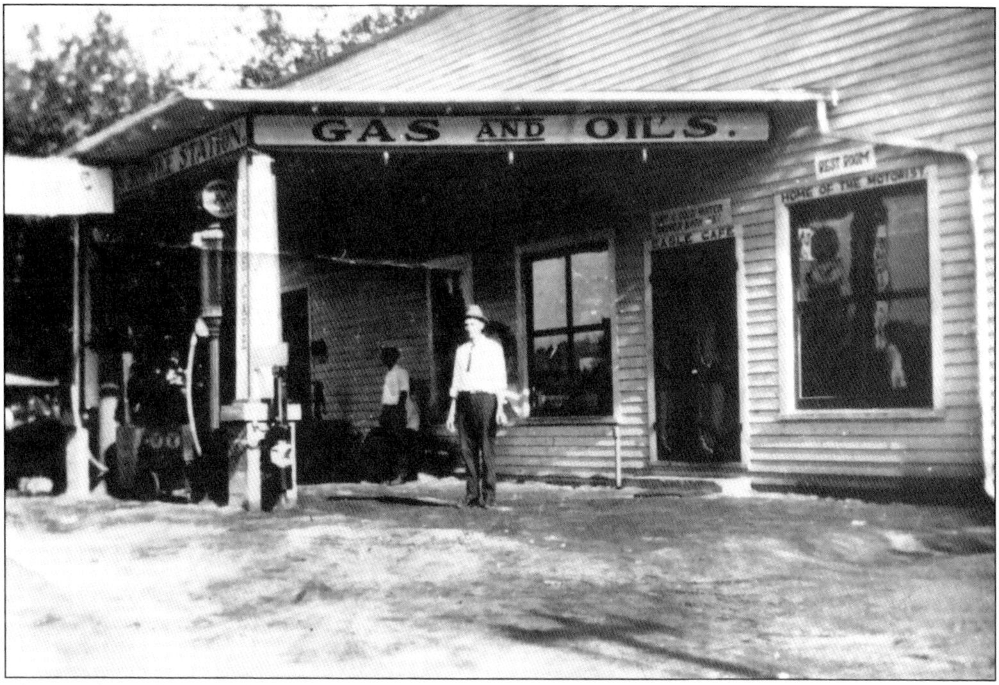

The Eagle Cafe in Yadkinville in 1923. As the number of cars on the roads increased, many local restaurants and stores added gas pumps, including the Eagle Cafe. (AS)

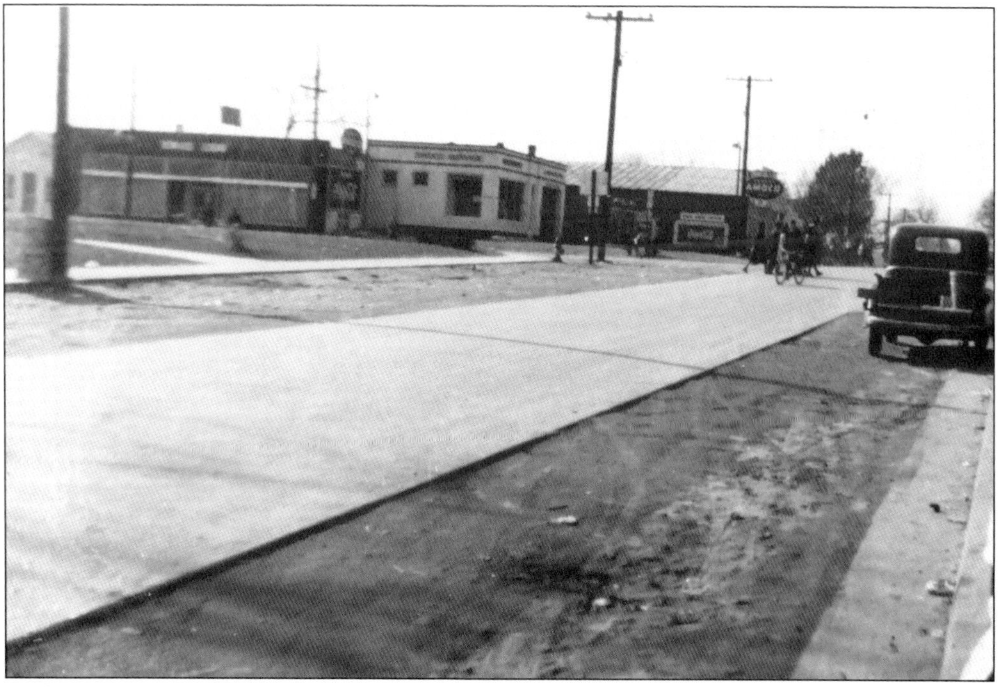

Looking west on Main Street toward Highway 601 about 1945, the office of Atty. J.T. Reece is visible at far left. Next is Howard Logan's store, and the Amoco service station is on the corner. Logan Motors faces Main Street north of the intersection. The shoulders of the road along Main Street are unpaved and there are no traffic lights at the intersection. (SO, LW)

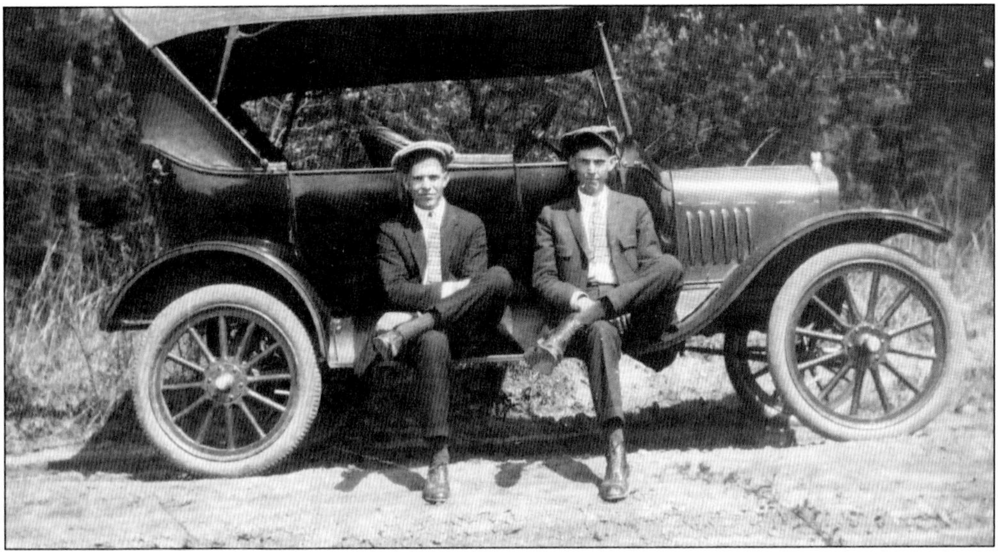

Joe and Freer Matthews sit on the running board. Perhaps they are out of gas. (IMR)

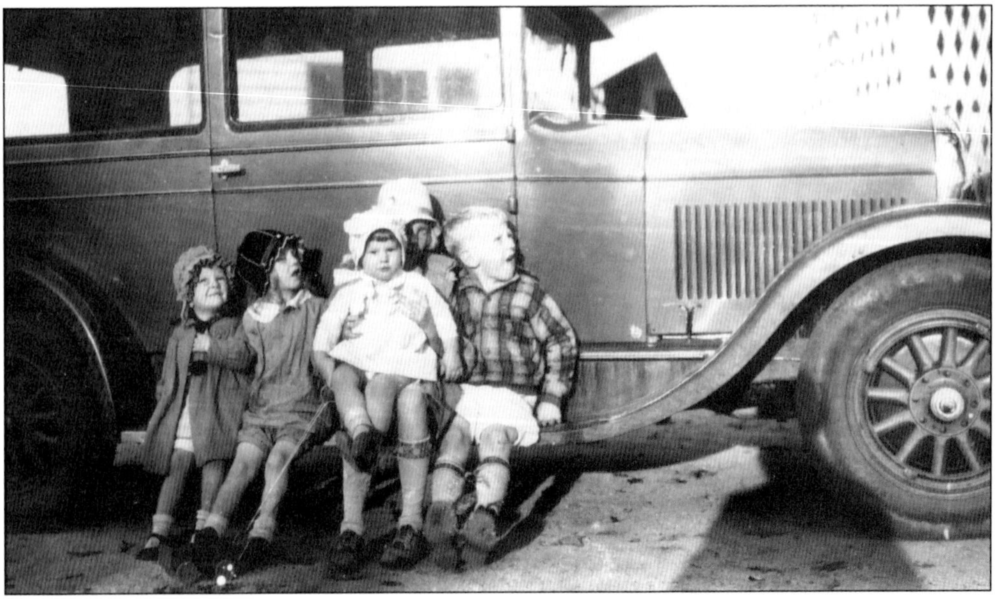

The children of Neal Davis with their cousin, Jessie Leigh Davis (the baby in the center), on the running board of the family Chrysler, c. 1928. (NMD)

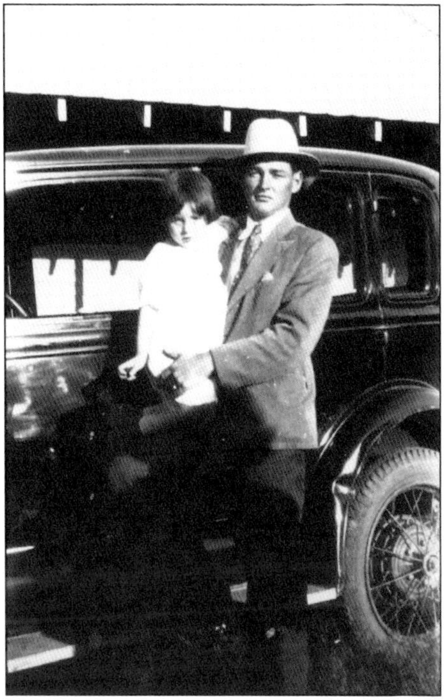

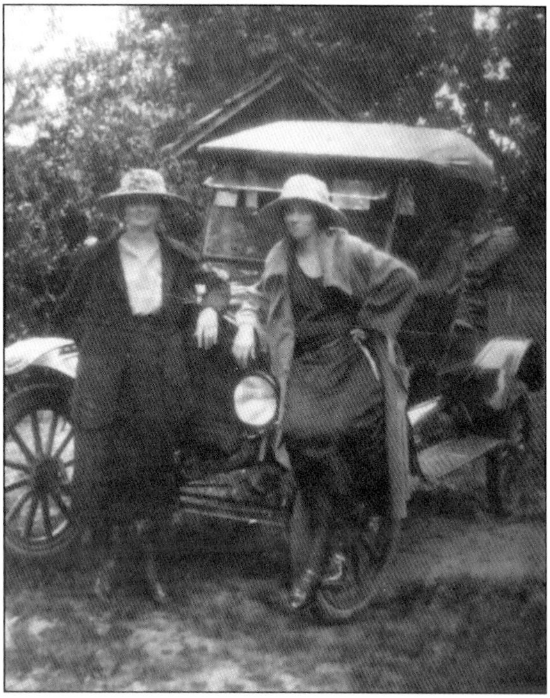

Top Left: Eli Mosteller holds his baby sister beside a 1929 Ford. (EM)
Top Right: Vallie and Nova Shore appear to be taking it easy after arriving at the J.W. Shore homeplace. This photograph was taken in the 1920s. (NH)

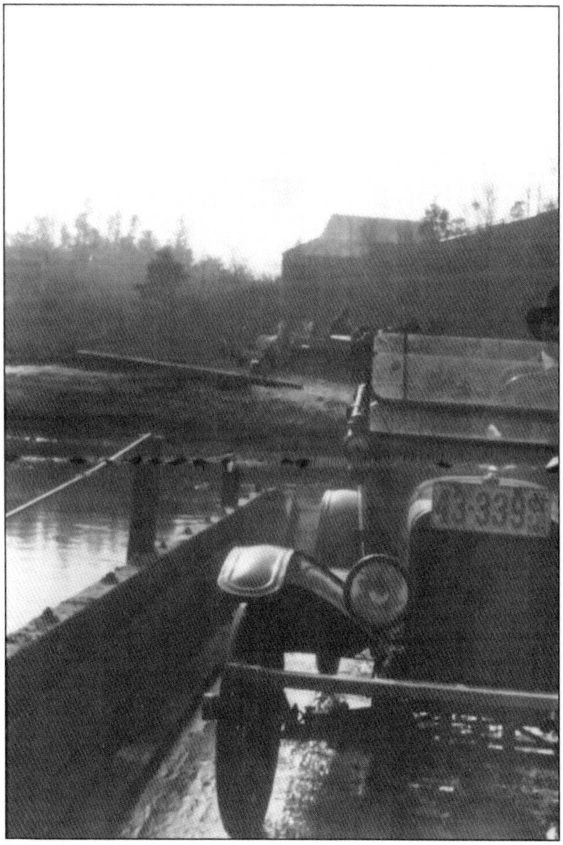

Nat Martin taking the car across the river on the Shoals ferry, c. 1920. (JN)

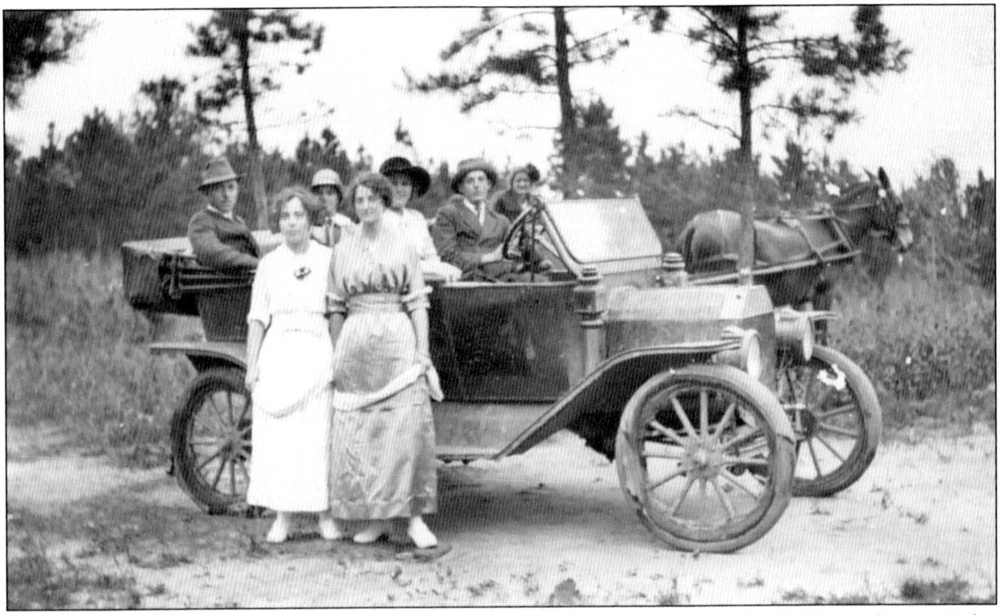

Martin Mackie is in the driver's seat and Julius Mackie is in the back of this early car. Julia (Mackie) Draughon is standing on the right. Notice the worn-out tires on the car, and the mule in the background. (HHM)

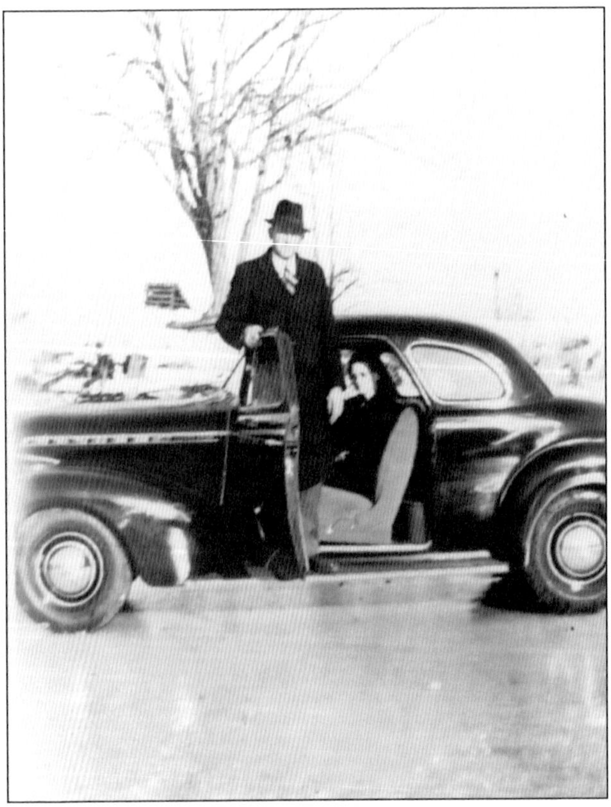

Gene and Nova Shore drove their car out on the ice when Dobbins' Mill Pond froze over in 1941. (NH)

Three

Shelter from the Storm

Homes

The earliest homes were primitive log cabins. Some cabins were later bricked over or covered with clap-boards. As the county prospered in the years before the Civil War, mansions dotted the landscape, most situated near the Yadkin River. Several of these beautiful, white-columned homes have been inhabited for over one hundred years; others are falling into ruin.

The typical farm home was a one-room log structure, often with a two-story addition. Sometimes a front porch was added. An outhouse, a well house, a smoke house, an ice house, a corn crib, a barn, and other buildings were built nearby. Early homes were often roofed with wooden shingles, and fire was a constant danger, so the kitchen was usually detached from the main house. Later, tin was used as roofing material, so kitchens could be built as part of the main house. Open hearths were used for heating the house as well as for cooking before the advent of wood stoves and kerosene-burning heaters.

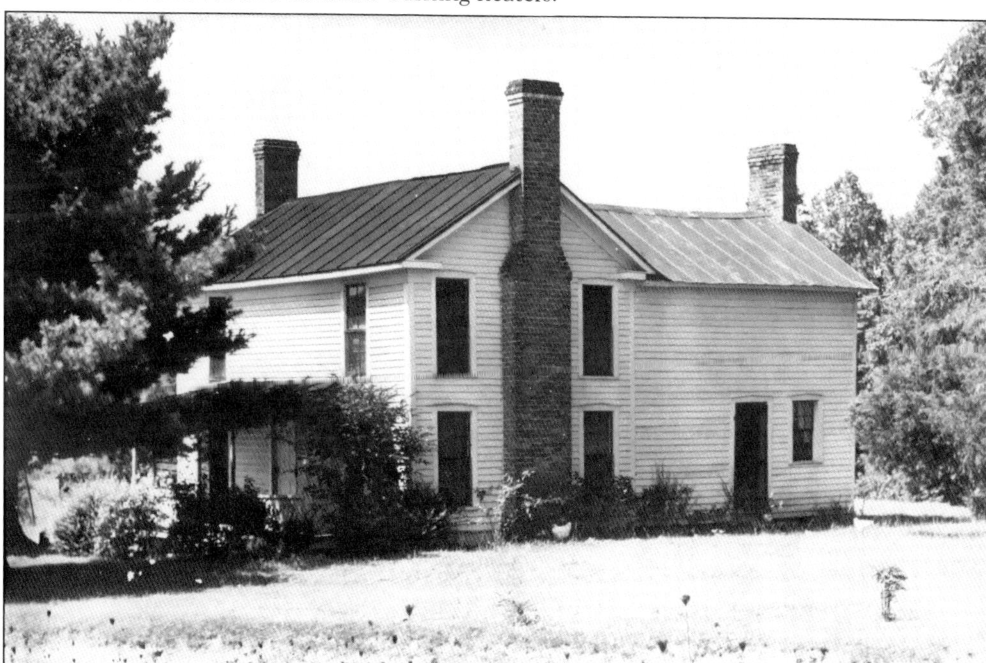

The John J. Angel (1813–1891) and Keziah Davis Angel house near Boonville. The two ran the Angel Hotel in Boonville. The house is no longer standing. (DMcL)

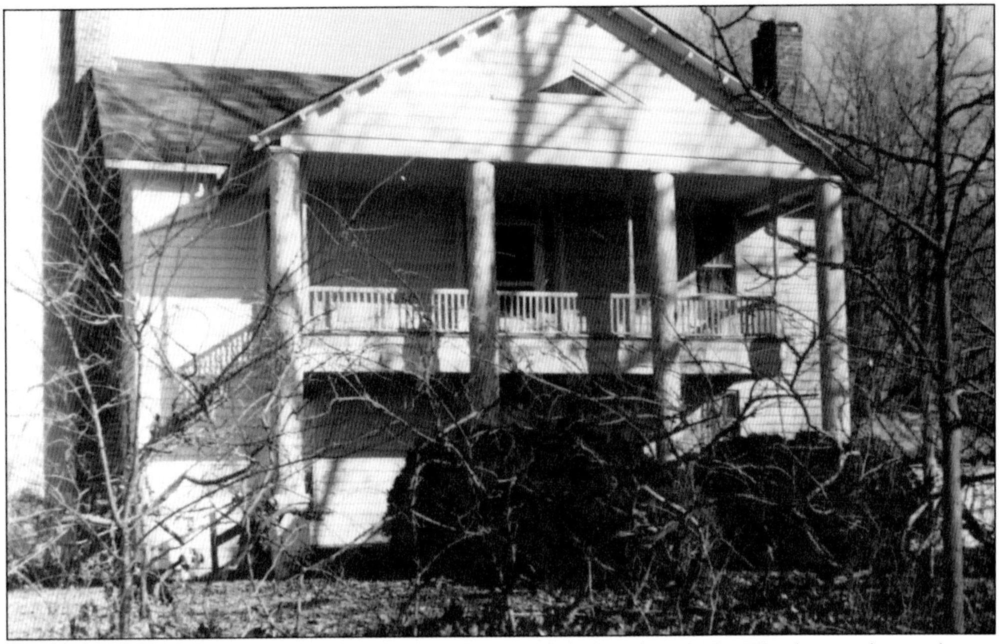

The Shore-Hoots house was built in 1884 and remodeled in the 1910s. The house, located near the Forbush Elementary School, was built for David L. Shore (1846–1920). The portico was added by the next owners, Henry Winfield and Rachel (Cranfill) Hoots. They were the parents of Zeno Hoots, a benefactor of the Lula Conrad Hoots Memorial Hospital, which was named in honor of his wife. (LW)

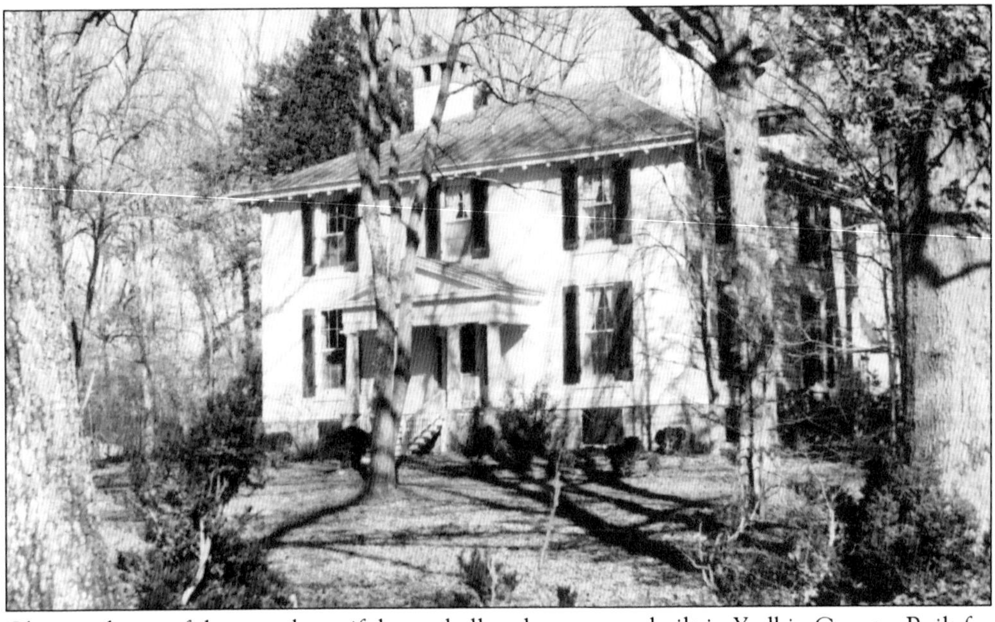

Glenwood, one of the most beautiful ante-bellum houses ever built in Yadkin County. Built for plantation owner Tyre Glen, the house was completed in 1851 after five years of construction. In 1860, Glen owned 3,500 acres along the Yadkin River near Enon, and was one of the county's wealthiest citizens. Glenwood was a hub of social activity, and the Glens played host to such notables as Governor Zebulon B. Vance and Chief Justice Richmond Pearson. (LW)

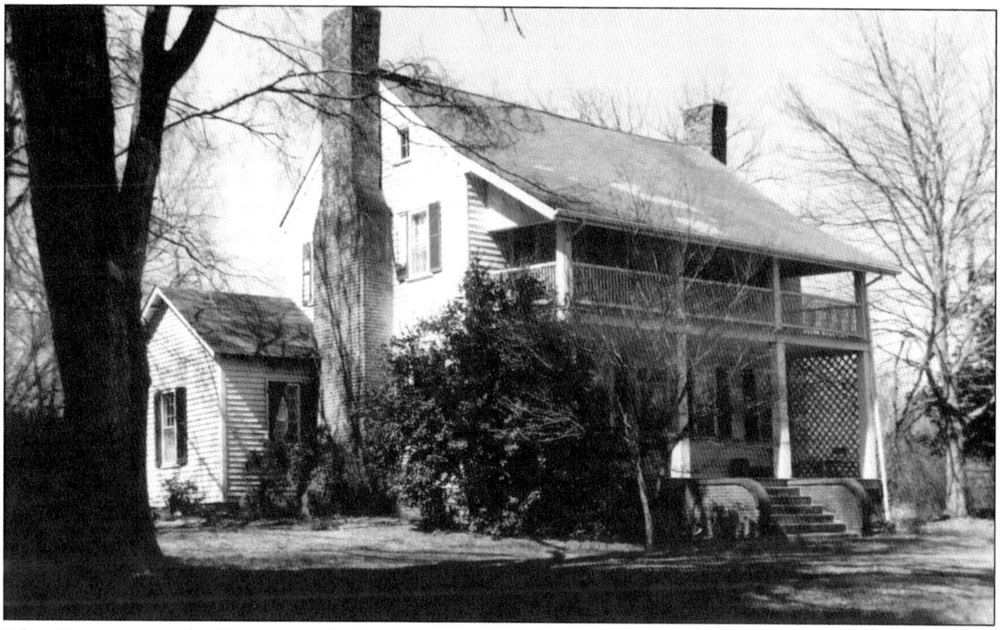

The Georgian-style Clingman-Sofley house at Huntsville was built by Henry Young about 1801. A later owner, Peter Clingman, referred to the house in his will as the "White House," probably because it was painted white. United States Congressman and Confederate Brigadier General Thomas Lanier Clingman lived here as a boy: it was said he had political aspirations to live in the "other" White House too. (LW)

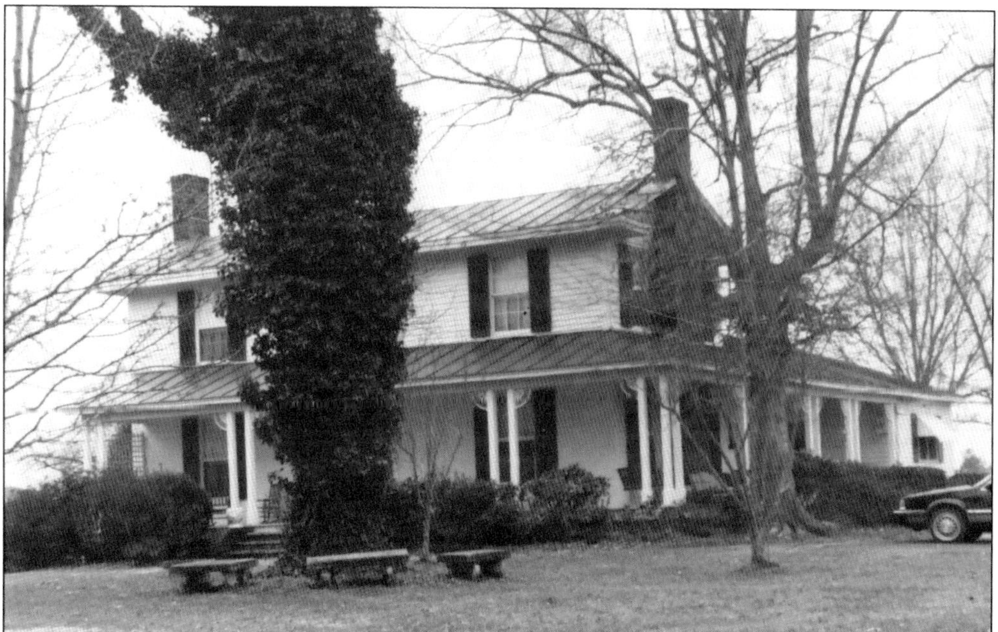

The Gray-Hartman-Holden house, located on the old Mulberry Fields Road just west of Huntsville, was built by slave trader Joseph Gray in 1860. He sold it to J.D. Hamlin, who operated a tobacco factory at Huntsville. Today, the house is occupied by the Holden family and is famous for its gardens of day lilies. (LW)

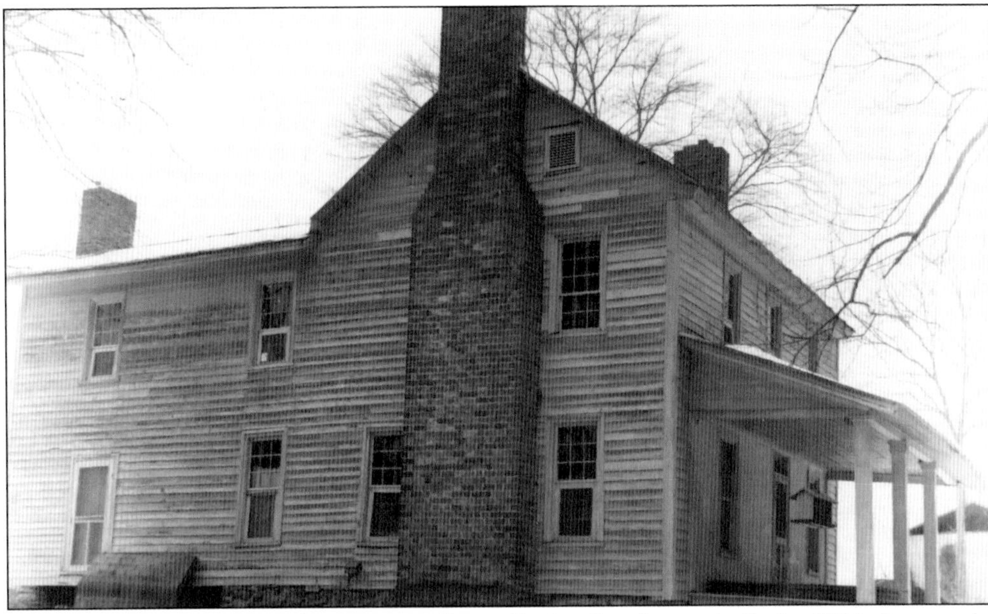

The Kelly-Harding-Brown house, near Speer Bridge Road, was built in 1836. It was the birthplace of Dr. Thomas Renny Harding (1855–1929), the son of William and Jane Speer Harding. In October 1855 William sold the house and took his family on the long journey to Texas. Within a year they had returned to Yadkin County, after deciding they did not like the Lone Star State. Fifteen-year-old Keziah Harding (1840–1864) kept a diary of the trip. (LW)

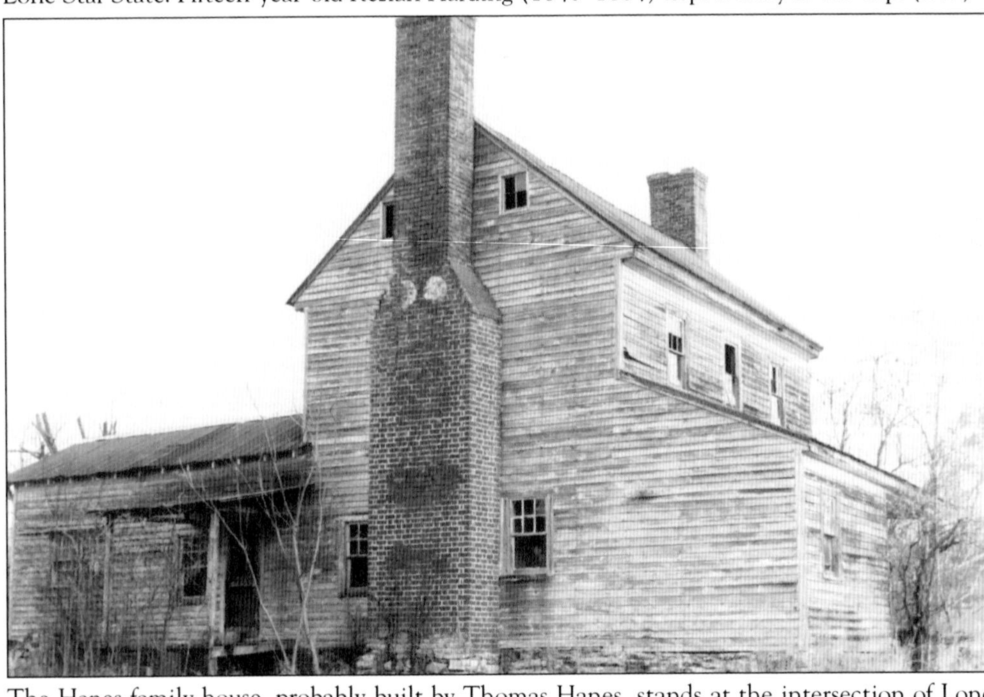

The Hanes family house, probably built by Thomas Hanes, stands at the intersection of Lone Hickory Road and Highway 21, and is now the best preserved Federal-style building in the county. Note the painted designs on the chimney: in the circle is the date "1823." A small cemetery nearby has inscriptions that date back as far as 1818. (LW)

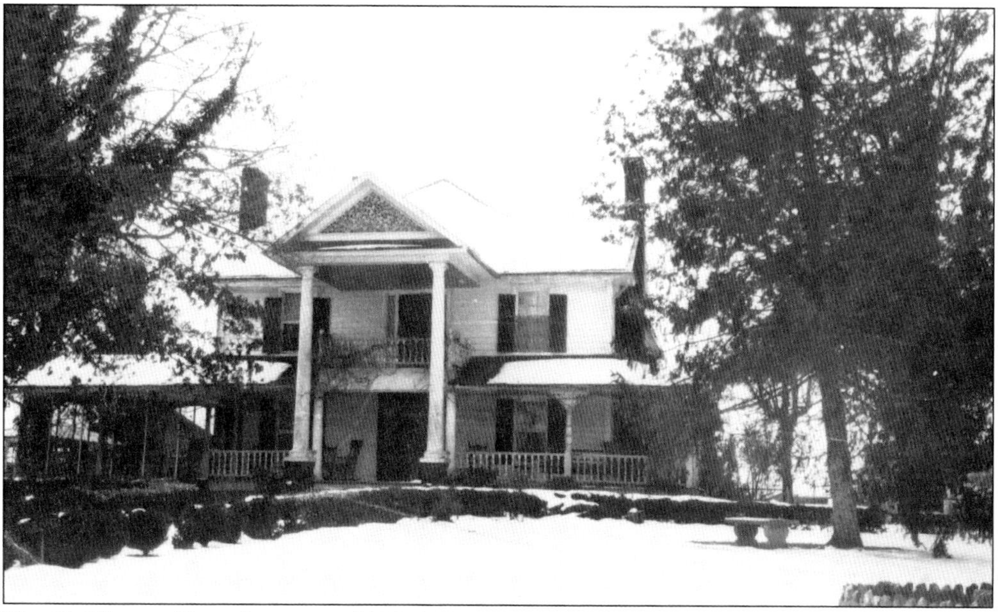

The Eli Thomas Davis home on old Highway 421 was built in 1881 and remodeled about 1890. This house burned on Easter Sunday in April 1948. The house that was built on the site still stands today. (NMD)

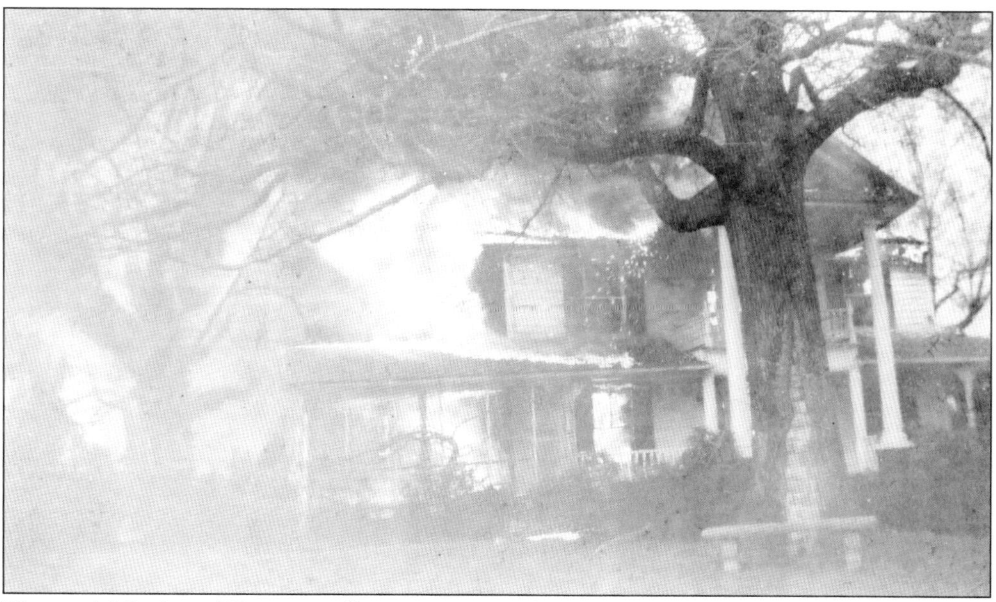

Thomas Miller Jr., of Hamptonville was returning from Easter services in Winston-Salem when he saw the Davis home (above) burning. He stopped and took a number of photographs. Few items were saved from the burning home. (NMD)

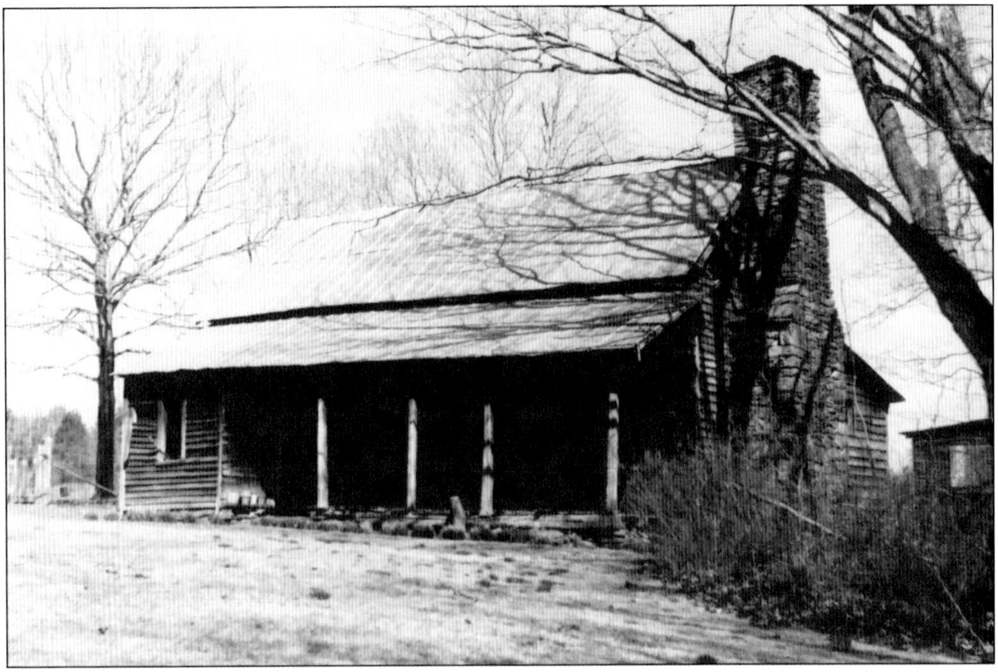

The Craft-Ray-Allred house, near Hamptonville, is a log and frame structure with a dry-laid, fieldstone chimney on the right. It is a one-story building with a sleeping loft, a design typical of early nineteenth-century houses. Nathan Charles Craft bought the property in 1827 and transferred it to his son in 1847. Jackson Ray acquired it in 1886. (LW)

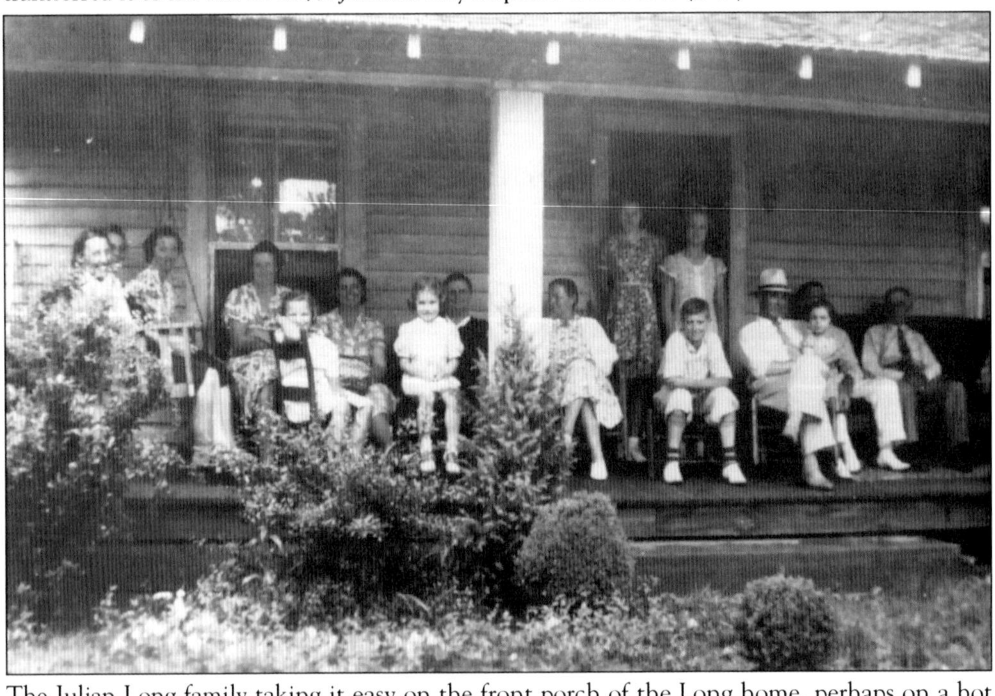

The Julian Long family taking it easy on the front porch of the Long home, perhaps on a hot Sunday afternoon. Julian (1873–1959) and Nancy E. Gentry Long were the parents of Jasper Long, a longtime postal worker and the Long family historian. (MMS)

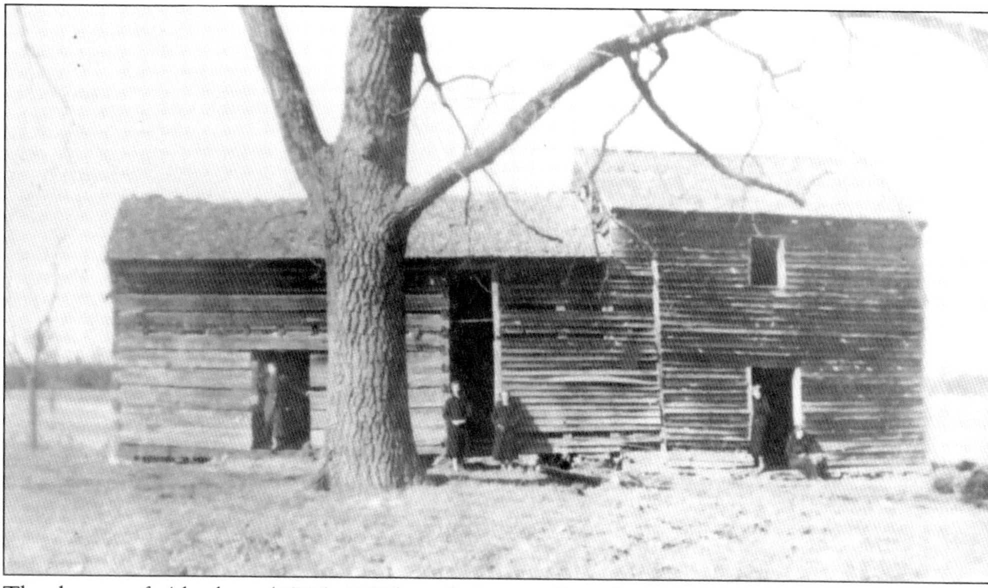

The home of Absalom (1795–1875) and Amitta Poindexter Matthews (1811–1886) near Smithtown. In the early nineteenth century families would add on to a basic log cabin as their numbers increased. Absalom and Amitta married in 1830 and had a large family. The log part of the house on the left may predate their marriage. The house was passed down in the family and was later known as "Uncle Frank's Place." (IMR)

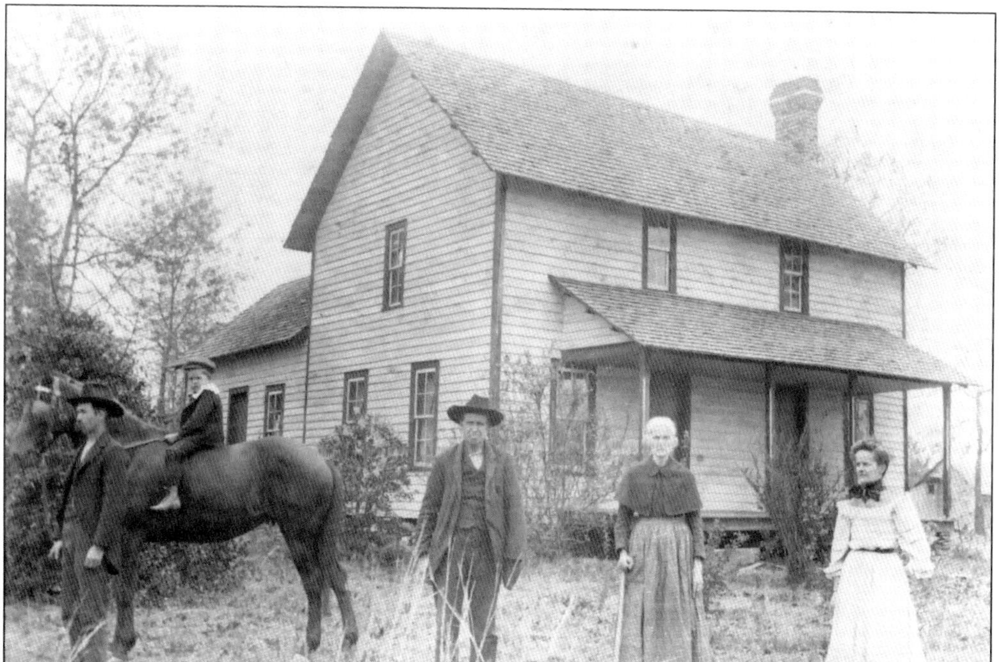

The William Fleming house was built about 1897 in the Smithtown area. The group pictured here includes: Robert L. ("Bob") Matthews; Joe Matthews (on the horse); William Fleming and his wife, Frances ("Frankie") Fleming; and their daughter, Annie C. (Fleming) Matthews, the wife of Bob Matthews. Annie and Bob were married in 1899. (IRM)

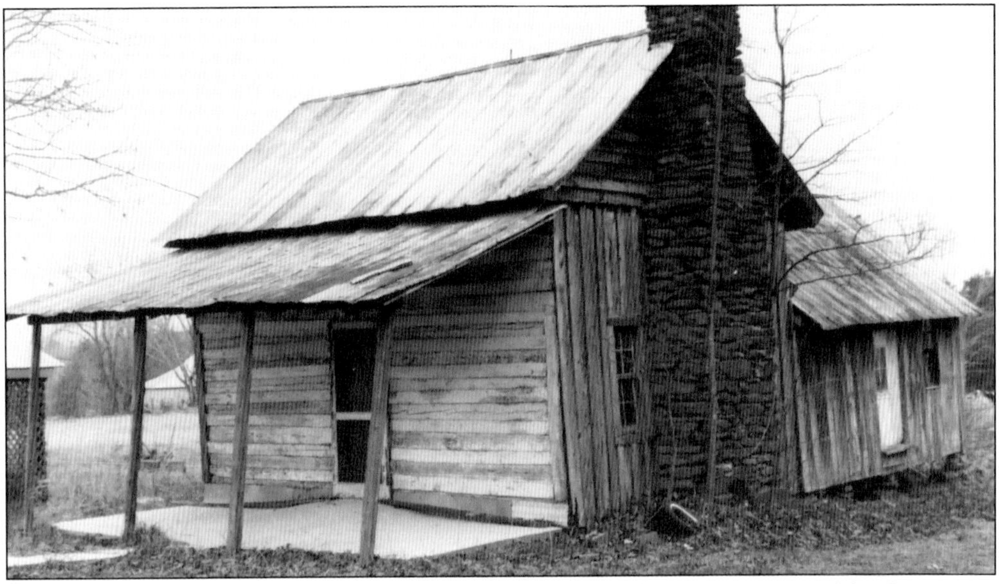

The Thomas Lee Casstevens home, built about 1897, housed three generations of the Casstevens family. It is a one-story log house with a sleeping loft. One of the original dry-laid, fieldstone chimneys is still standing. Lee married Alice Melton in 1895, and raised a large family here. Their son, John Dalton Casstevens, and his wife, Truler (Weatherman) Casstevens, lived in the house, and their children were born here. "Dalt" raised tobacco and ran a dairy. He built a two-story brick house nearby in 1946. (LW)

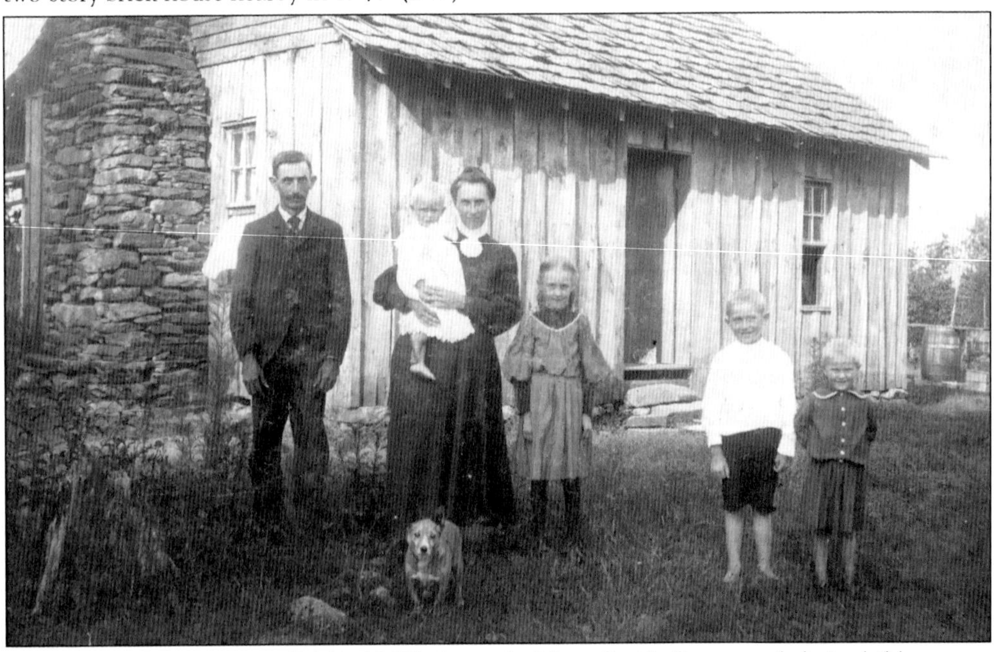

Reverend Robert L. Speer (1869–1950), his wife, Mina Smith Speer, and their children pose in front of the Cartwright home in 1907. The house may have been near what was once called "Hinshaw" and the site of the old Cartwright cemetery. The Speer children are: Lillie (beside her mother); Arvil; Callie; and baby Howard. The dog's name was not noted. Note the shingled roof, the rock steps, and the rain barrel at the corner of the house. (AS)

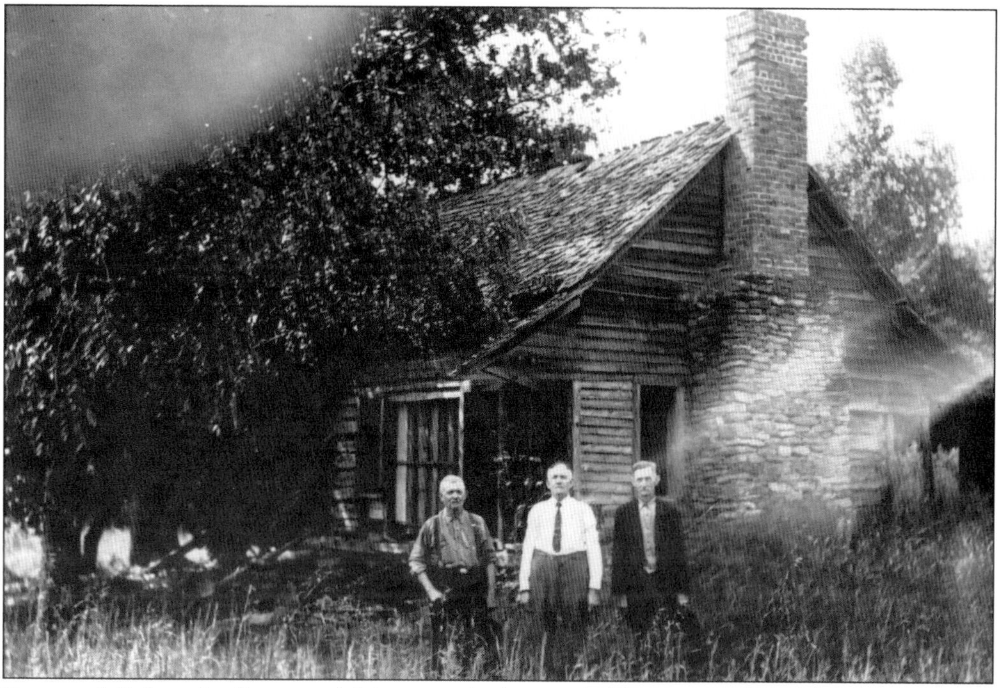

Reverend Robert L. Speer and his sons, Arthur and Clinton, at the old Sylvester Speer homestead near the Speer graveyard. This house was sold about 1879 by Sylvester T. Speer, who was sheriff of Yadkin County from 1862 to 1865, and county commissioner in 1870. The early Providence Methodist Church was located near this house. (AS)

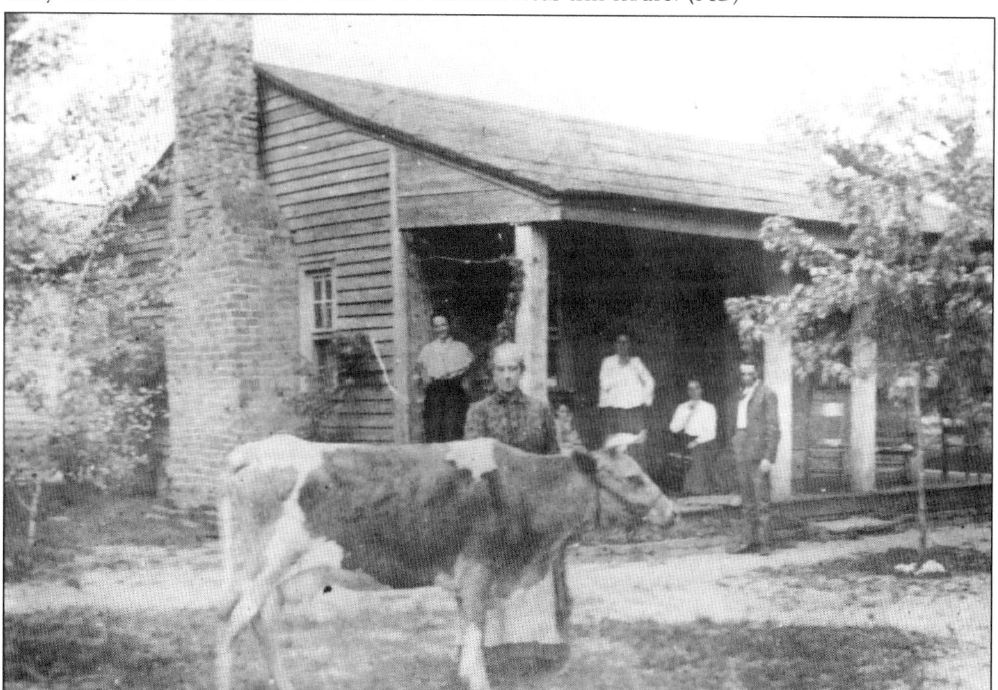

A c. 1899 photograph of the house that Sylvester ("Vet") Speer bought "on the branch near Bob Holcomb place." It was probably off Haire Road, near Yadkinville. (AS)

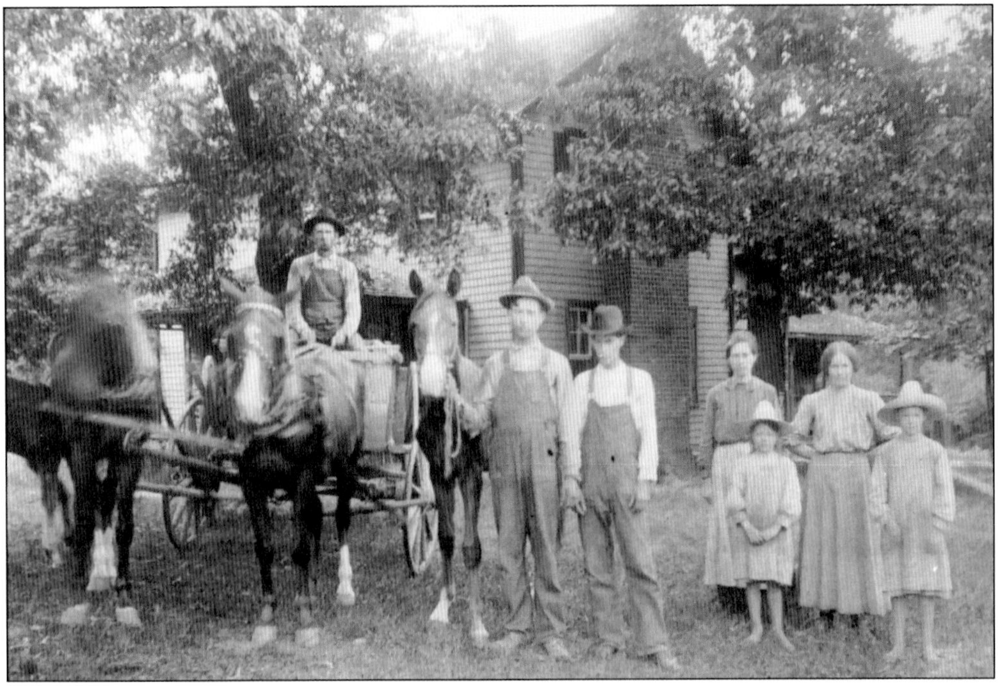

The Ben Shore homestead on Old Stage Road was built in 1870. The men in this 1912 photograph have been cutting wheat. They are: Leander Grant Allgood (on the wagon); John Glenn Allgood (holding the horse); and Pinnix Shore. The women are, from left to right: Turnie (Allgood) Shore; Sarah (Allgood) Reavis; Mucie (Allgood) Hoots (at the back); and Lelah (Allgood) Reavis (the larger child). (JA)

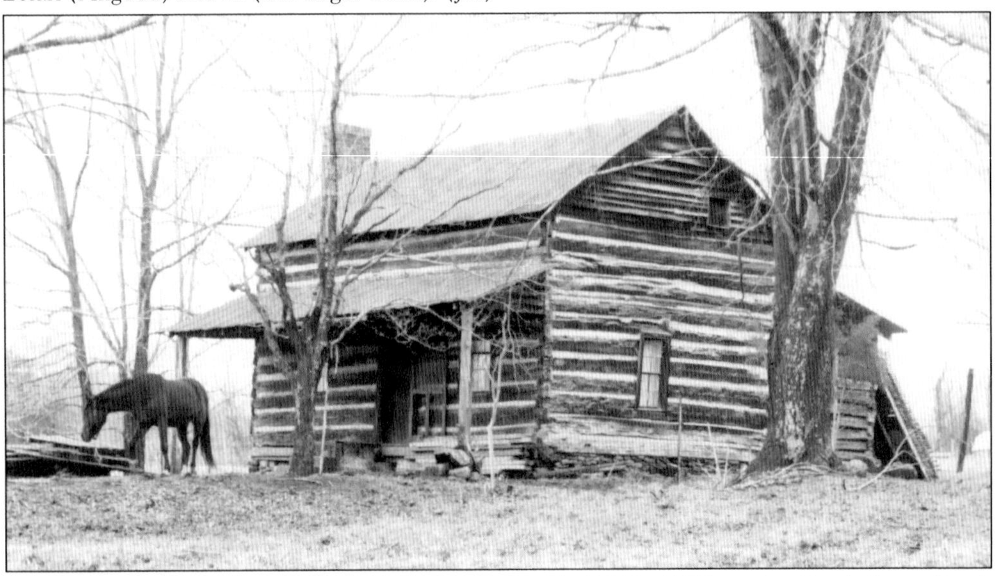

The Gough-Reynolds house was built by James Gough (1810–1878) in the South Deep Creek area about 1830. An earlier log house (dating from about 1794) that belonged to James' father, Thomas, stood nearby. The Gough-Reynolds house was near a spring and close to Spiker Creek. It was later occupied by Ephraim A. Reynolds (1862–1918) and his wife, Emma Steelman Reynolds (1860–1954). The house was restored by Weymouth Allgood several years ago. (LW)

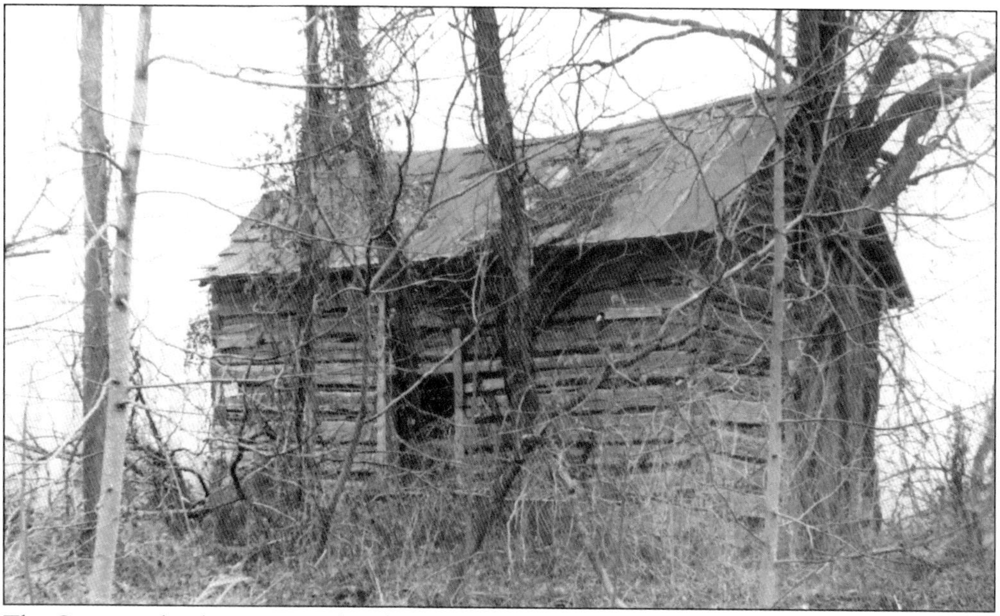

The Sizemore log house sits a few feet off Highway 601 about 2 miles north of Yadkinville. Louise Sizemore lived there in the early years of the twentieth century. Although she only had one eye, she wove rugs on a loom. Her brother John, who was a cobbler, had a house across the present road. Another brother, Bill, also had a large house which sat across from the present Faith Fellowship Church. (LW)

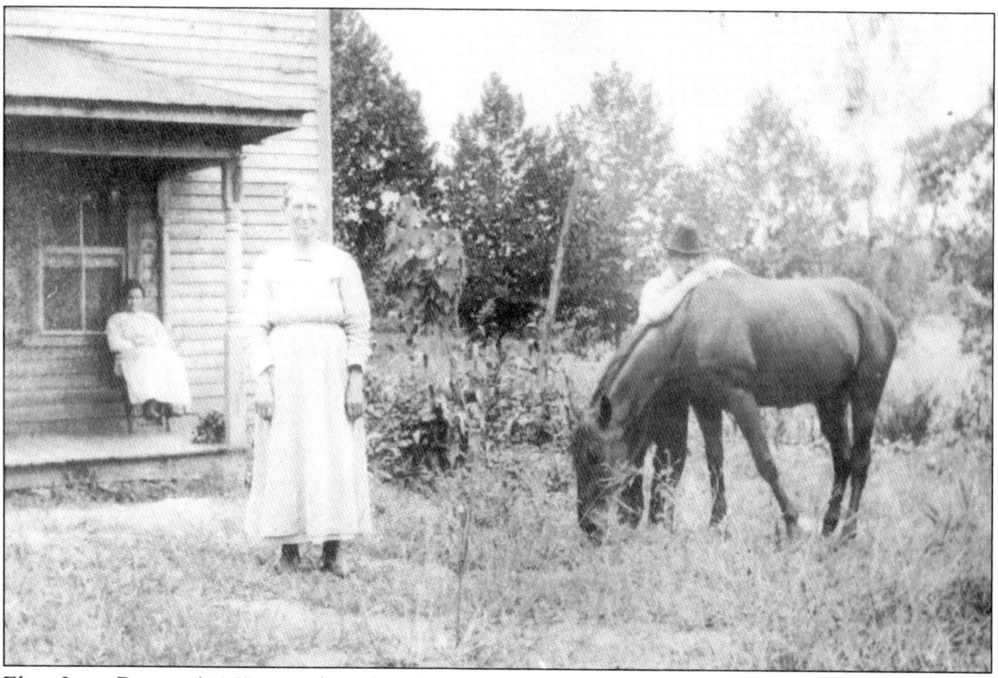

Eliza Jane Brown (1857–1918) and William Pleas Brendle (1847–1922), the parents of John Emory Brendle (1883–1965), are shown here outside the William Pleas Brendle homeplace about 1900. This house was located near North Oak Ridge. (LBH)

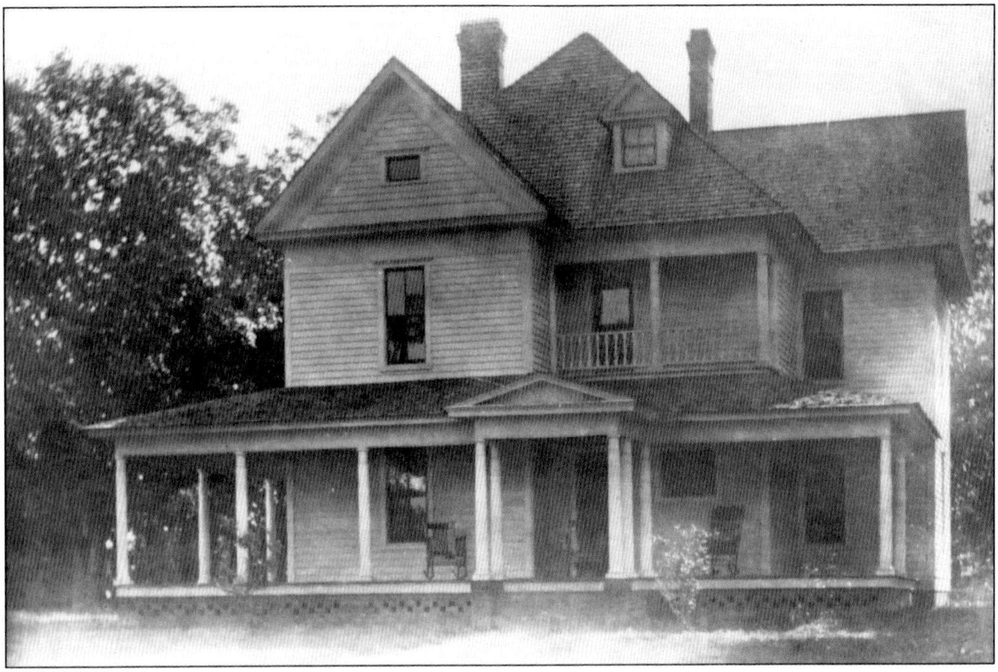

The home of Reverend Franklin and Ollie Carter Warden was located near Deep Creek Friends Church, where Warden was the minister. It was typical of many houses built between 1900 and 1920. It burned in 1942. (RW)

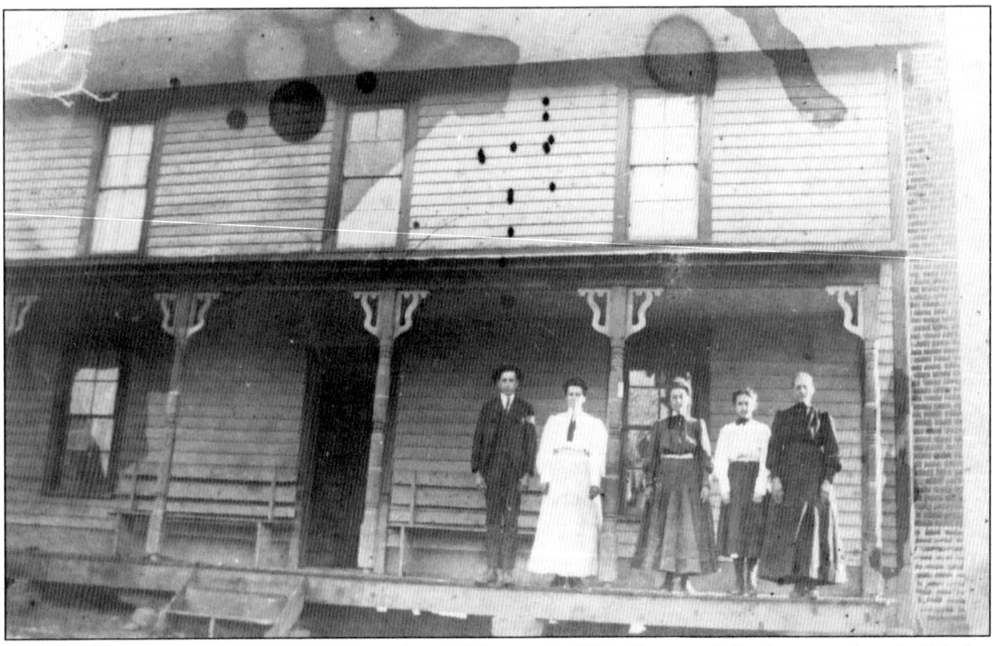

This was the Carter homeplace from the 1880s until 1976. Some of the logs used to build the house were rolled from the nearby Holcomb-Carter brick house. The house was later enlarged. This photograph, taken about 1910, shows Mary Ellen (Carter was her maiden name also) Carter (at the far right) with her children. From left to right are Thomas Andrew Carter, Roxie Rodena (Carter) Adams, Annie "Dusty" Carter, and Mary (Carter) Hanks. (WC)

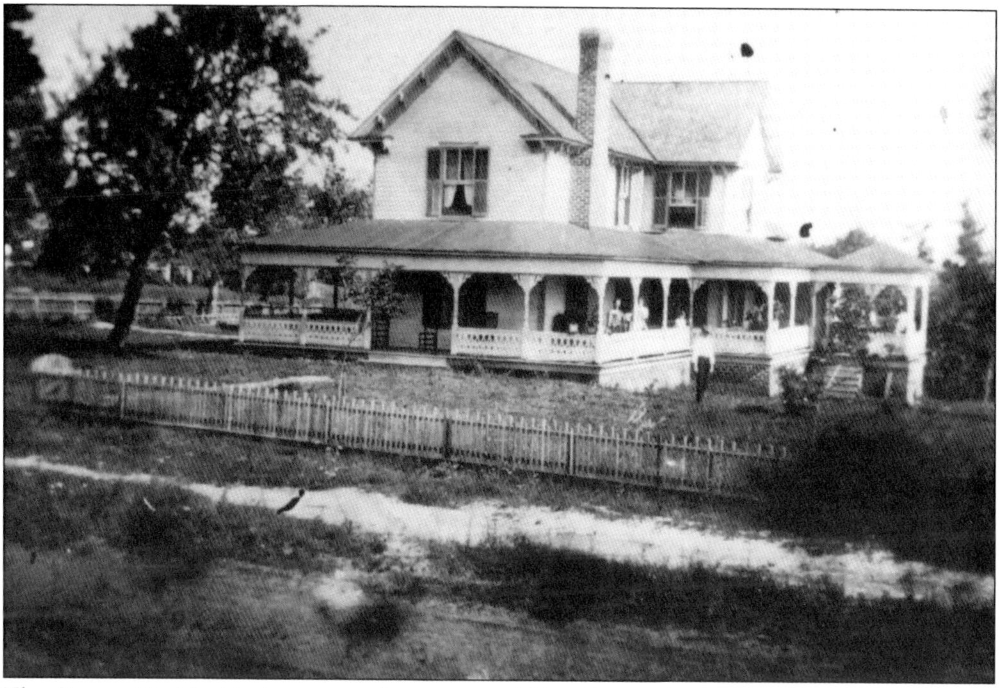

The Henry H. Mackie house, at the corner of Van Buren Avenue and Virginia Drive in Yadkinville, as it appeared *c.* 1900. Mackie was a Yadkinville merchant. He died about 1923. (DMcL)

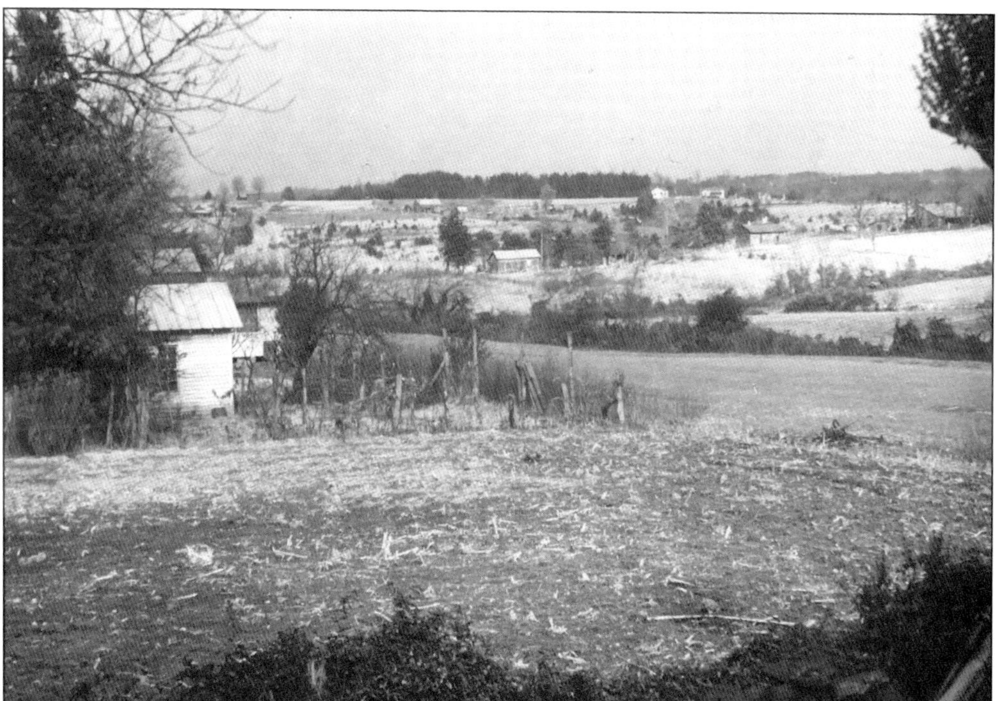

The black community homes on the north side of Yadkinville, as seen from in back of the Garner house on Highway 601. (EGS)

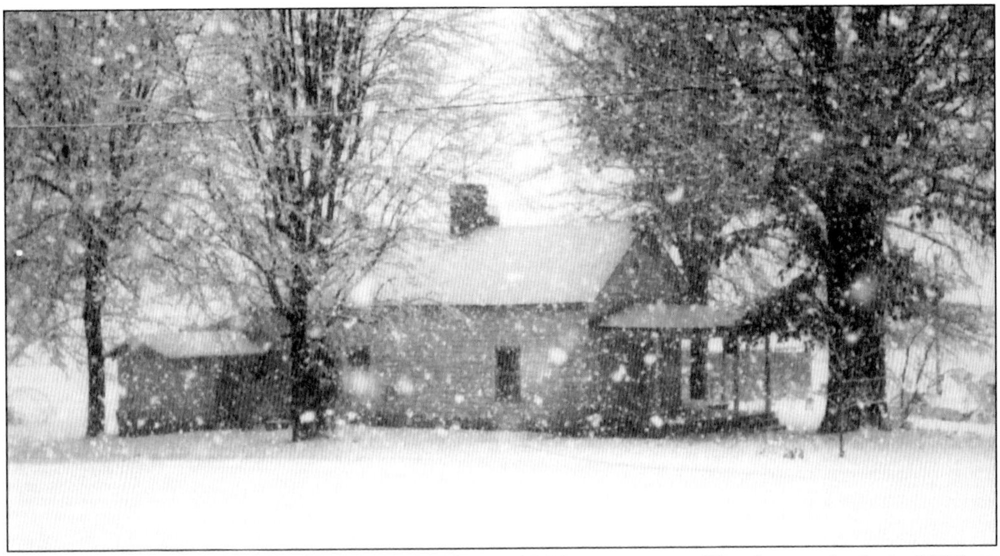

The John Henry Hauser Jr., home pictured in a 1986 snowstorm. The house, built in 1913, is located south of Yadkinville on Highway 601. (VS)

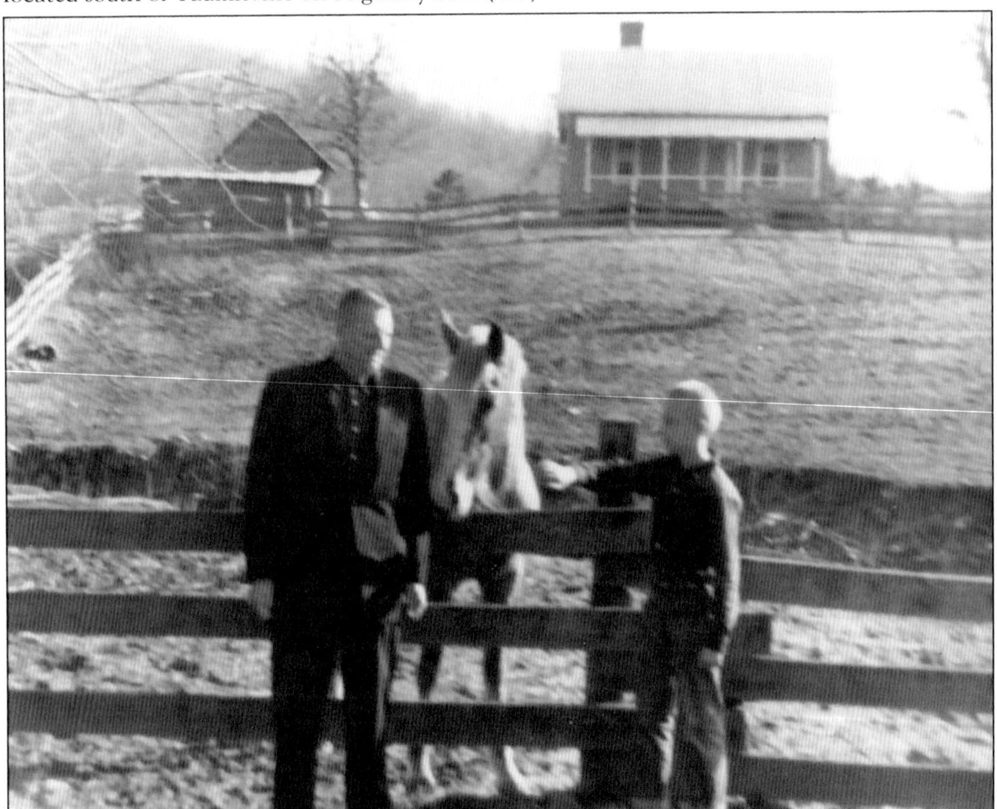

The childhood home of Edna (Bray) Reece on Center Road near Star Peak. Edna was born in 1905 to John L. and Lela Finney Bray. In the foreground of this photograph are Richard H. Parsons and his son Ricky. An ash hopper, used in making lye soap, once stood behind the house. (EBR)

Four

A Penny Saved
Agriculture

Historically, agriculture has played a major role in the economy of Yadkin County. Farm families grew practically everything they needed, from rye, wheat, oats, corn, flax, fruits, and vegetables. Cattle, chickens, and hogs provided meat, eggs, butter, and milk. Excess produce was traded at the neighborhood store for items that could not be made or grown.

Tobacco, once the main cash crop, was a year-round job. Beginning with seeding plant beds in February, the young plants were transplanted to the fields in May. Priming (harvesting) and curing occurred from July through mid-September. In the fall months the tobacco was removed from the sticks on which it had been cured, and tied into "hands." The hands were sold locally to plug tobacco factories, traded to merchants, or hauled to markets outside the county to be sold at auction.

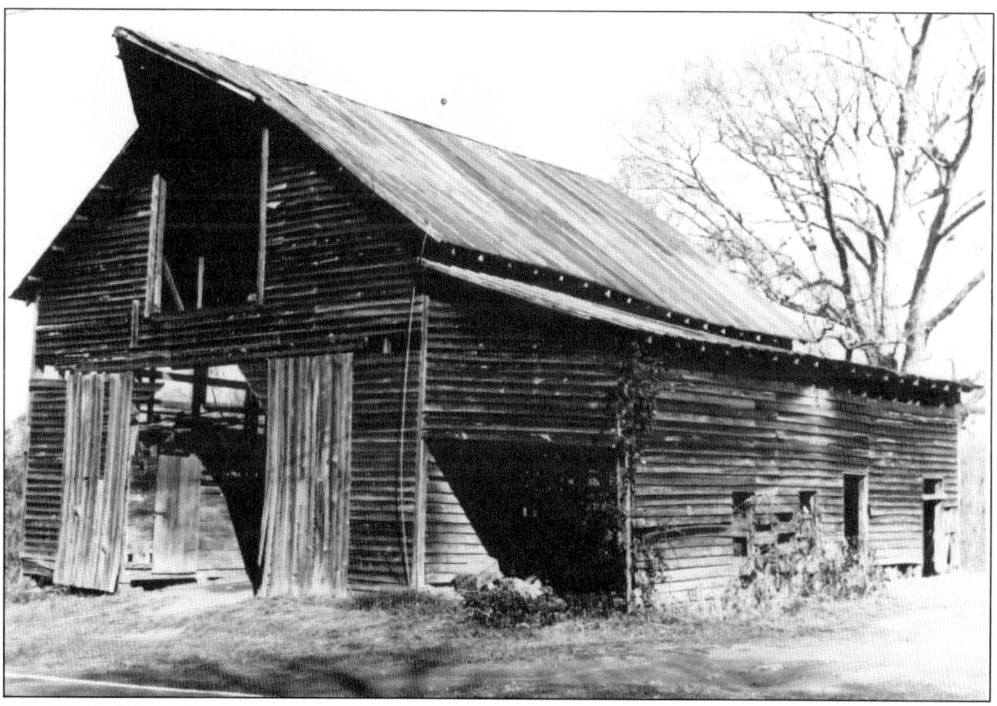

The Noah Myers barn, near Courtney, was typical of many barns throughout the county. It was large, with stalls for animals and an upstairs hay loft. The tractor could be parked in the shed on the side. (LW)

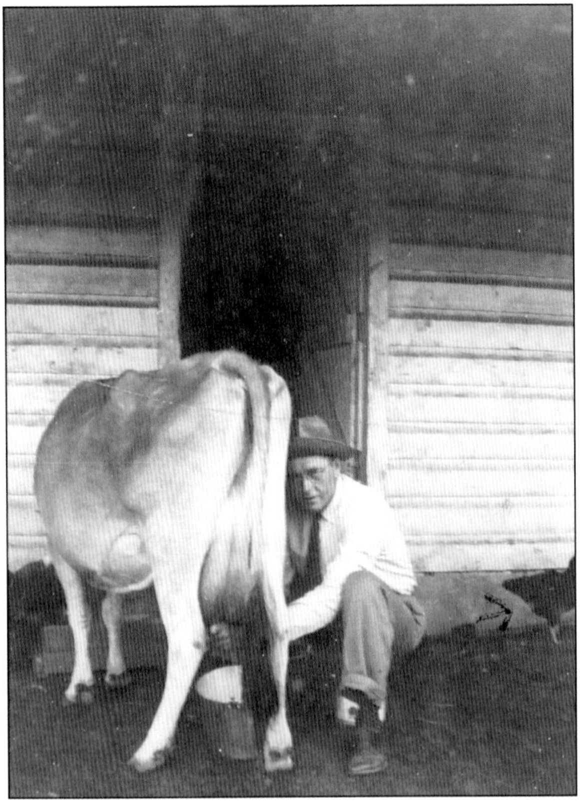

Wendell Hinshaw is milking a cow, a chore that had to be done even on Sundays. (LBH)

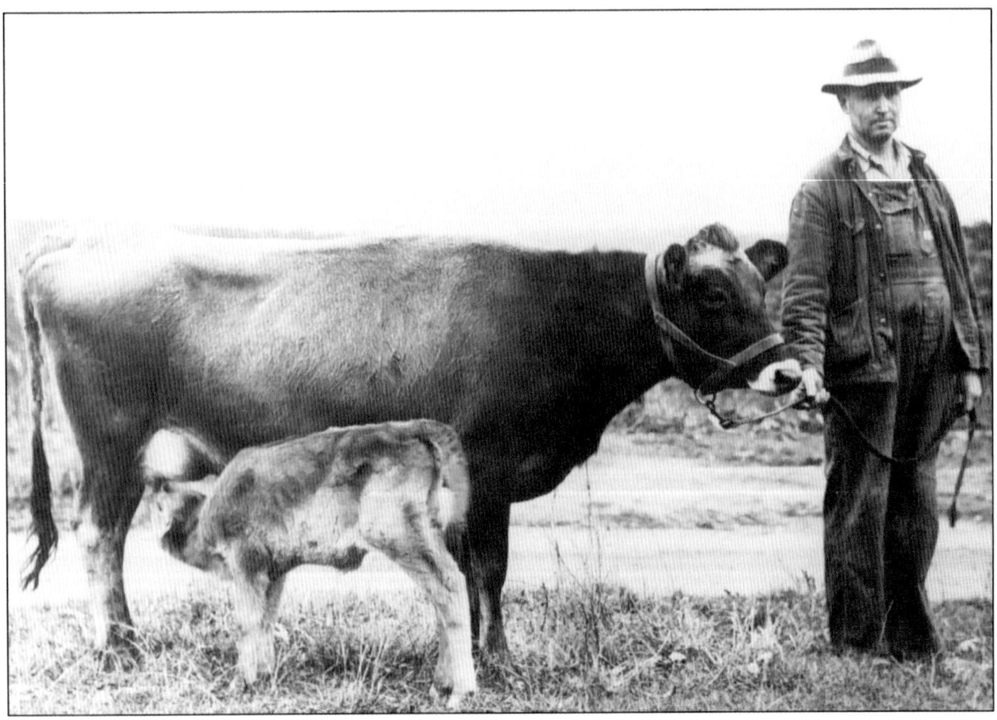

Luther Shore pictured with a cow and her calf in 1945. (MMS)

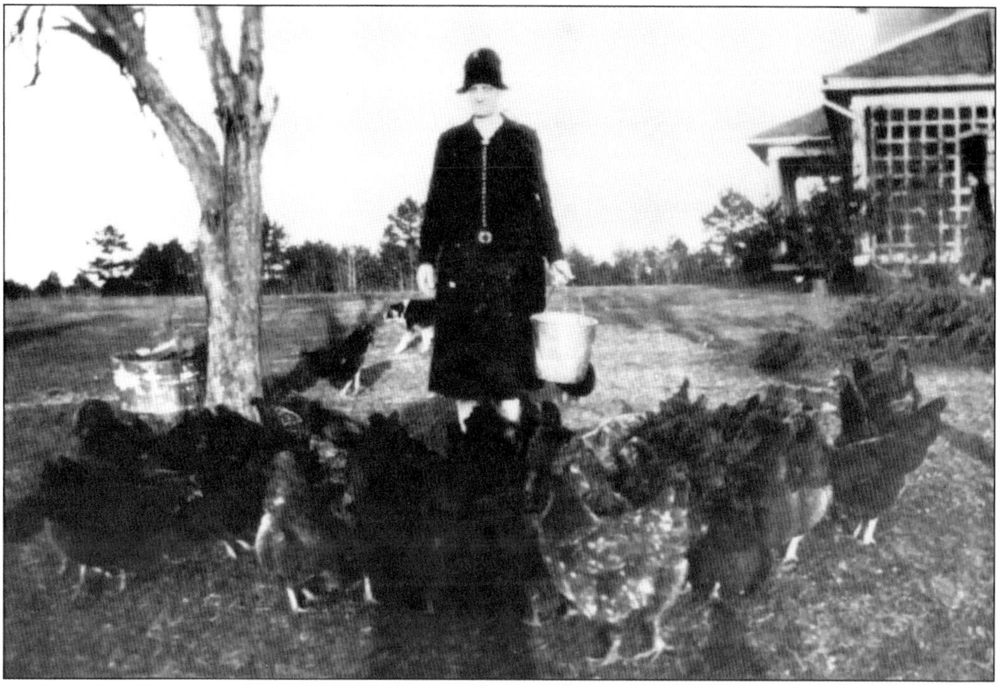

Feeding the chickens was usually a woman's chore. Ella Davis Doub, who lived near Baltimore Church, is shown here feeding her Rhode Island Reds. (MDL)

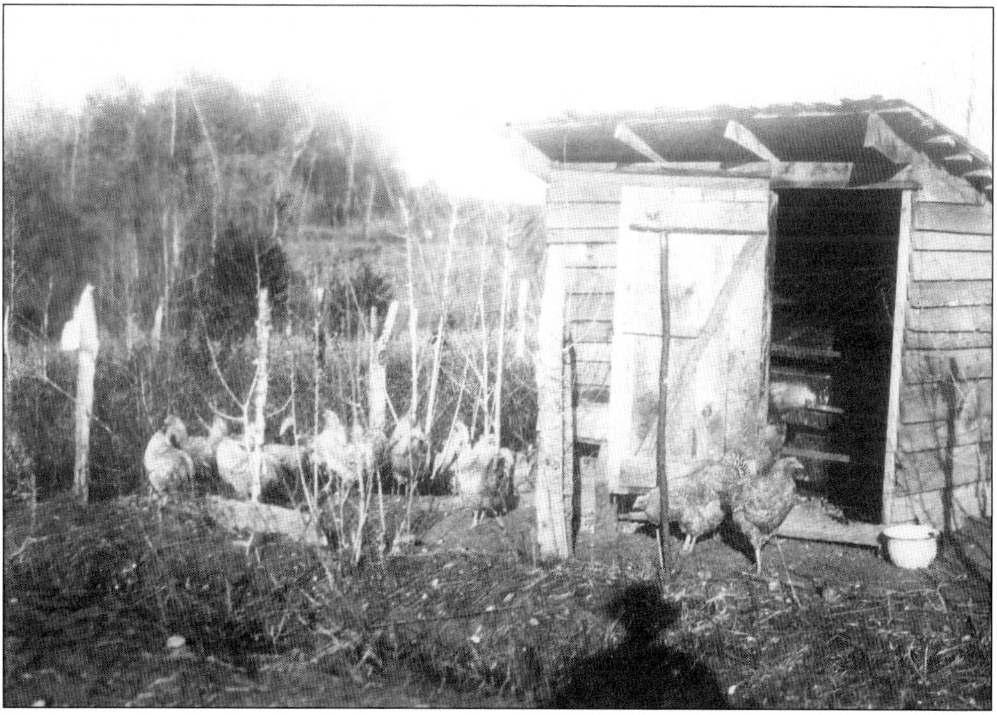

While some families let the chickens wander around the yard, others, such as the Shermer family, had a chicken house. The fenced enclosure in this *c.* 1920 photograph was to protect the chickens from predators such as foxes. (MSP)

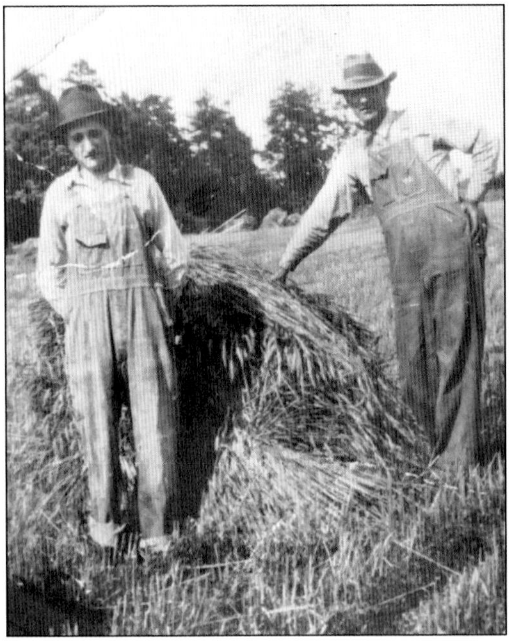

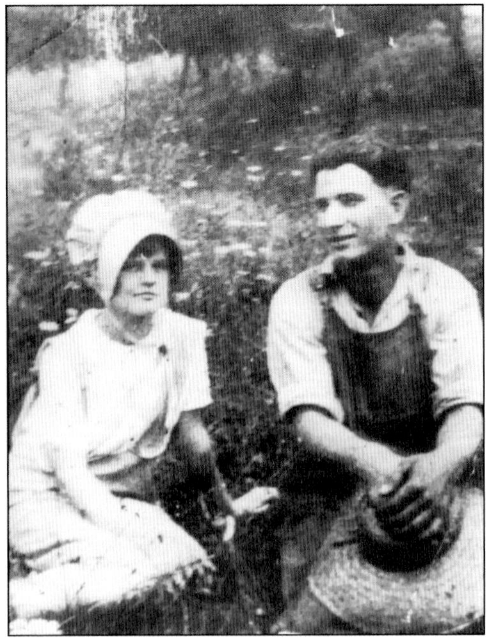

Left: Tom C. Hauser and his father, John Henry Hauser Jr., had just finished cutting wheat when this photograph was taken in the summer of 1937. (VS)
Right: Valena Jolly and Worth Brown are taking a break from work. Note the bonnet and straw hat: standard headgear for farming in the late 1920s. (EM)

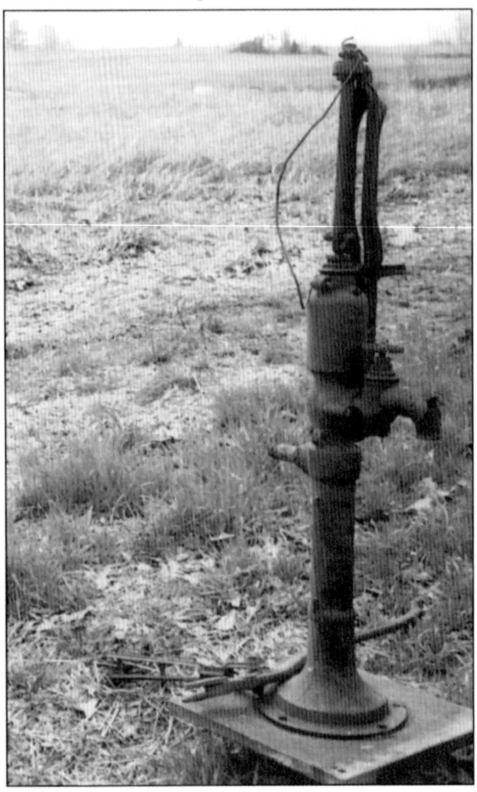

An old water pump stands idle beside a winter field. (CDC)

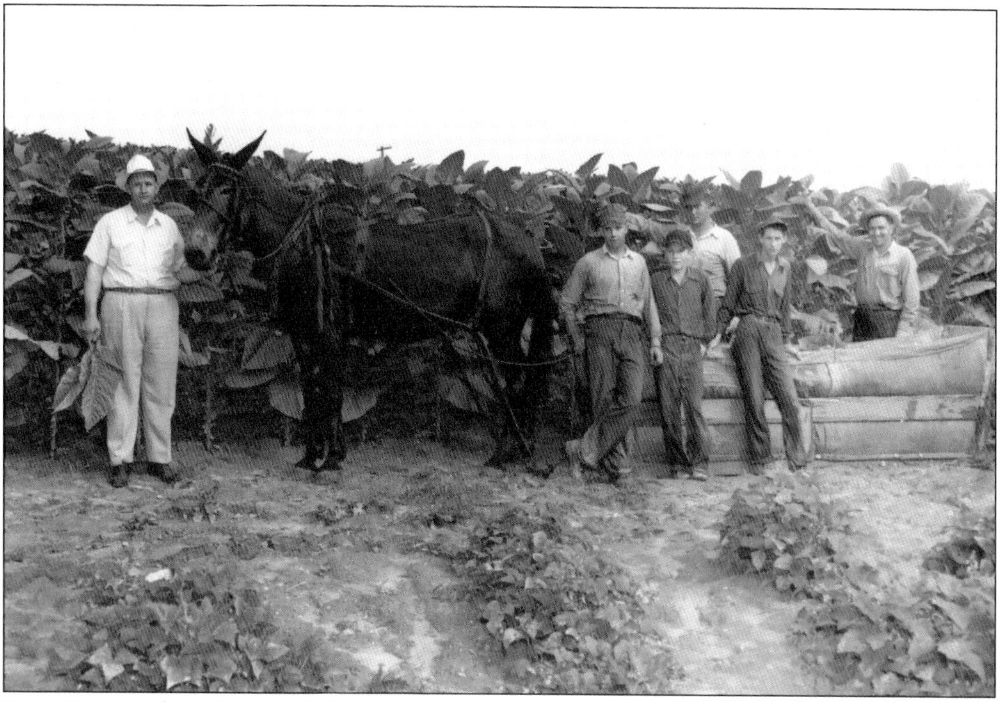

Troy Davis and a tobacco priming crew stop to have their picture taken. The mule pulled the homemade sled that carried the primed tobacco. When full, the sled was taken to the tobacco barn, where the tobacco would be tied on sticks and hung in the barn for curing. (LW)

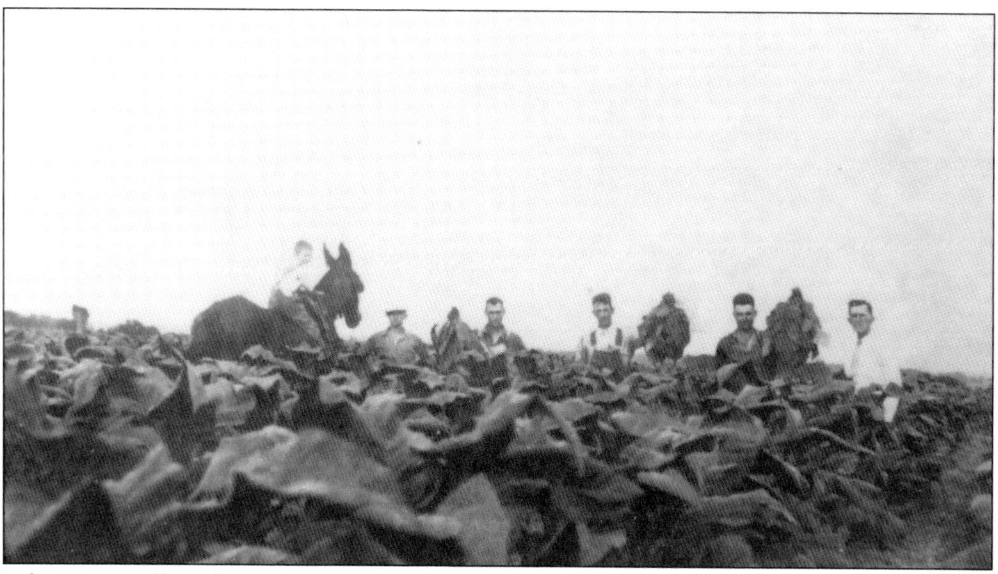

Life was not all work and no play for this youngster, who was allowed to ride the mule as his father primed tobacco. (MLH)

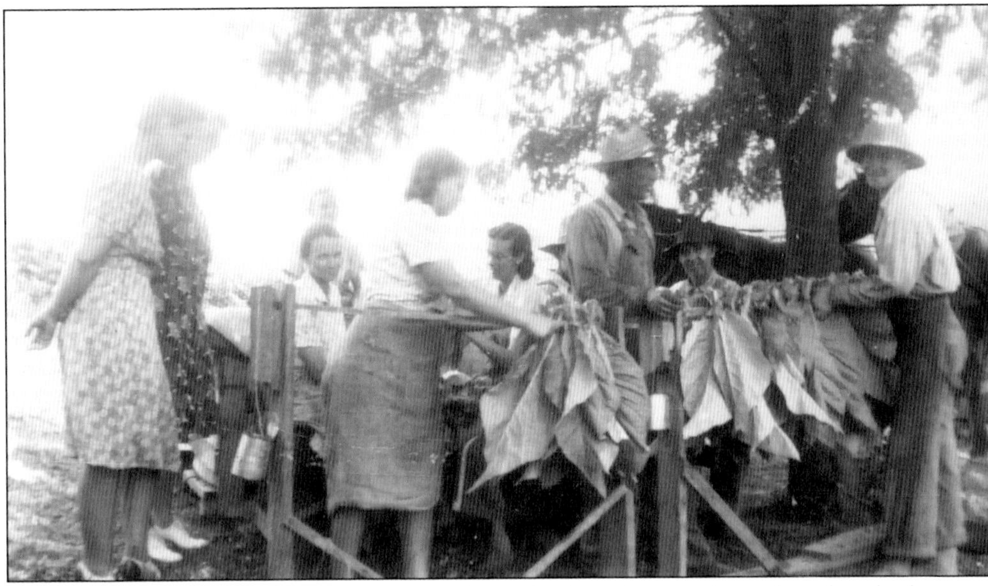

Some visitors watch tobacco being tied on the sticks. It took several people to hand tobacco to a fast stringer. (EBR)

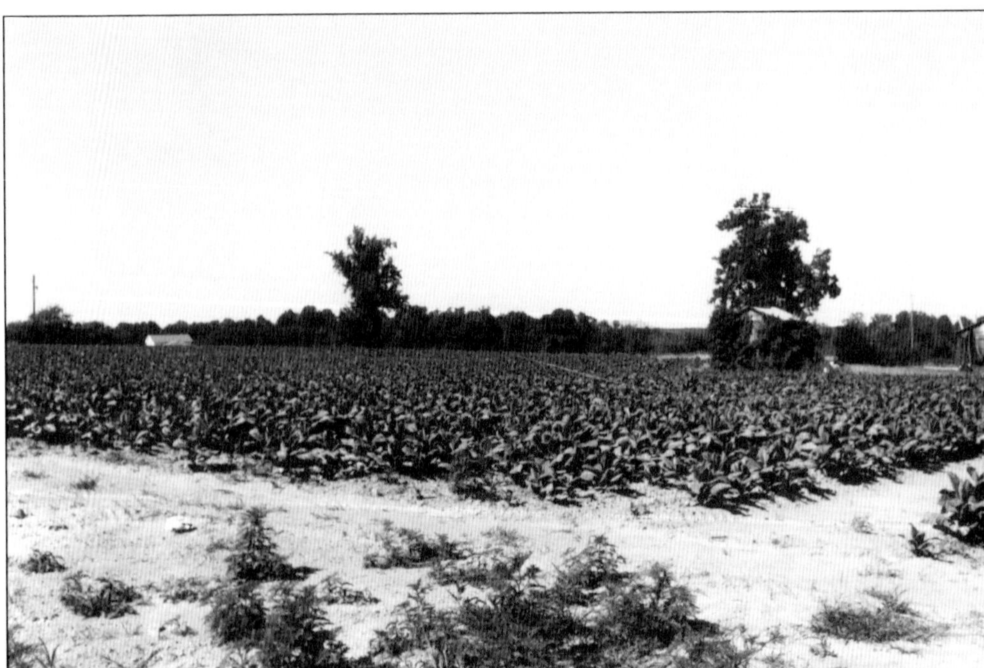

An old tobacco barn sits in the middle of the tobacco field near Yadkinville. Pilot Mountain is barely visible in the background. (FHC)

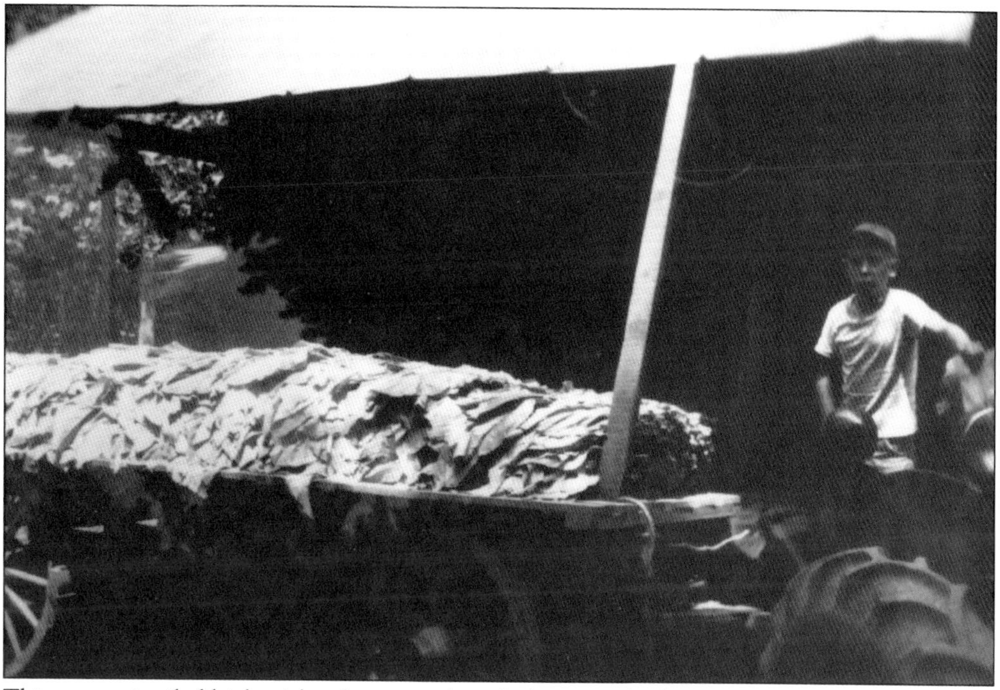
This wagon is piled high with tobacco ready to be hung in the barn and cured. (EGS)

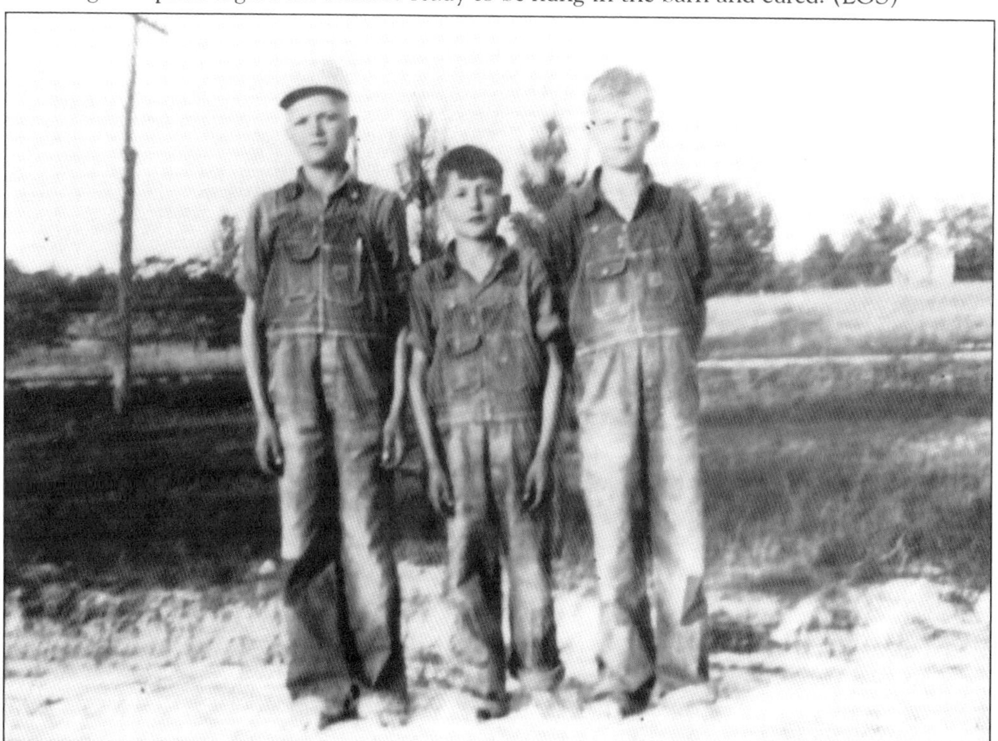
The sons of Thomas Andrew and Allie C. (Speer) Carter are shown here c. 1936. From left to right are: Thomas Ray, Frank Locksley, and Pinkney Lee C. (Speer) Carter. (WC)

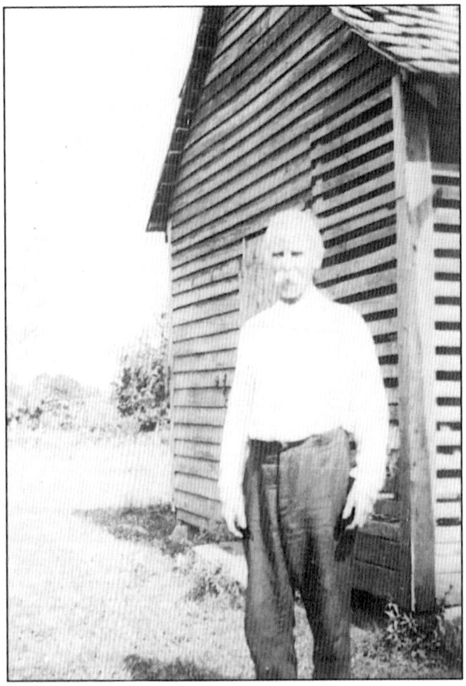
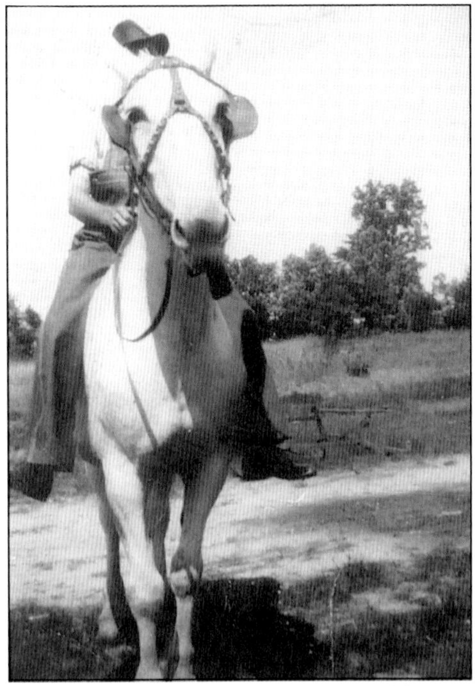

Left: Samuel E. Joyner stands in front of his corn crib at the old Joyner homeplace on Old Stage Road about 1935. (VC)
Right: Tom C. Hauser rides bareback on an old white mule. (VS)

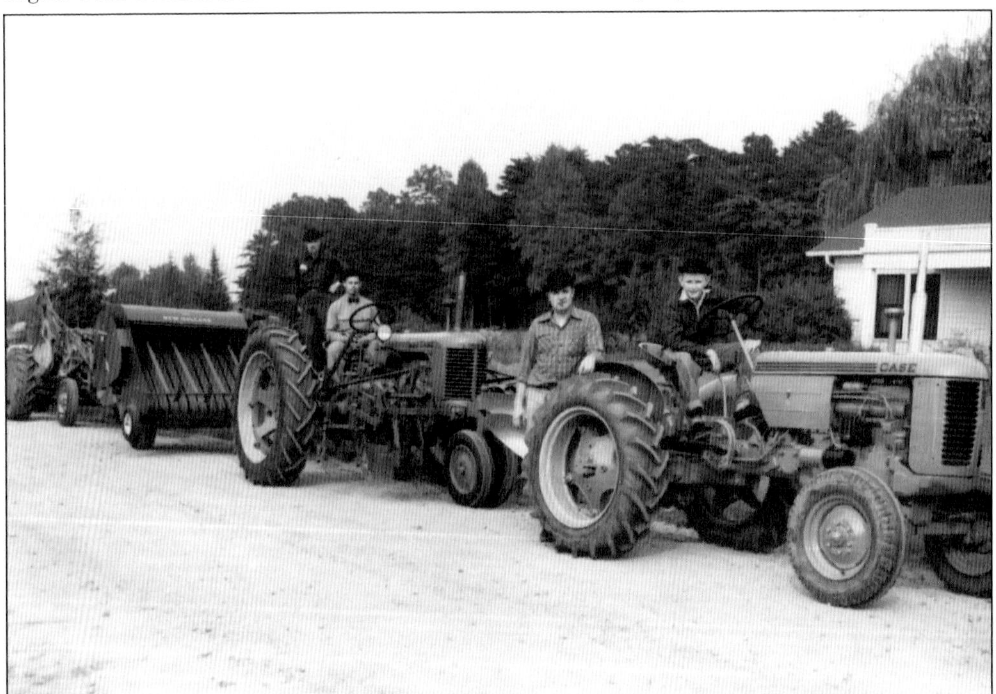

The latest in farm equipment was displayed in a parade during the 1950 Yadkin County Centennial Celebration. J.D. Welborn sits on the Case tractor at the far right. (SO)

Five

FROM LITTLE ACORNS GROW

Business and Industry

Gristmills, taverns, and general stores were among the earliest businesses in Yadkin County. Some early industries, such as mining and iron and gold smelting, were short-lived because the extraction of ore became too expensive.

Advances in transportation brought new businesses and industries such as gas stations and automotive repair shops, but these same advances were also responsible for putting ferry operators, blacksmiths, wheelwrights, and buggy manufacturers out of business.

Tobacco farming created several spin-off businesses in Yadkin County, such as plug tobacco factories, tobacco basket factories, and a company that employed women to put strings in the little cotton sacks used to hold smoking tobacco.

At one time every family made their own clothing from flax, cotton, or animal skins. Today, the spinning wheel and the loom have been replaced by factory processes.

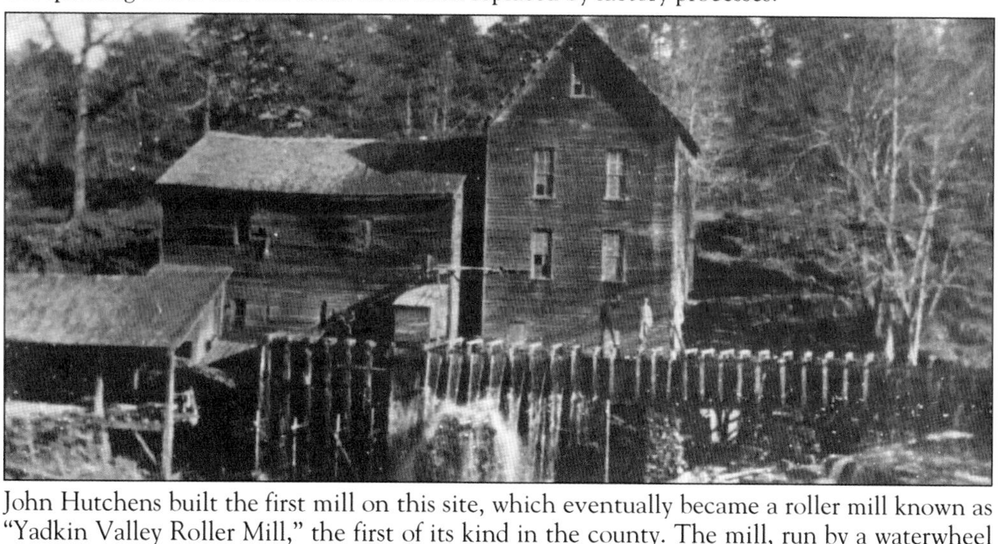

John Hutchens built the first mill on this site, which eventually became a roller mill known as "Yadkin Valley Roller Mill," the first of its kind in the county. The mill, run by a waterwheel powered by South Deep Creek, was purchased in 1891 by Benjamin and Isaac Shore, and in 1931 it was acquired by Joe Styers. Some of the millers were Abe Dixon, Evan Shore, Ike Willard, and Johnny Shore. The last owner was N.P. Bryant. The race which carried the water to the wheel burst in 1949, and the dam across the creek washed out in 1956. This 1934 picture, taken from the north bank of the creek, shows Ike Warren and two unknown men. (BW, AB)

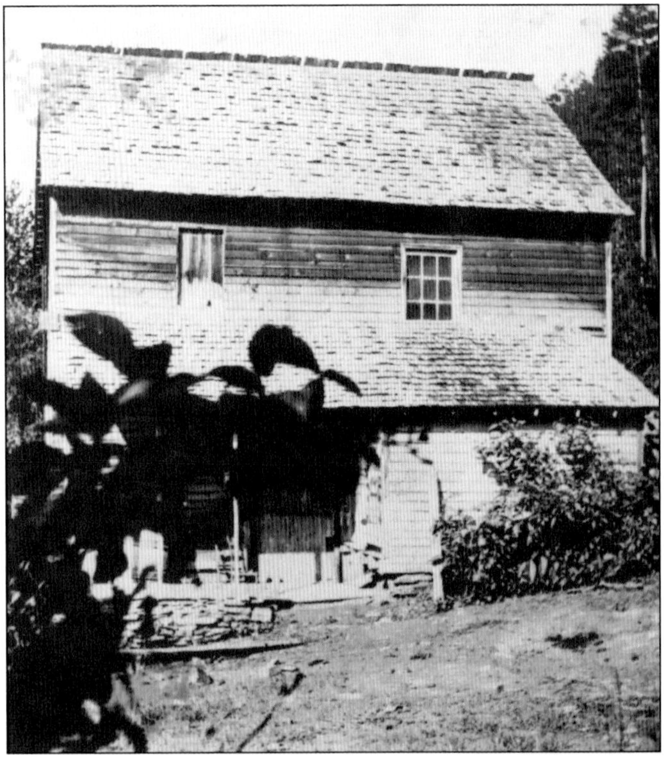

The T.C. Hauser Gristmill, built about 1837, stood near Swisher Creek, a half mile south of Yadkinville near Highway 601. The mill passed to T.C. Hauser's son, John Henry Hauser Sr., who operated it for many years. (VS)

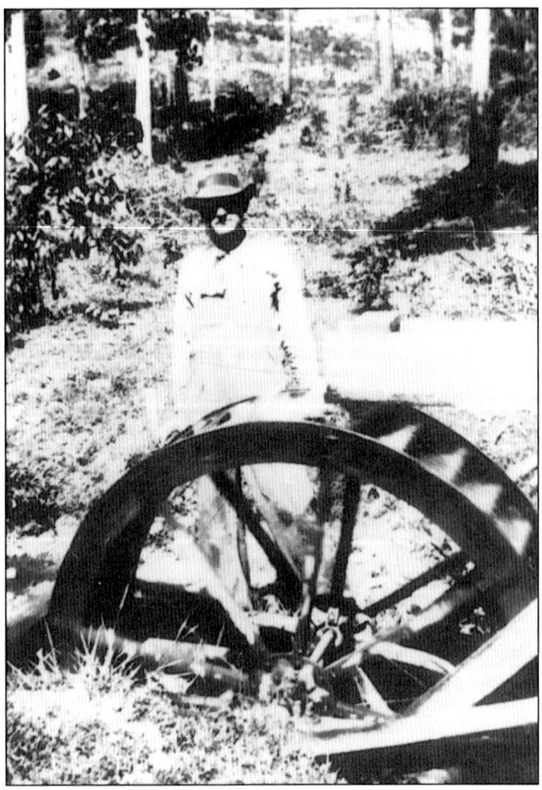

In this 1937 photograph, John Henry Hauser Jr. stands beside a waterwheel that was used to generate electricity for his home. These were the days before the REA brought electricity to rural areas. (VS)

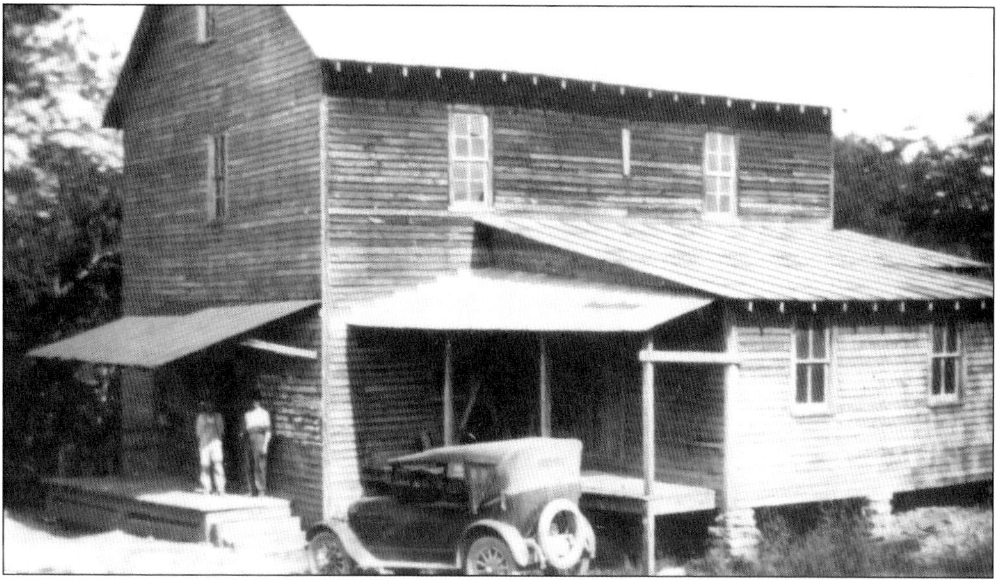

Vestal's Mill (sometimes called Potts' Mill) on South Deep Creek, as it looked in August 1925. The mill burned in the 1940s. (MC, LW)

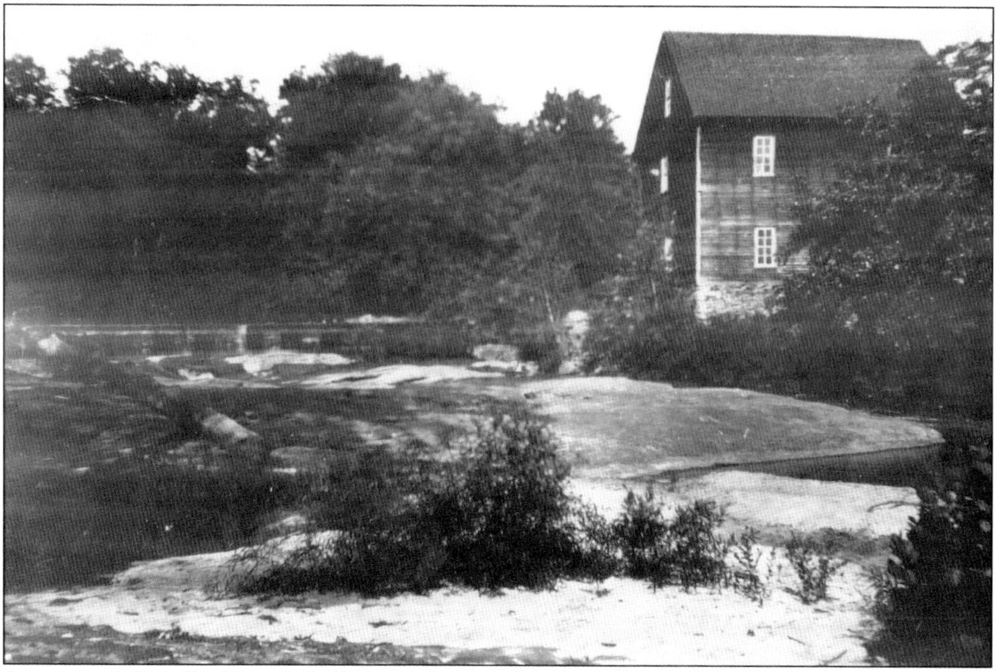

A view of Vestal's (Potts') Mill from the creek. The mill was originally built by William Davis. (AS)

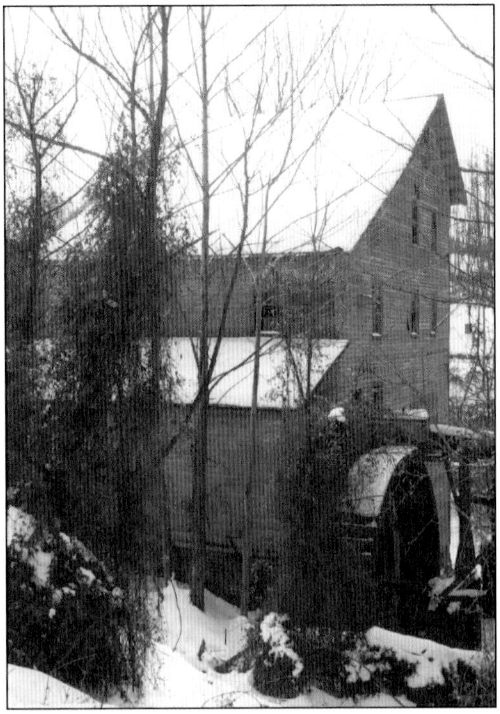

Butner Mill, near Flint Hill, also has a long history. A mill had been located on the site or nearby since the late 1700s. The mill was restored by Robert Allgood. (LW)

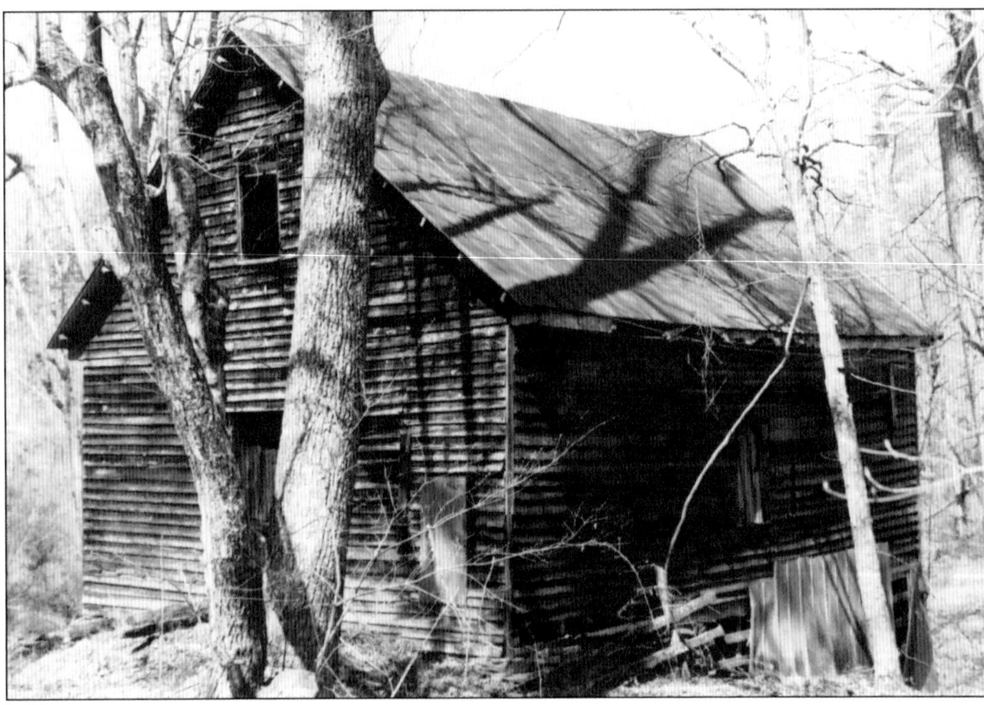

The Casstevens-Caudle Mill was probably established by John Casstevens (1779–1841), who passed it to his four sons in a will in 1840. A grandson, John Mecans Casstevens (1834–1903), ran it for many years and lived in a log house nearby. Lee Sprouse later acquired it, then Frank Caudle. The flood of 1940 destroyed the dam. (LW)

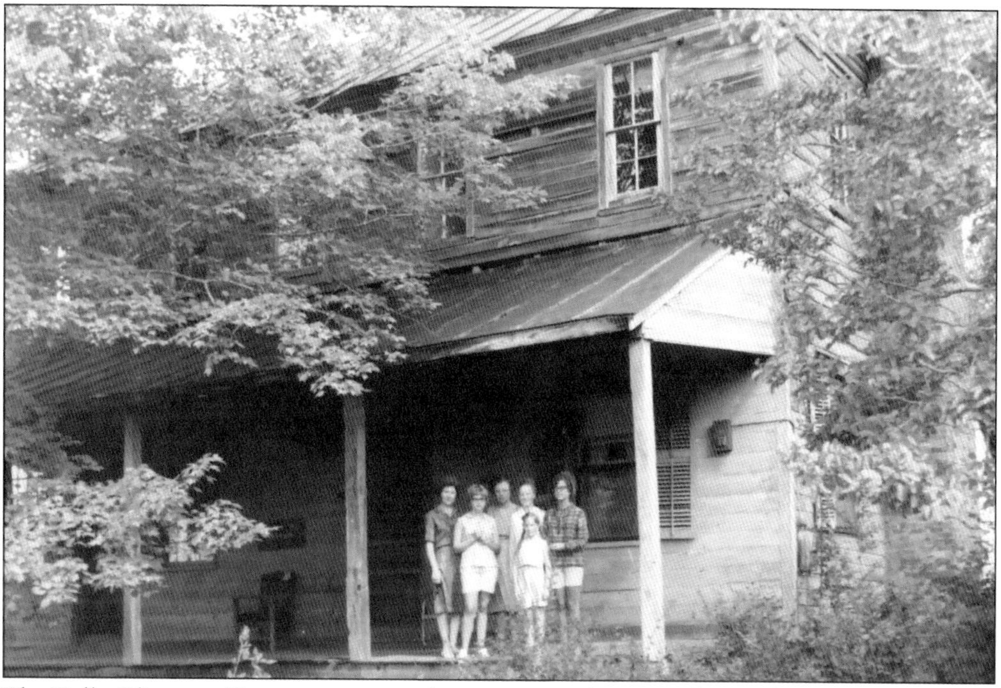

The Kelly-Clingman Tavern once served as a stagecoach stop and post office as well as a hotel and tavern. John Kelly ran it until his death in 1816. He also acted as postmaster. The tavern sits just outside the town of Huntsville on the Salem to Mulberry Fields Road, about a mile from the Shallow Ford. Mrs. Polly Wood, Ann Clingman, Judy Baity, and Barbara Sain are among those standing on the porch.

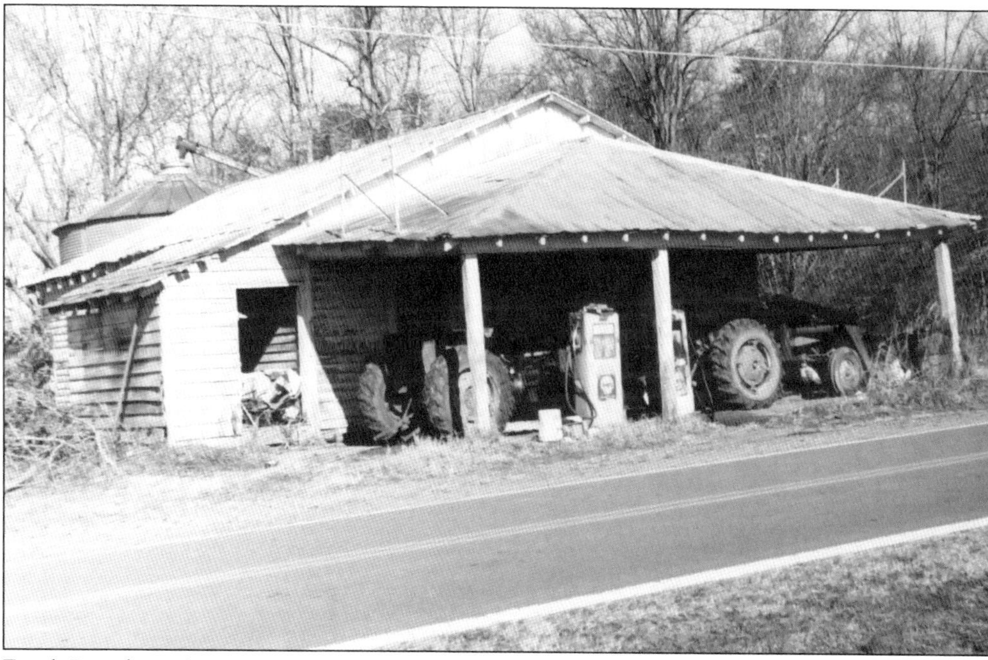

Frank Poindexter's store in Huntsville was typical of many country store-gas stations that dotted the county. (LW)

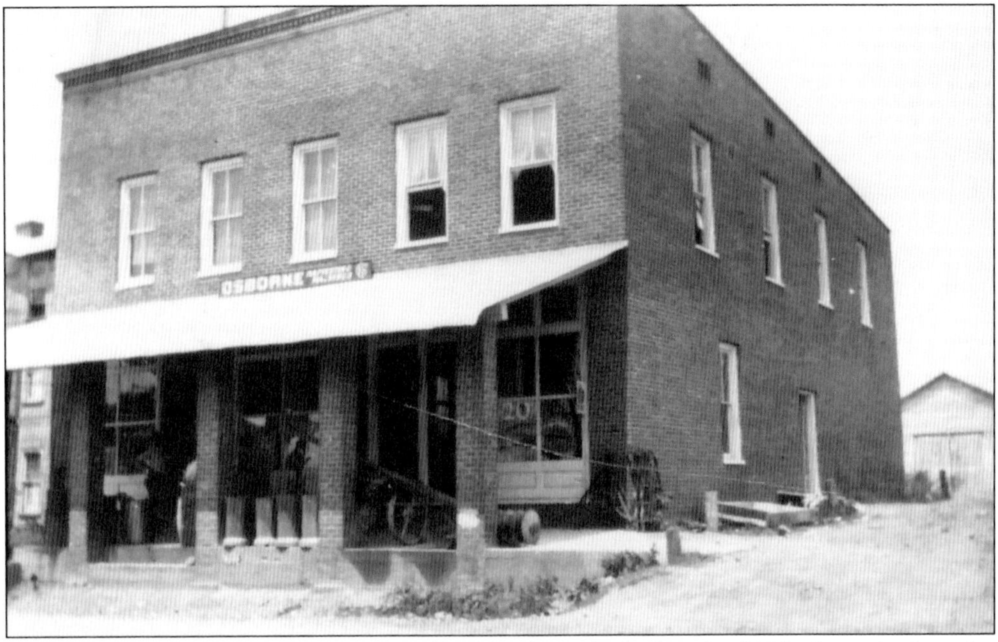

The Davis Bros. Store on Main Street in East Bend as it looked in the 1930s. It was built in the early 1900s. Rosebud (Morse) Garriott's dental office was upstairs. The store was reopened by John and Barbara Norman as a gift shop and old-time country store. (JN)

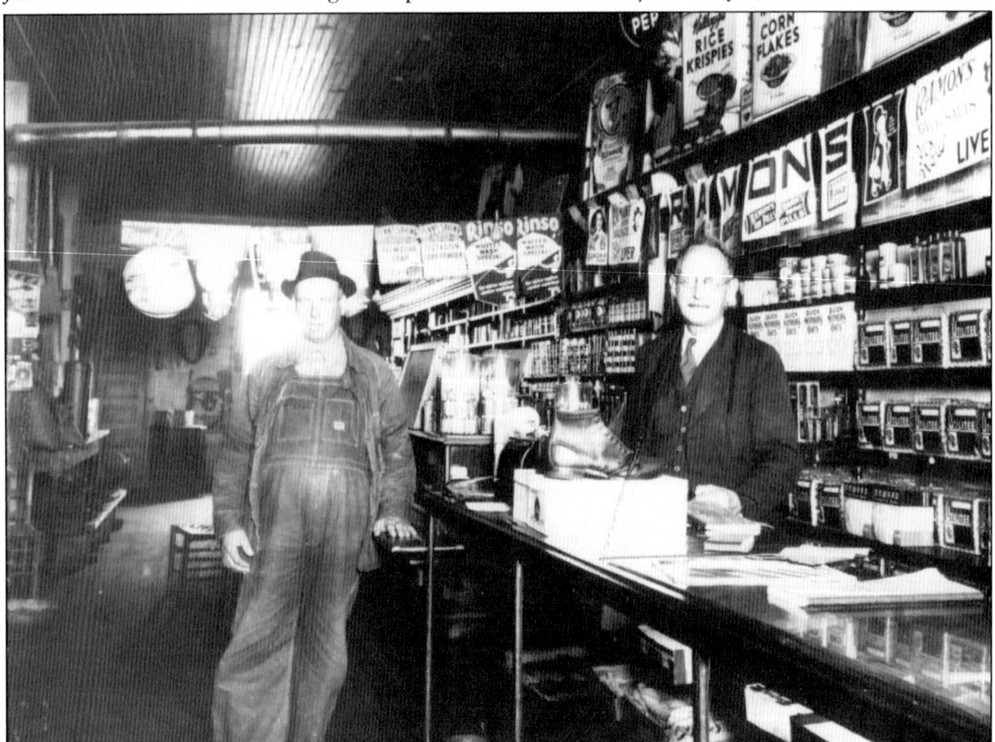

The interior of the Davis Bros. Store with one of the owners, Henry E. Davis, behind the counter. Note the items that are stocked for sale: they range from cereal to shoes. (JN)

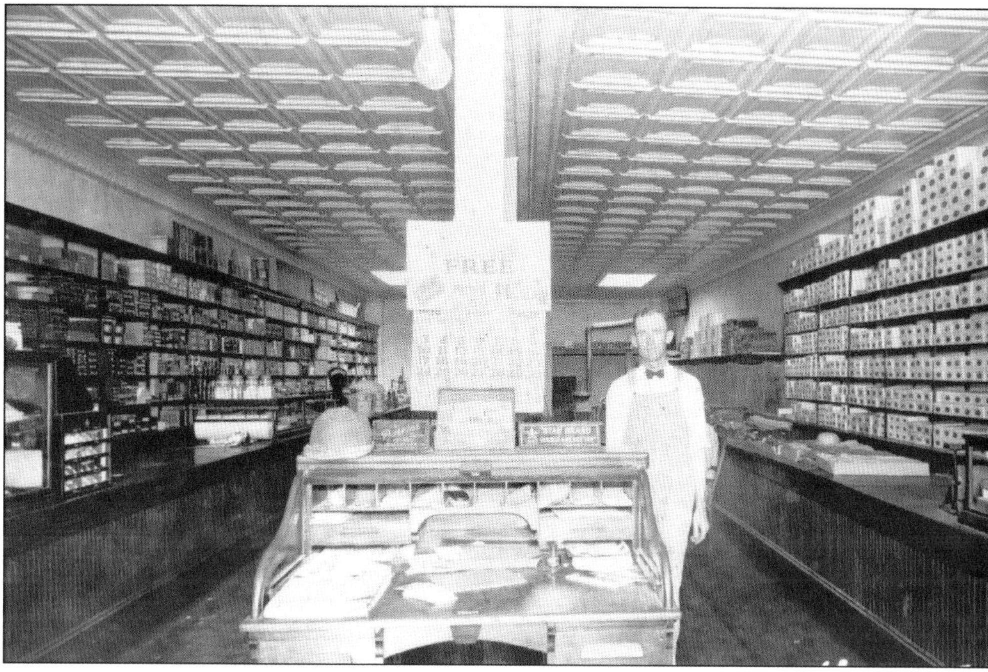

Arvil Speer working as a clerk in the J.H. Dobbins & Son, General Merchandise Store, in 1926. The store was located on the east side of the courthouse—Jackson Street—in Yadkinville. (AS)

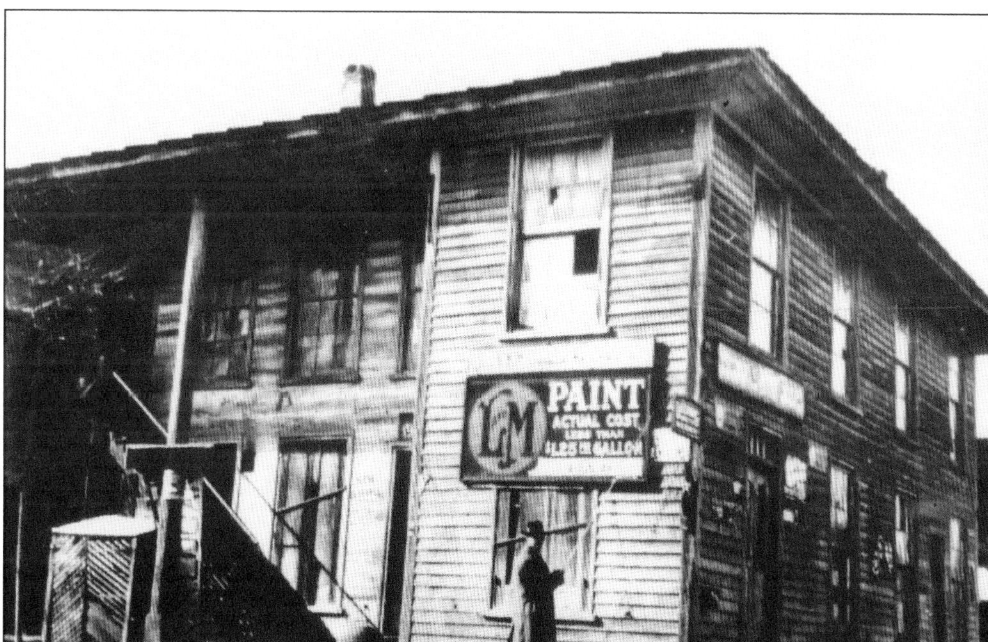

T.C. Hauser's (later J.A. Logan's) store was built by Hauser on the west side of the courthouse in 1853, when Yadkinville was first established. An interesting note found on this photograph states that the unidentified man is pointing to the "Lynch and Bitting bullet hole," a reference to some long-past event that has been forgotten. (LW)

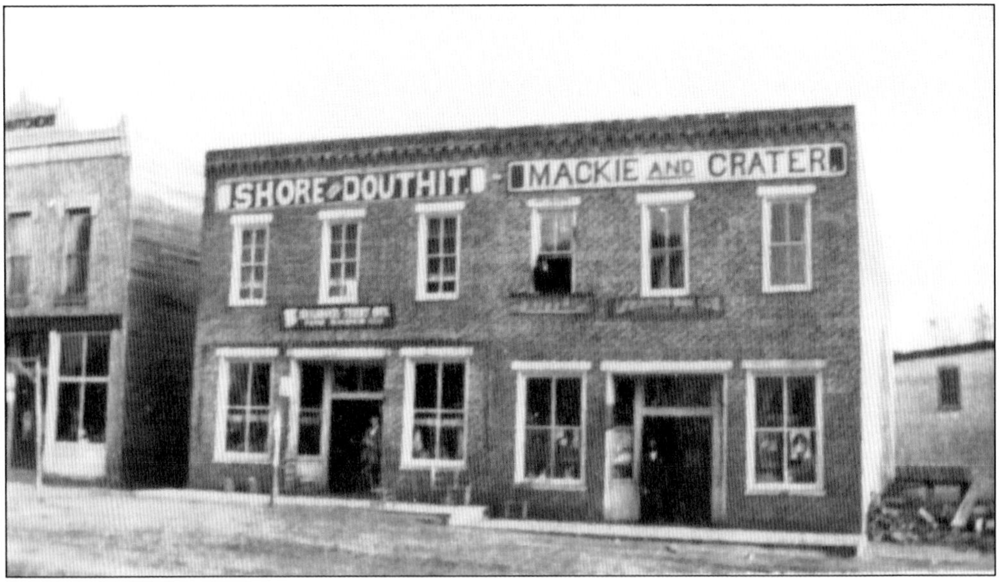

These store buildings on the south side of the courthouse—East Elm Street—still stand today. Originally they housed the stores of Shore & Douthit and Mackie & Crater. More recently, the one on the left was the John D. Holcomb & Son Store, and the one on the right, the law offices of Zachary, Zachary, and Zachary. Note the wooden "sidewalks" in this photograph. (HHM)

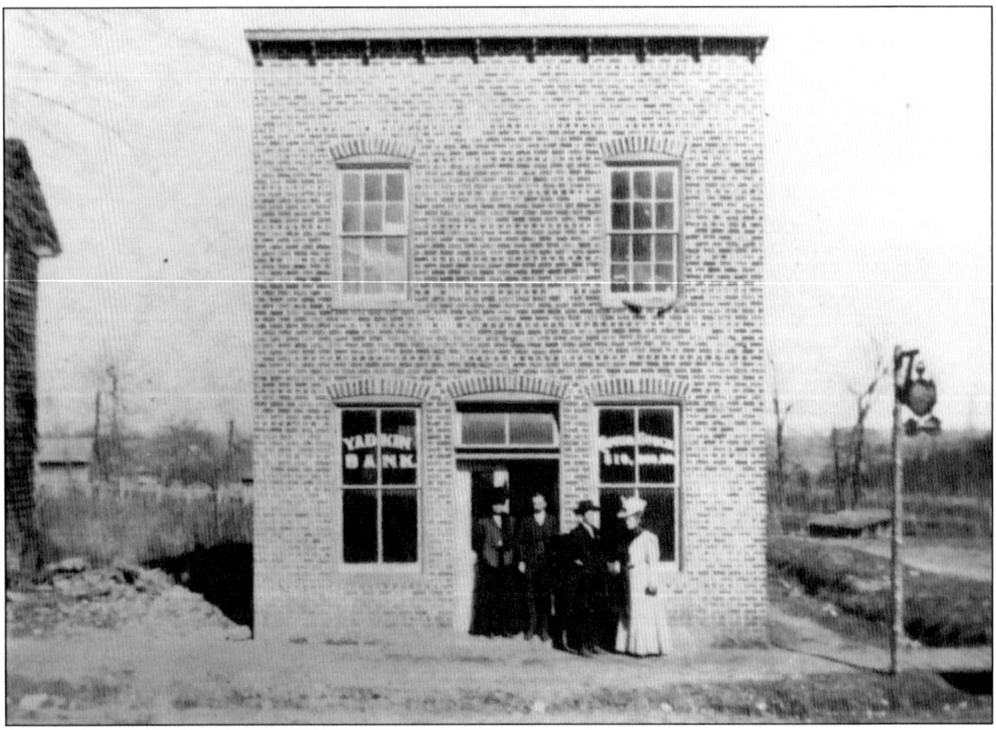

The first Bank of Yadkin building on the northwest corner of the intersection of Jackson and Main Streets in Yadkinville. Established in 1905 with John Q. Holton as the president, it was the first bank in the county. The building served as a bank until 1917, when the bank moved to new premises across the street. (HHM)

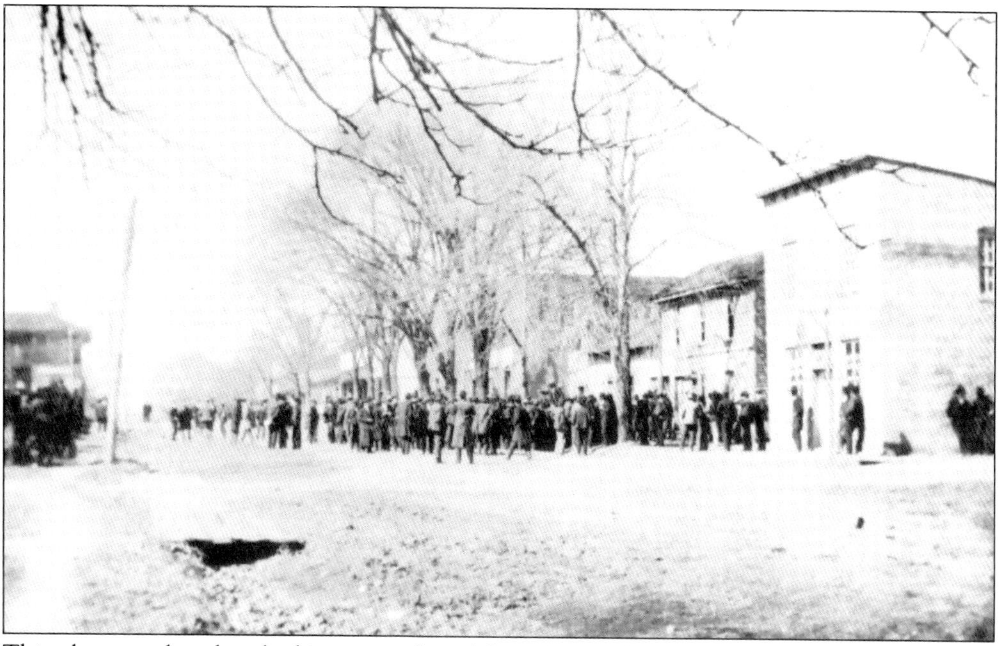

This photograph, taken looking west along Main Street, shows the Bank of Yadkin (the first building on the far right) and other early Yadkinville businesses as they looked about 1916. Note the unpaved street lined with large elm trees. (HHM)

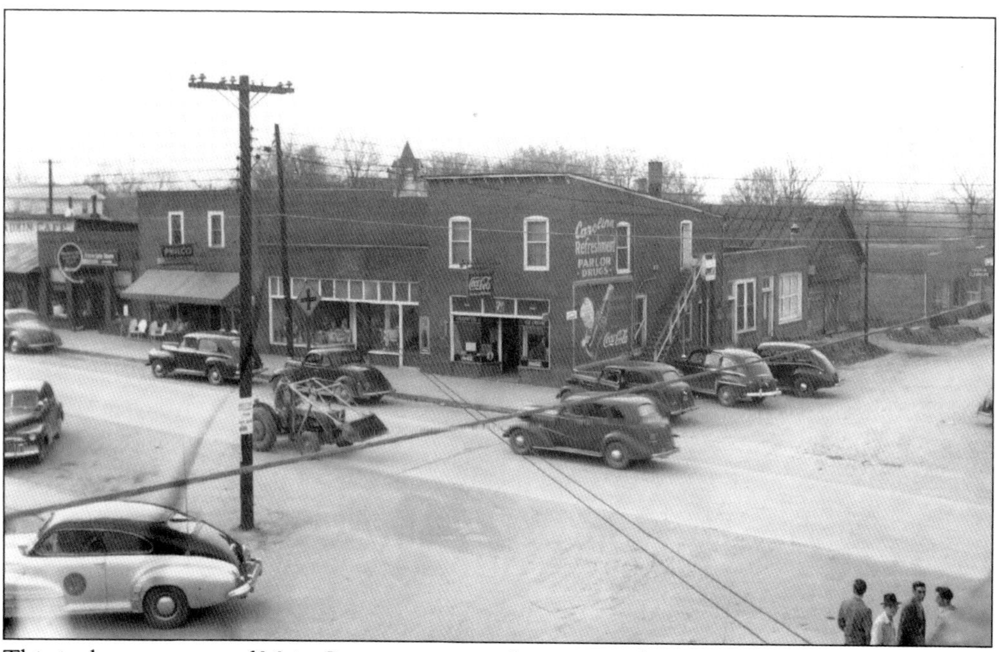

This is the same area of Main Street as seen in the picture above, but by the 1940s, the stores have changed. They are now the Yadkin Cafe, Western Auto, Brown's Department Store, and the Carolina Refreshment Parlor. Dr. Frank Walker's dental office was upstairs over the Carolina Refreshment Parlor. A Highway Patrol car is in the foreground. The steeple of the Yadkinville Baptist Church can be seen towering above the buildings in the center of the picture. (SO)

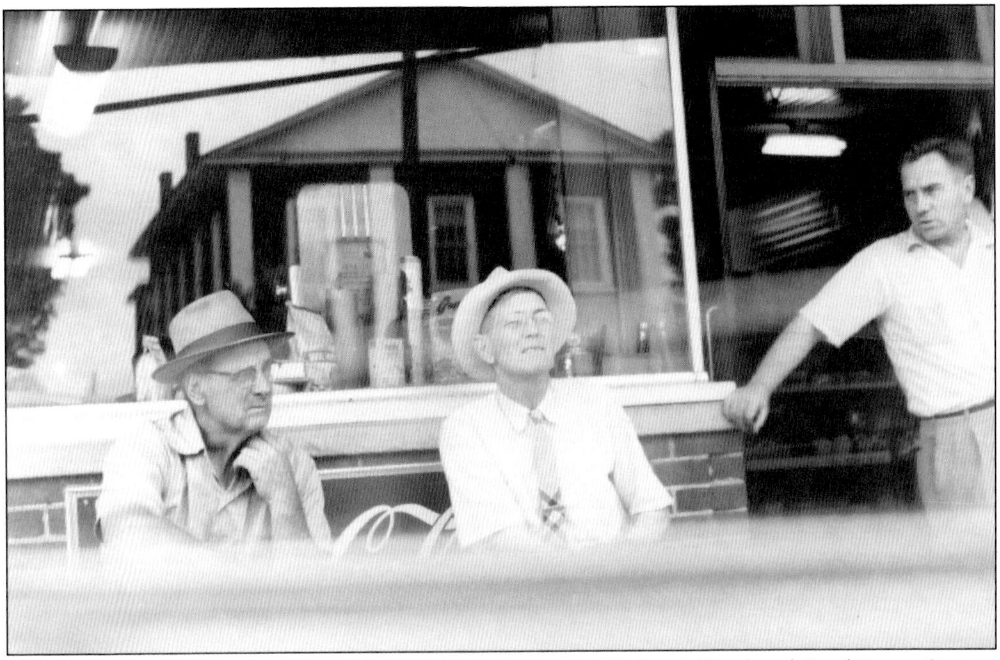

The old courthouse is reflected in the window of Long & Wishon's Feed and Seed Store. Sitting in front of the store are store owner Earnest Long and Attorney Thad Reece. Clyde Wishon is standing in doorway. (LW)

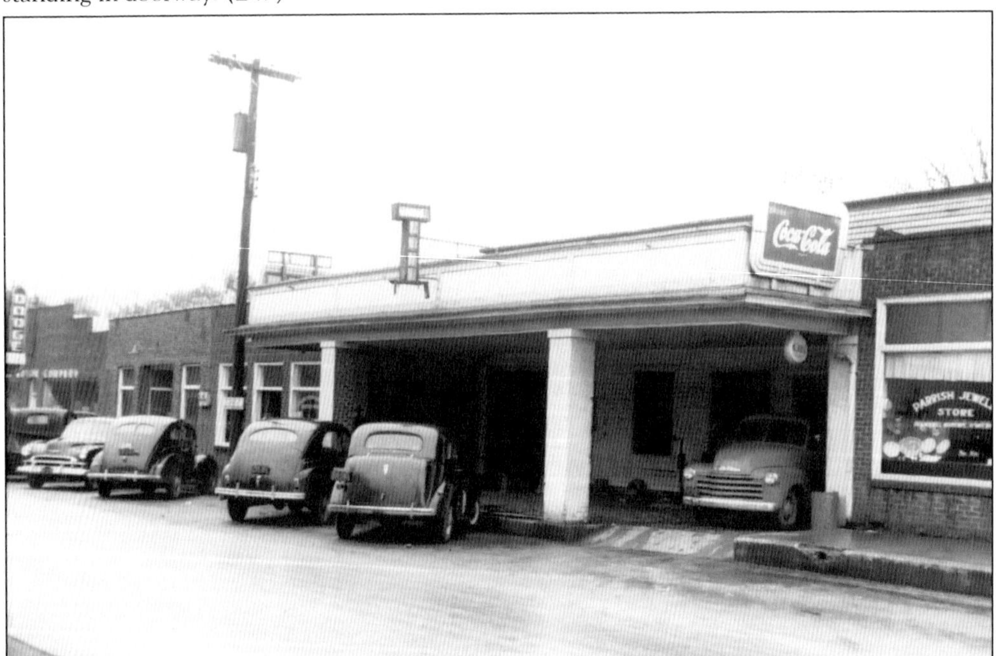

Gilbert Hutchens' Eagle Cafe on East Main Street as it looked in the 1940s. Before Yadkinville School had a lunchroom, the students walked to town to get a hot dog at the Eagle. The Parrish Jewelry Store, operated by Jack Parrish, is on the right. Gene Adams' Dodge-Plymouth dealership is on the far left. (SO)

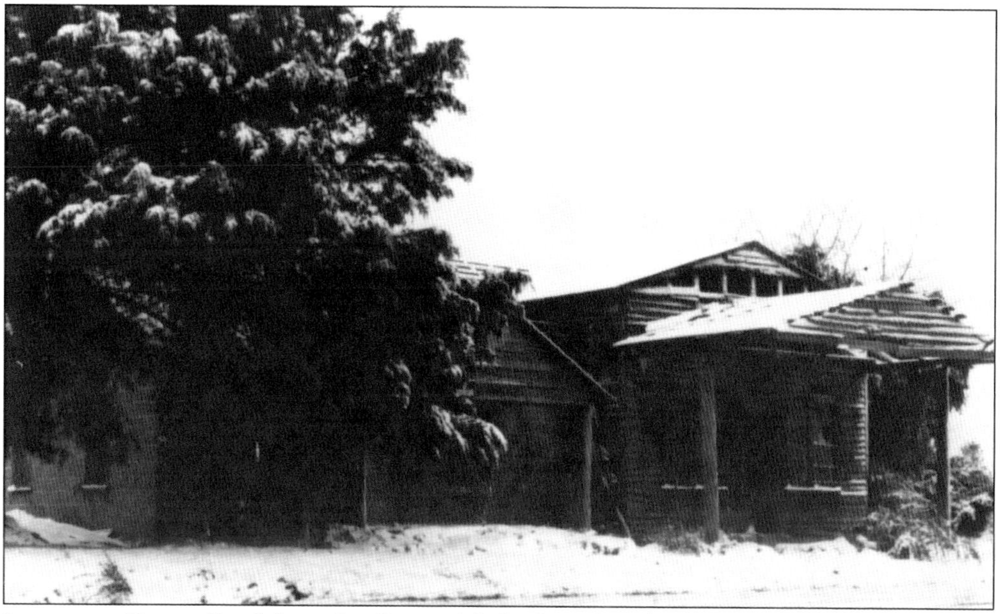

Just across Center Road from the Center Methodist Church was the Lee Sprouse Store. In the 1930s and '40s, people would come from miles around to talk or play cards and checkers at this popular gathering place. The store sold a variety of items, including peanut butter, which was sold by the pound from 5-gallon cans; soda pop, which cost between 3¢ and 5¢; and candy bars, which could be bought for 1¢. Local children would often trade eggs for these coveted treats. (NLG)

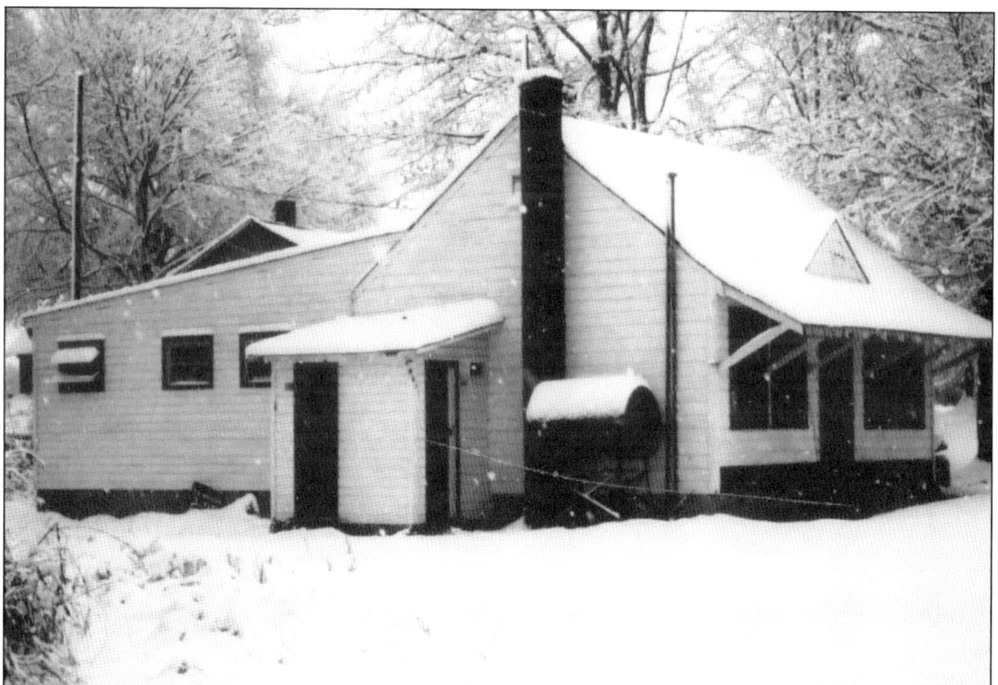

Tom Hauser's grocery store, located south of Yadkinville on Highway 601, was built in 1946. When this photograph was taken it was blanketed with snow. (VS)

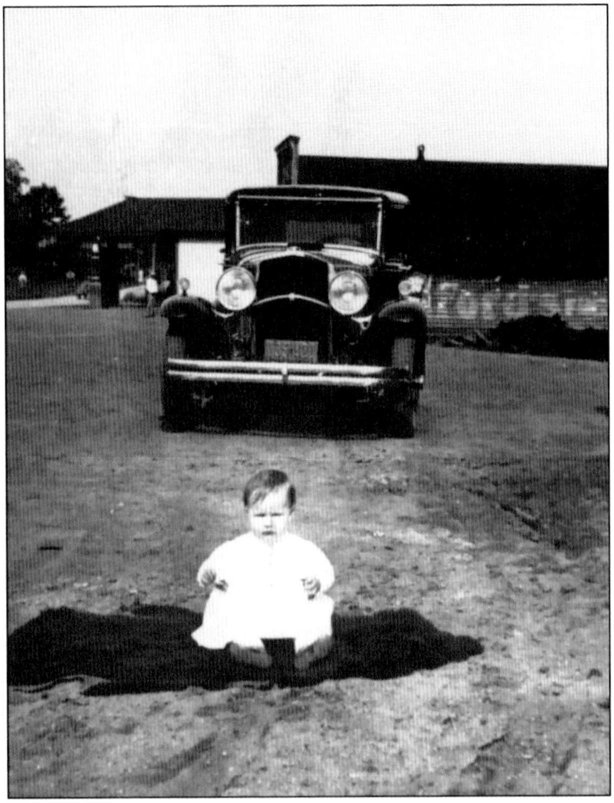

Claude P. Mackie and Jasper W. Shermer leased the building for the C.P. Mackie Store from Frank Eddleman in 1924. The store, on the west side of Speer Bridge Road, was a combination grocery, shoe, and hardware store. Grain, feed, kerosene, and large barrels of vinegar were stored in adjoining sheds. On the east side of the road was a building belonging to Gray Eddleman, who ground grain with a large tractor. Mackie later bought the building, and added hand-operated gasoline pumps. Seated on the sheepskin rug in this photograph is Ruth Hutchens. (MM)

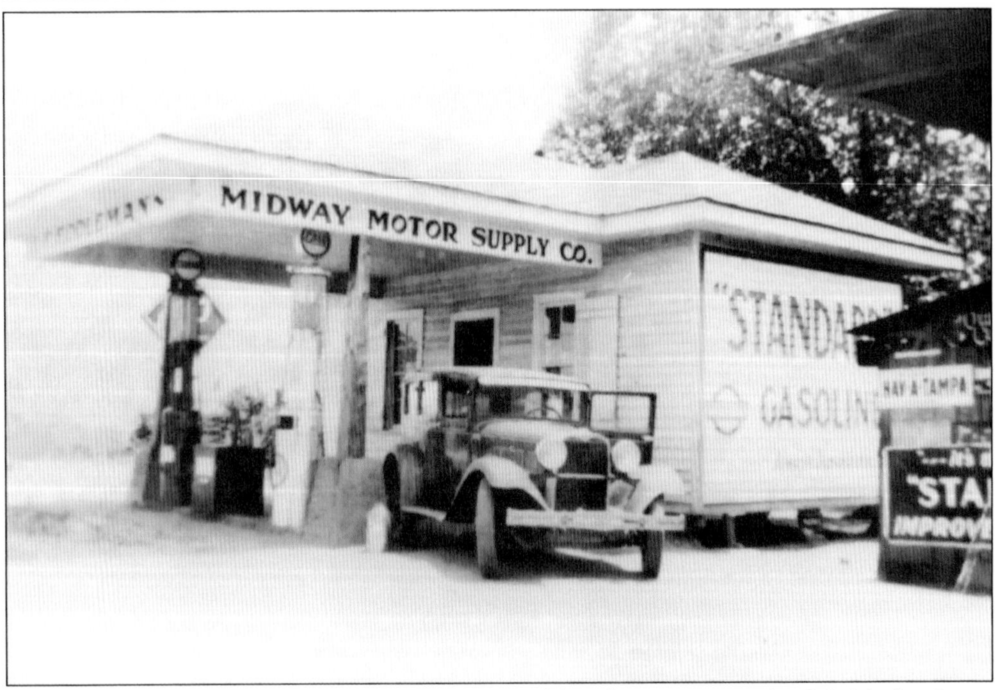

Gray Eddleman's Midway Motor Supply Co. was on old Highway 421 near the C.P. Mackie Store. Note the old gasoline pumps and the Standard Gasoline sign on the building. (EG, LW)

Tommy Garner and friend at Garner's Service Station at Brooks' Crossroads, near Hamptonville. Joe Brooks' store and gas station can be seen in the background. To the right of the photograph was the J.W. Garner Store. (EGS)

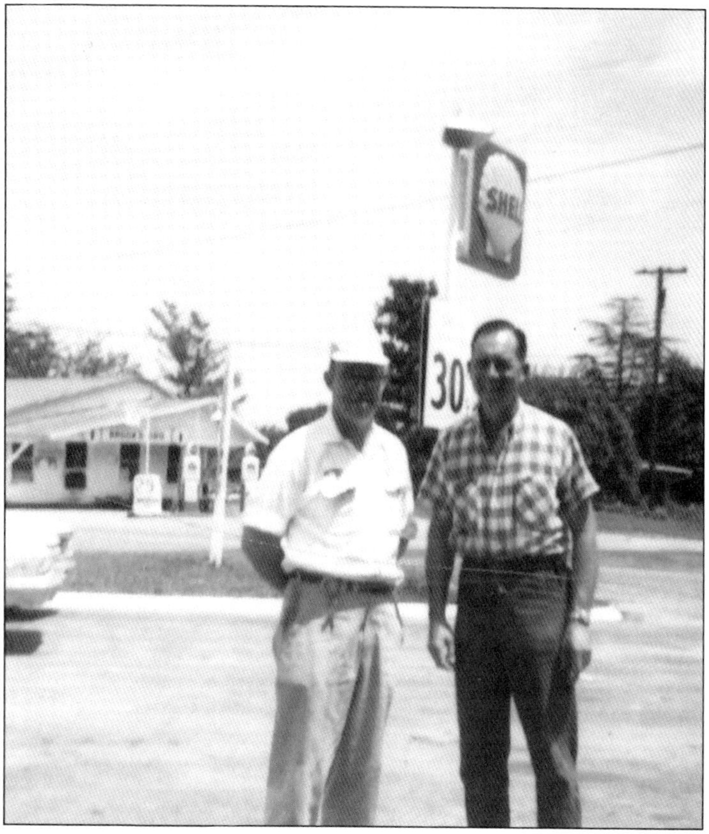

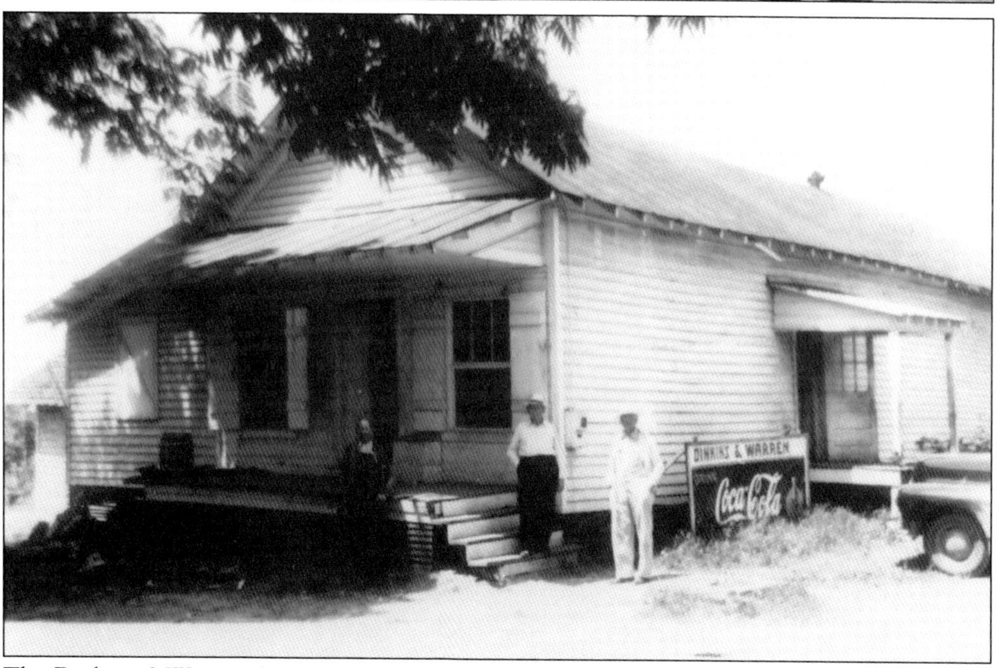

The Dinkins & Warren Store on the Shacktown Road was run by Harrison Dinkins and Isaac Columbus Warren. Warren, with only one leg, is seated on the porch. (JMD)

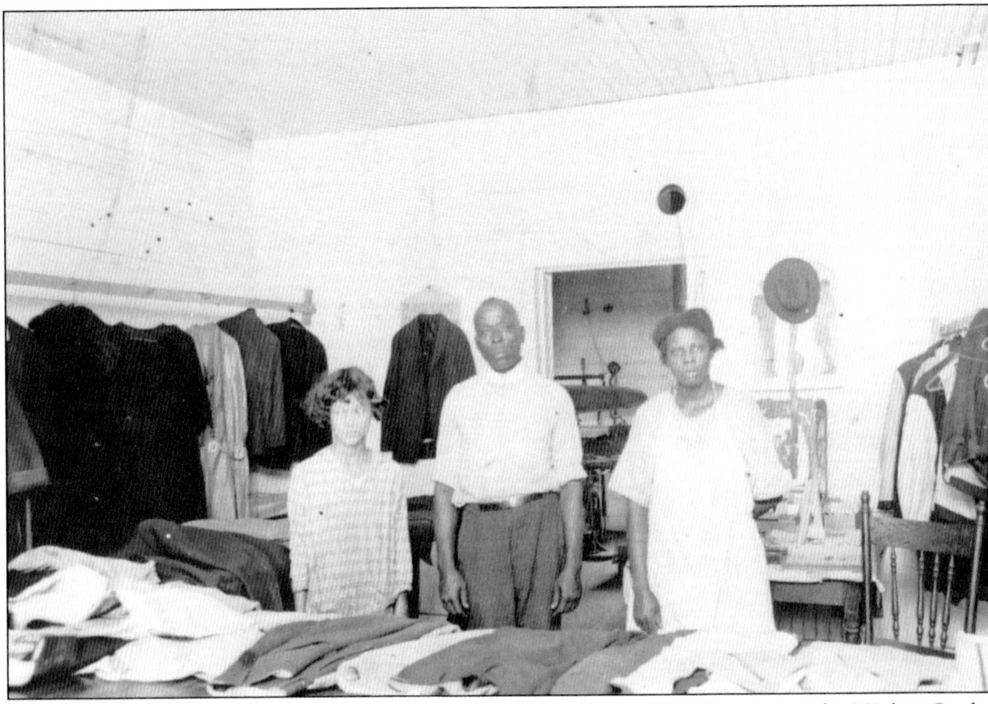

The Sanitary Dry Cleaning Parlor on East Main Street in Yadkinville was run by Walter Scales in the 1930s. (RH)

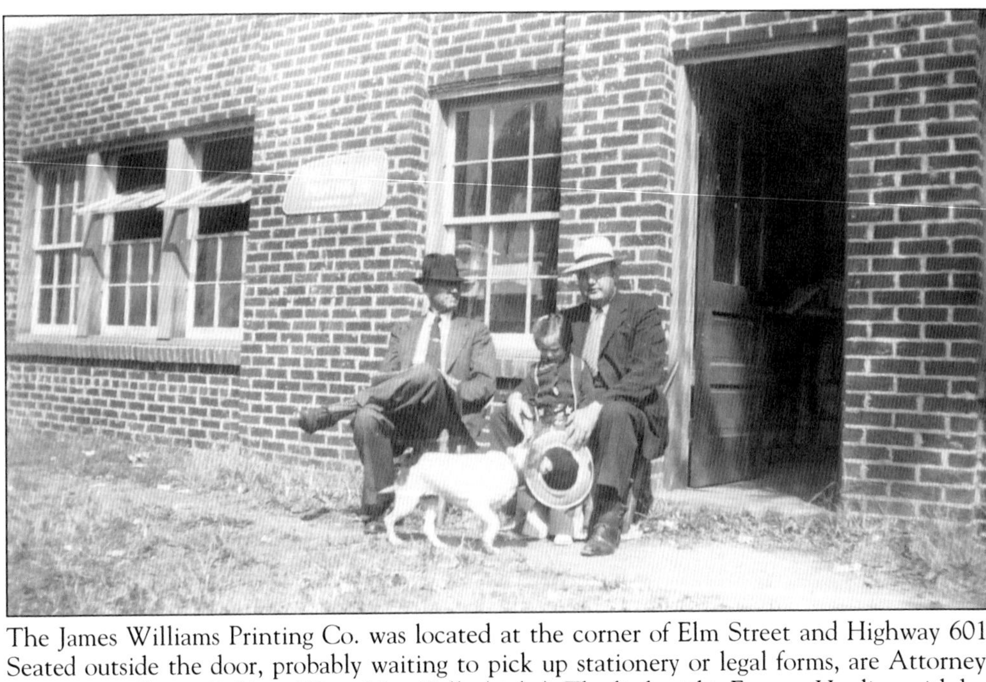

The James Williams Printing Co. was located at the corner of Elm Street and Highway 601. Seated outside the door, probably waiting to pick up stationery or legal forms, are Attorneys S. Carter Williams (left) and David Lee Kelly (right). The little girl is Frances Harding with her dog, "Flopsy." This photograph was taken in 1939 or 1940. (FHC)

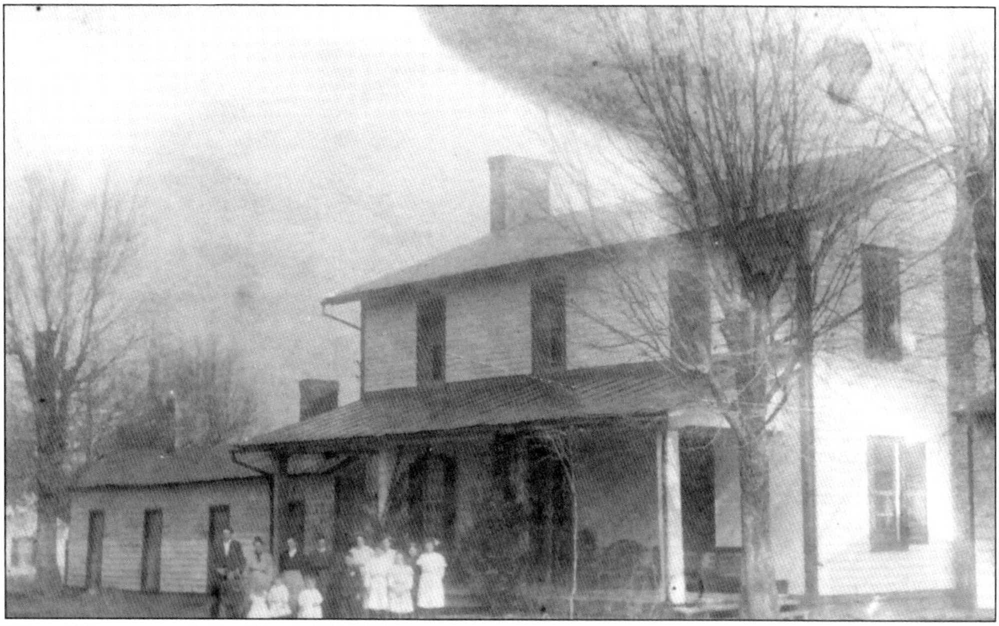

This old picture of the Shore Hotel shows the rooms that once stood on both sides of the hotel. Some rooms were rented to court officials and out-of-town lawyers during court week. (HHM)

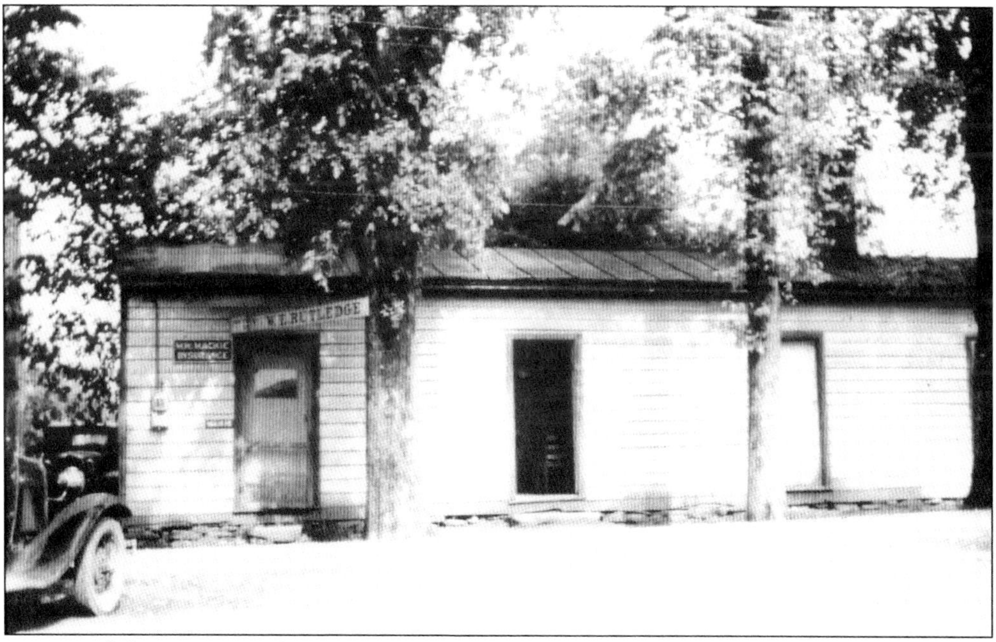

A view of the rooms on the south side of the Shore Hotel. W.E. Rutledge, the editor of the newspaper, and M.W. Mackie, an insurance salesman, shared an office. This building was on the site of the present office of the *Yadkin Ripple*. (LW)

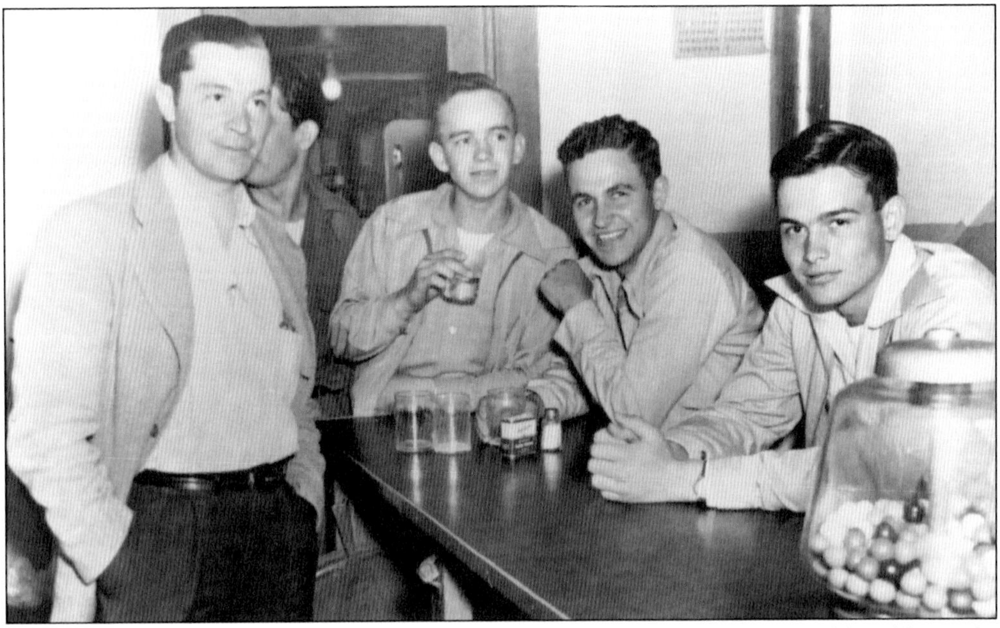

Located on Highway 601 about 2 miles north of Yadkinville, Jim's Grill is one of the oldest cafes in the county. It has always been popular, and it is still in business today. At the counter in this 1947 photograph are, from left to right: Lennie Shore, Carl Underwood, Glen Holcomb, and Charles Holcomb. Jim Pardue, the owner, cooked the best barbecue in the state, and his place was a favorite spot for teenagers to go after a Friday night basketball game in the 1940s. (RY)

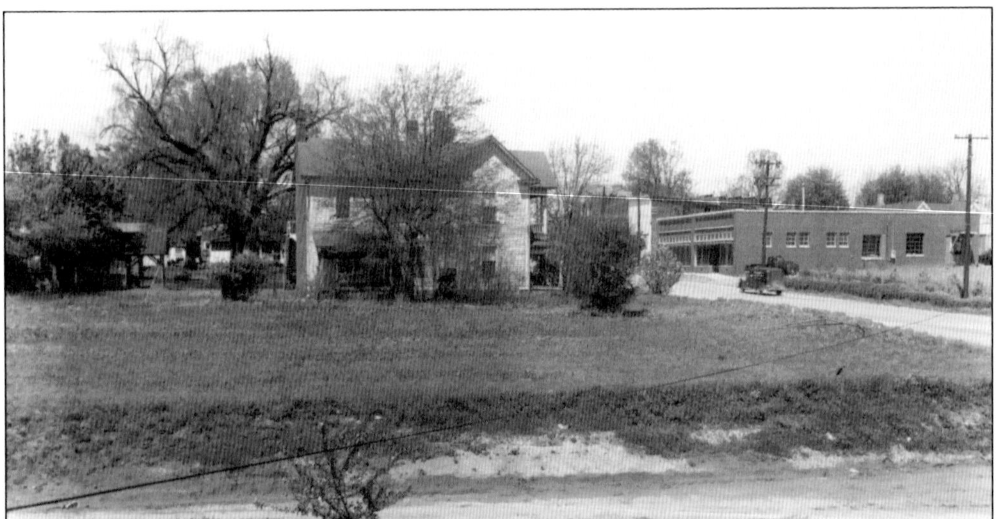

The Attorney D.M. Reece home on Highway 601 is on the left in this photograph. The house was also once the home of John and Stella Reece. It was demolished in the 1960s, and the First Baptist Church of Yadkinville now occupies the lot. The now-vacant Freezer Locker building across the road was a grocery store and frozen food storage facility, in the days before everyone had a freezer at home. In 1979, the Yadkin Arts Council leased the building and for several years it was used as a theater for plays and other events. (LW)

Six

Government by the People

Institutions and Agencies

After having been part of Rowan County, and later of Surry County, Yadkin County citizens were glad to have a county of their own, with a county seat and courthouse closer to their homes. In 1850, the legislature empowered the county to purchase 50 acres of land for a county seat, and to erect a courthouse and a jail. The first jail was completed in 1852, and the courthouse was finished by 1853. A public well was built at the same time.

From the very basic local government institutions of a county court and jail, tax collector, coroner, surveyor, clerk of court, and register of deeds, county services have continued to expand into the areas of education, transportation, health care, and other social services, as have state and Federal agencies and programs.

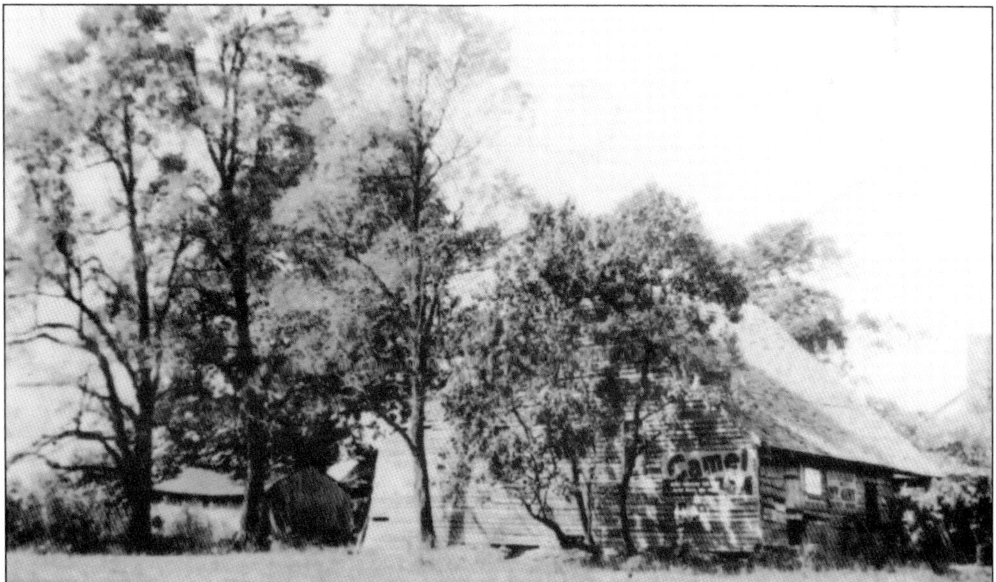

Theophilus C. Hauser ran this store c. 1833 just east of his home on old Highway 421 at Dowelltown, just outside of the present Yadkinville city limits. After the county was established late in 1850, court was held here until a courthouse could be built. Hauser later built a store on the west side of the new courthouse. (AS)

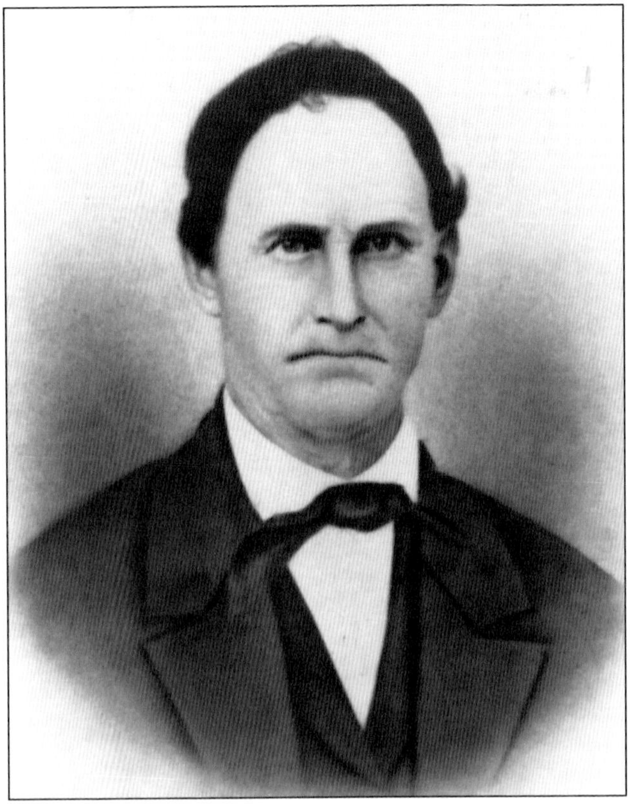

William White (1803–1867) was contracted to build the first courthouse for the sum of $11,000. The first step was to buy land so that the plan to build a town with a courthouse in the center could be realized, and 50 acres were purchased for $100 from Robert Mackie. It was ordered on July 5, 1853, that, "hereafter the court shall be held at the court house in the Town of Yadkinville and that all court papers shall be made returnable there." Historical records also show that William Whitaker was paid $32.35 to dig a public well for the townsfolk of Yadkinville. (DMCL)

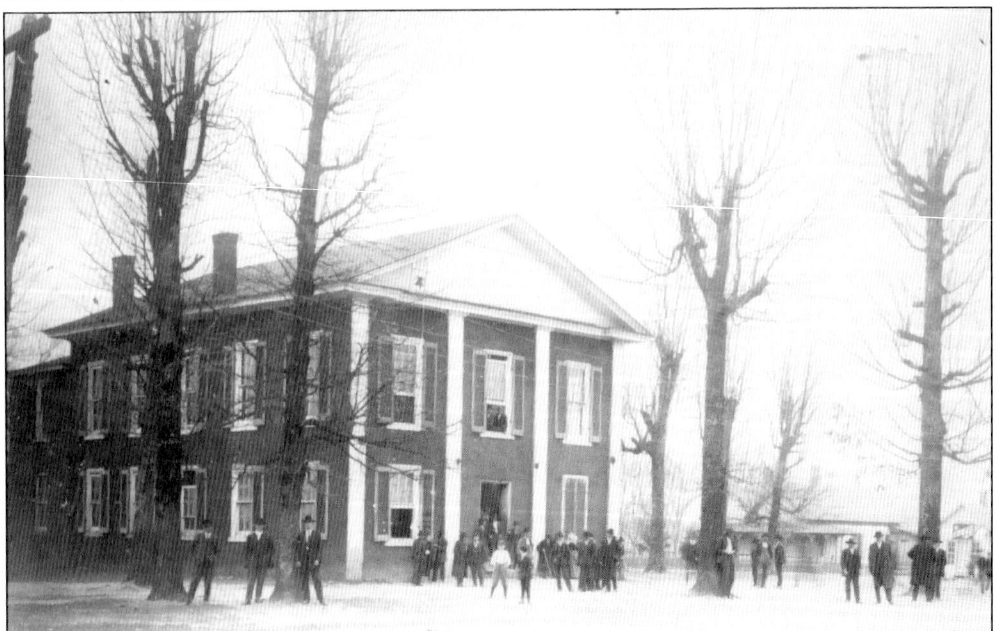

This is the west side of the old courthouse about 1910, probably during court week. Note the shutters on all the windows. The Harding-Hauser-Holcomb house and a small office, which was probably used by Drs. T.R. Harding and B.B. Hauser, are in the background. (HHM)

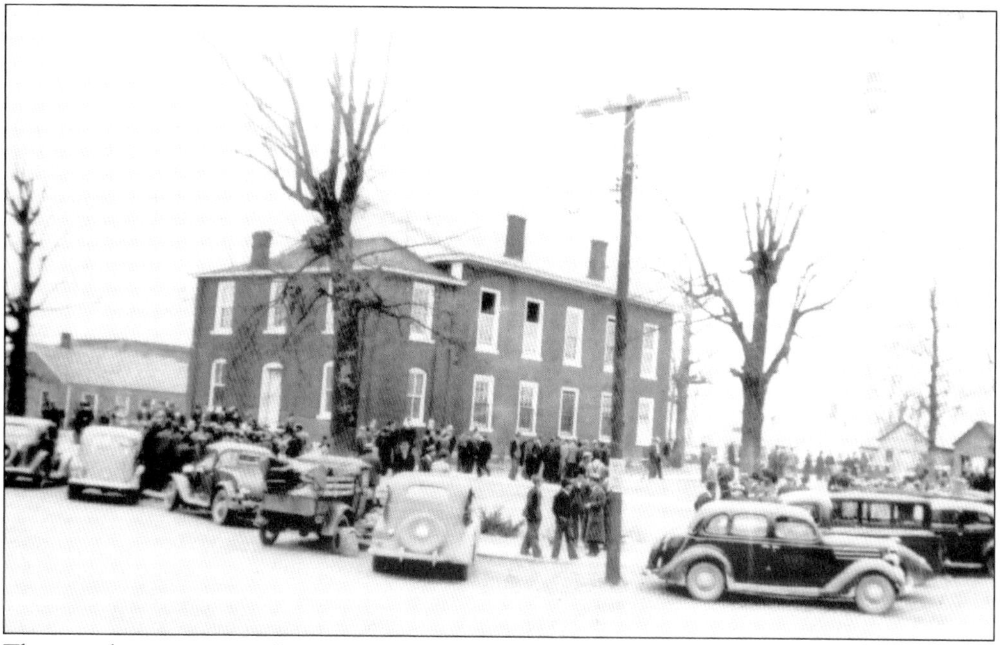

The courthouse was usually crowded during court week, as can be seen in this 1939 picture, which shows the north and east sides of the building. (AS)

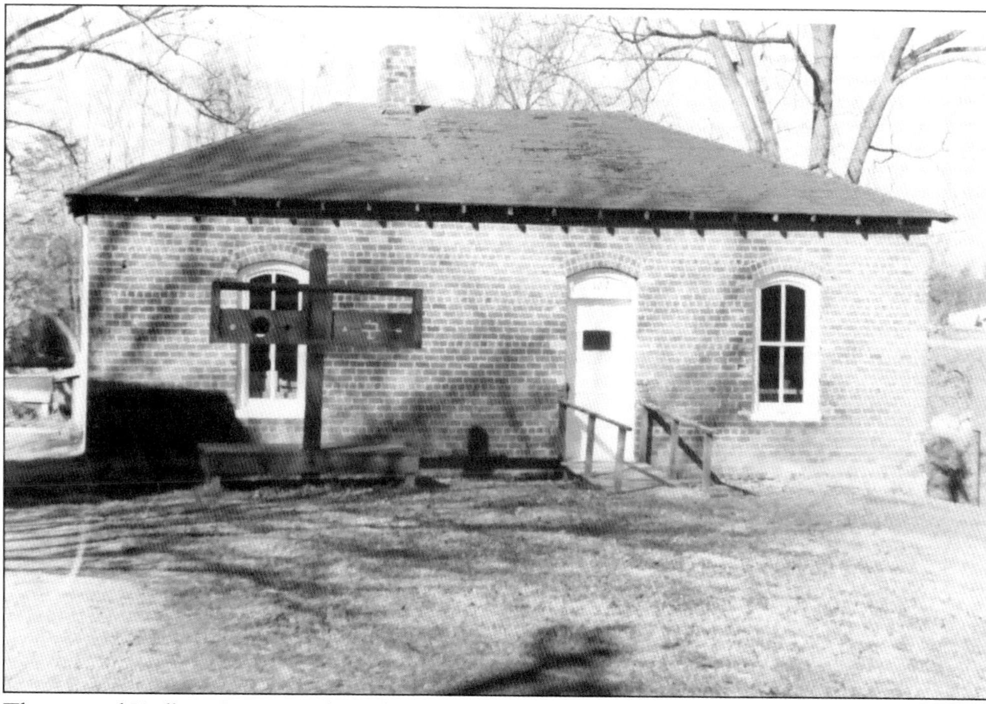

The second Yadkin County Jail was built in 1892 after the first jail, built in 1852, burned. The second jail was made with the best fireproof materials available at the time, and it featured a cement floor, a metal ceiling (topped with 7 inches of concrete), and brick walls. The second jail, which is on the National Register of Historic Buildings, is now part of the Charles Bruce Davis Museum of Art, History, and Science, Inc. (LW)

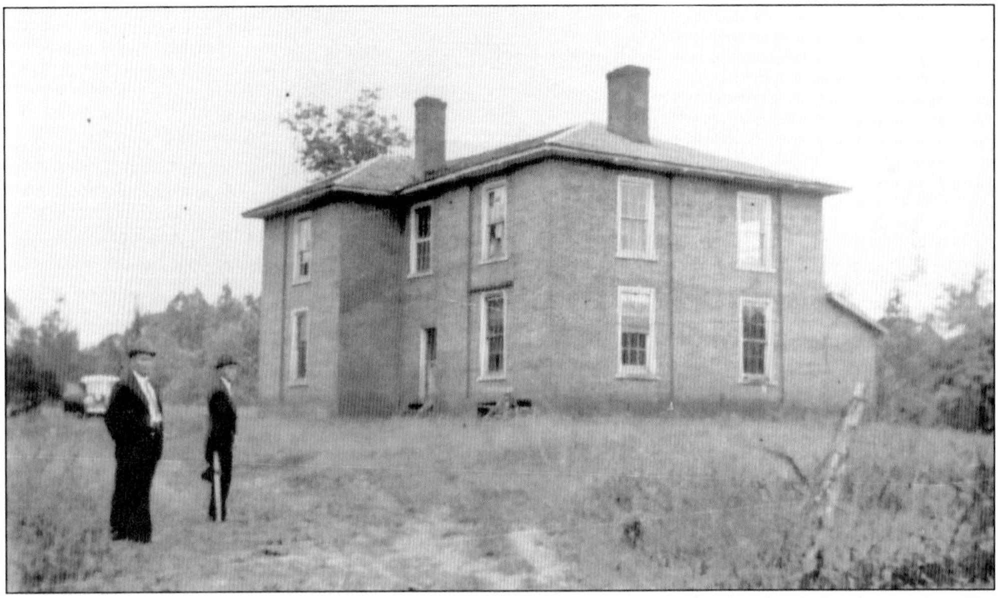

This 1918 photograph shows Arthur and Arvil Speer standing at the back of "Richmond Hill," the home of Judge Richmond M. Pearson. Pearson conducted a law school here from *c.* 1850 until his death in 1878, between his duties as state supreme court judge. Classes were sometimes held under a shade tree. Now restored, the house is open to the public. (AS)

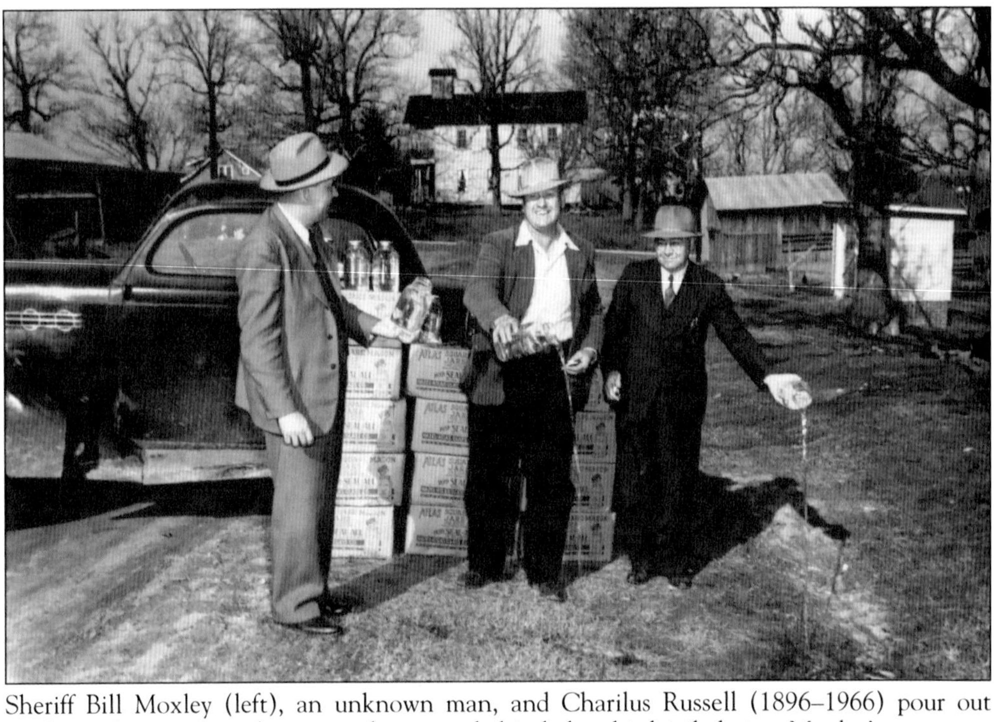

Sheriff Bill Moxley (left), an unknown man, and Charilus Russell (1896–1966) pour out confiscated moonshine liquor in the street behind the third jail during Moxley's tenure as sheriff (1946–1954). In the background the old Yadkinville Academy building can be seen. The Yadkinville Town Hall now occupies the area where the two small buildings stand on the right. (SO)

Postman Arvil Speer meets the train at Crutchfield to get the mail. (AS)

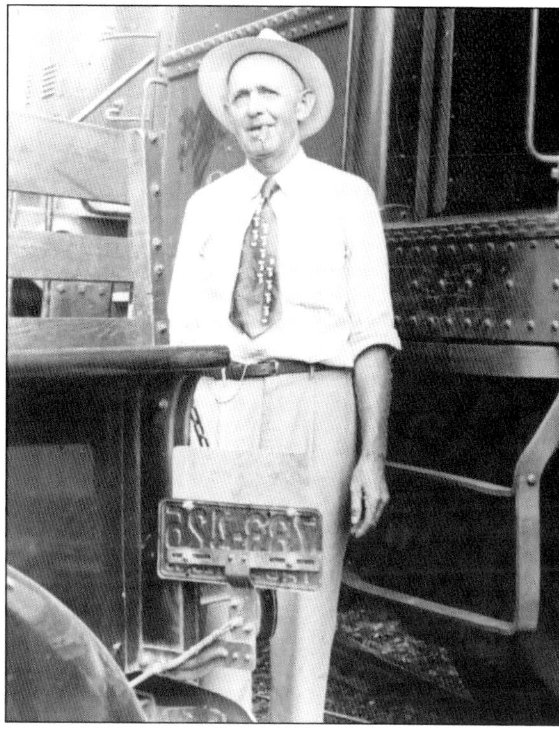

These postal workers at the Yadkinville Post Office are, from left to right: Jasper Long, Izetta (Steelman) Mackie, George Steelman, Arvil Speer, Edwin Poteat, Vic Reavis Steelman, Grady Royal, Mozelle (Lakey) Hinshaw, Eugene Joyner, and William F. Van Hoy. This photograph was taken between 1946 and 1950. (MLH)

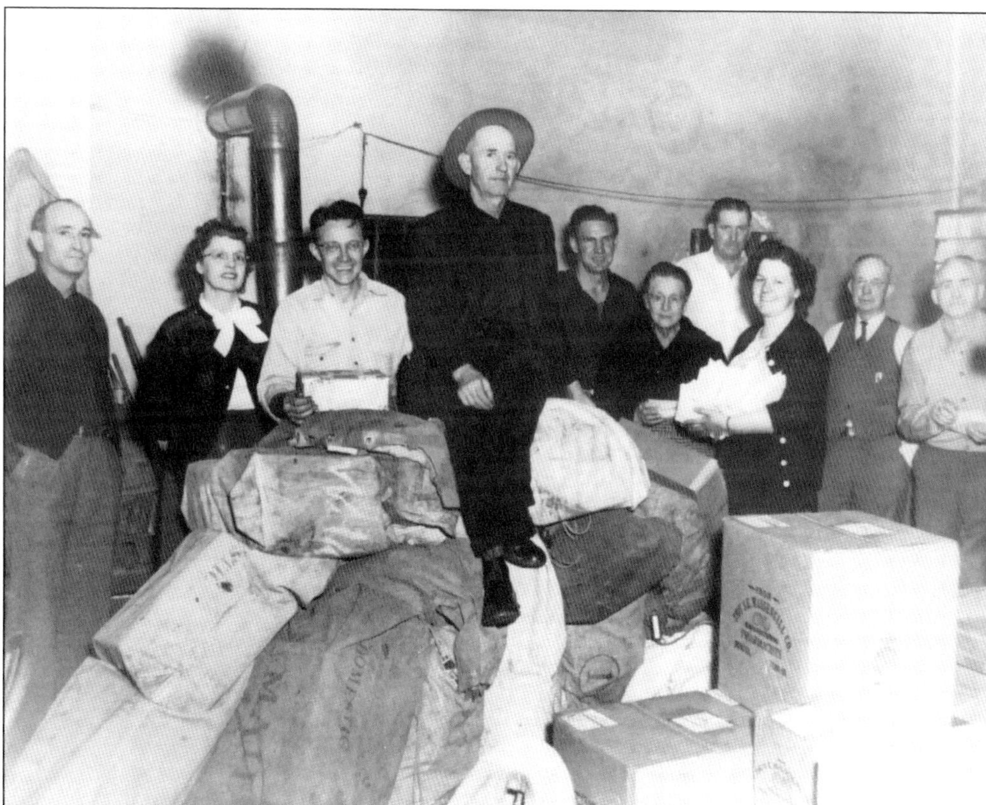

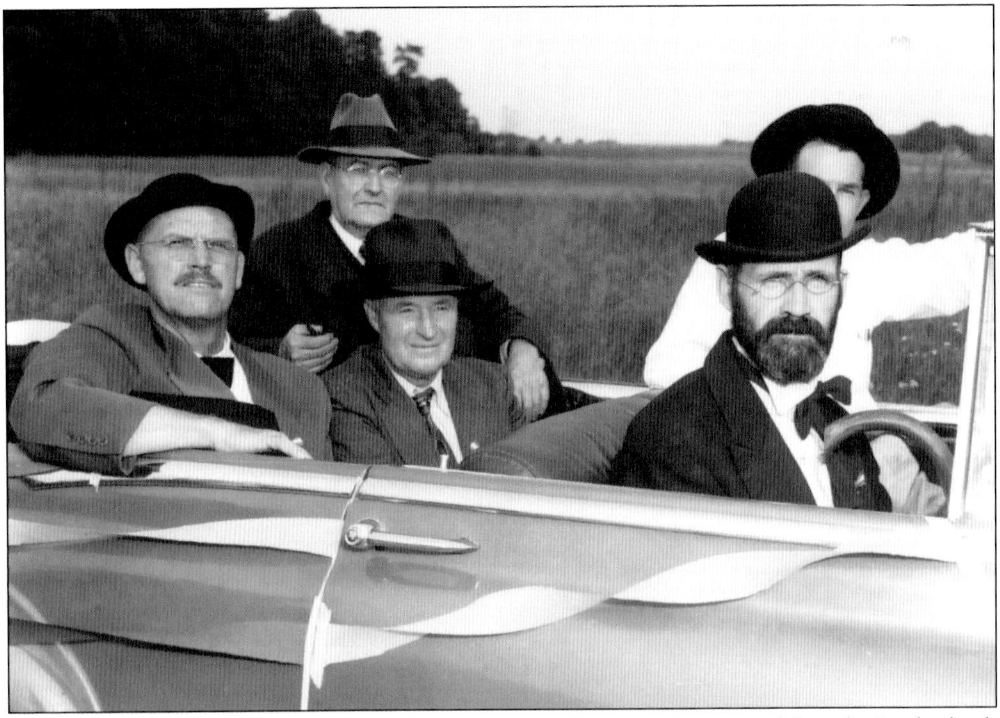

Some of the Yadkin County commissioners riding in the 1950 Centennial Parade. In the back seat are, from left to right: Arvil Norman, Walt Wagoner, and Sam Brewbaker. Marshall Shore is in the passenger seat in the front. The driver has not been identified. (SO)

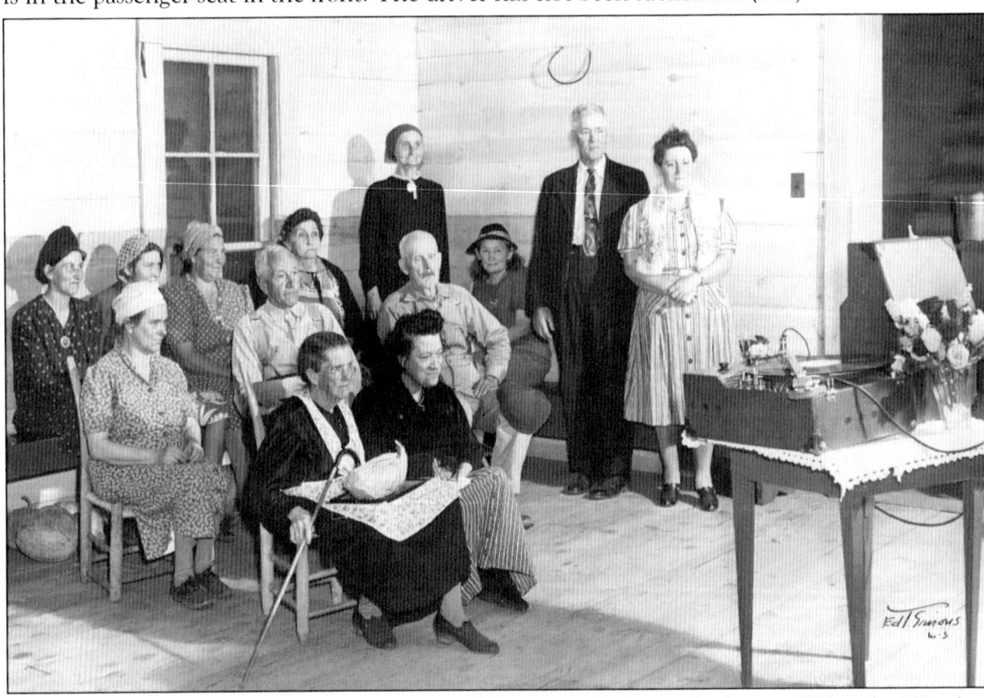

Inmates of the county home being entertained by a record player. Arthur and Blanche Warden, the custodians, are standing at the far right. (LMW)

Seven

A Mighty Fortress

Religion

Religion has always played an important part in the lives of Yadkin County people. Communities grew up around churches, and the church buildings often served as schools and community centers when they were not being used for worship. Week-long camp meetings and revivals were held which attracted people from miles around.

The Baptists established a church at Shallow Ford in the 1760s and Methodist churches flourished after the visit of circuit riders such as Bishop Francis Asbury and John Lee in the 1790s. By that time Friends churches were well established. A variety of denominations soon followed, including Presbyterian, Church of Christ, and Holiness churches. Some congregations first met in a "brush arbor," before they built a permanent church building. A few early churches had an upstairs gallery for slaves to sit while attending services. After 1865, the freed slaves established many churches of their own throughout the county, which remains predominately Protestant.

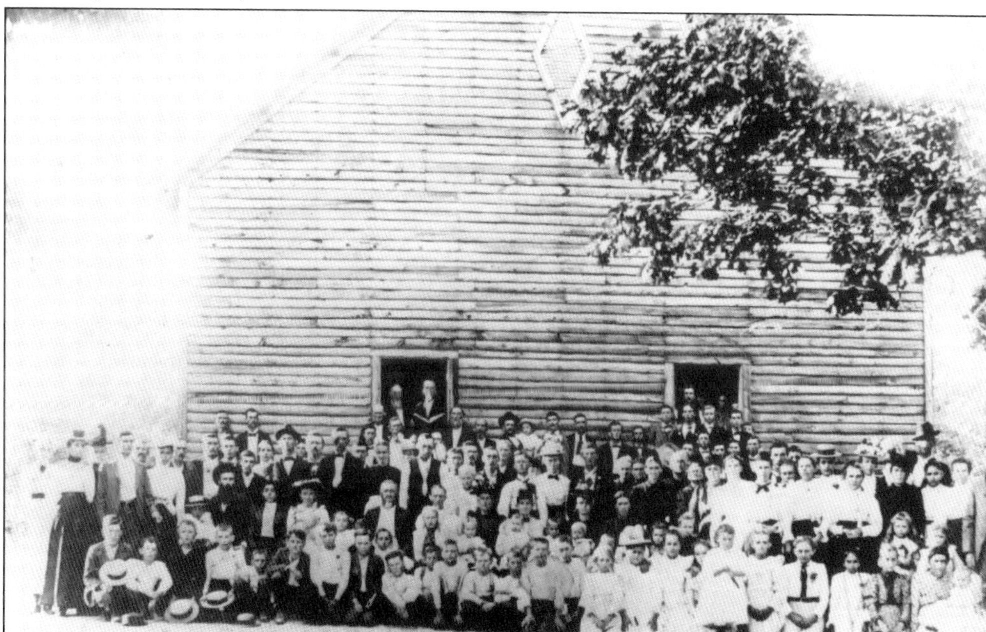

The South Oak Ridge Baptist Church and congregation about 1897. The church was created when the congregation decided to separate from the Cross Roads Baptist Church and build a new church in 1896. Reverend W.A. Myers was the first pastor and Charlie M. Reavis the first clerk. This structure was used until a new church was completed in 1932. (JC)

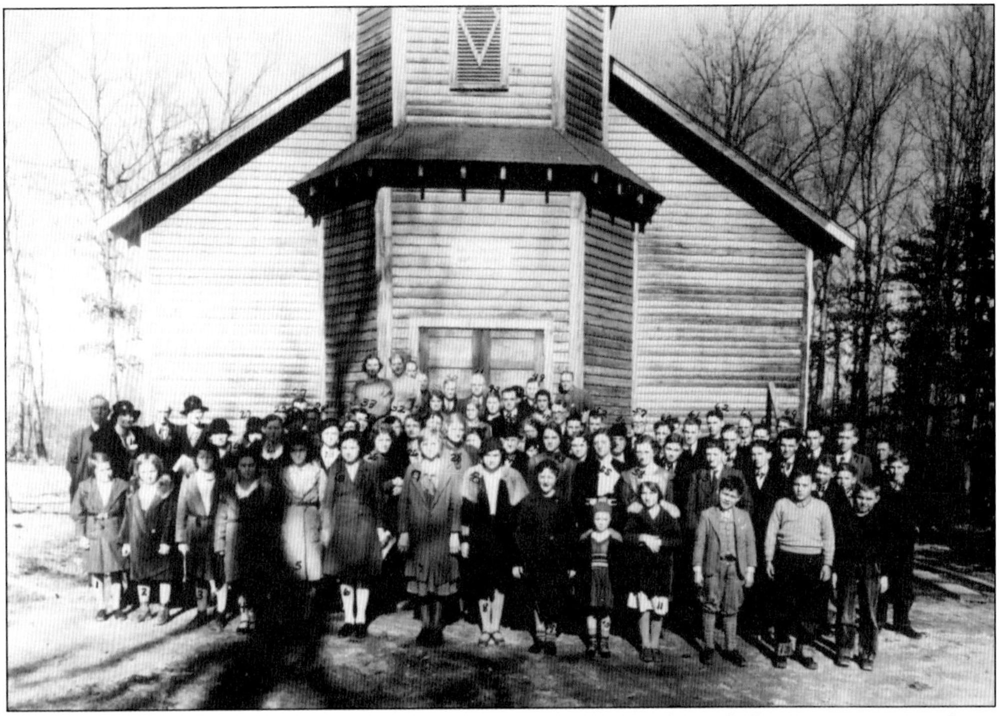

The second building of the South Oak Ridge Baptist Church and the congregation about 1932. (JC)

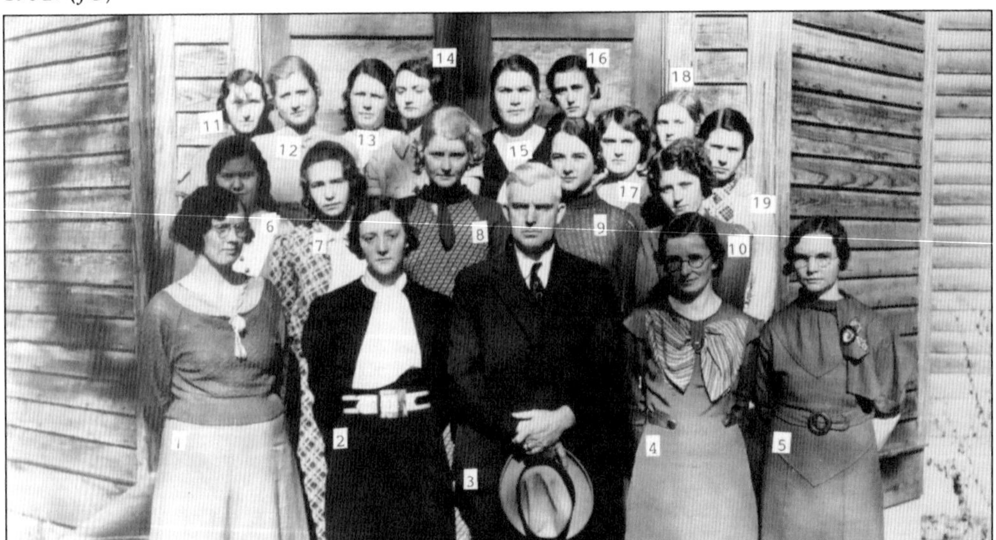

The Marshall Reavis Sunday school class of the South Oak Ridge Baptist Church. Those pictured are: 1) Eula Reavis; 2) Ida Mae Brandon; 3) Marshall Reavis; 4) Annie Reavis; 5) Ila Jester Reavis; 6) Zella Hutchens Todd; 7) Gertrude Steelman Cranfill; 8) Willie Mae Reavis Paxton; 9) Isa Mae R. Reavis; 10) Sylvia Wilkins; 11) Rena Reavis Holden; 12) Athagene Reavis Steele; 13) Lola Reavis Harris; 14) Francis Holden; 15) Mabel Holden; 16) Hilda Brandon Poindexter; 17) Bertice Holden Smith; 18) Lorraine Wilkins Holden; and 19) Lizzie Reavis Brandon. (JC)

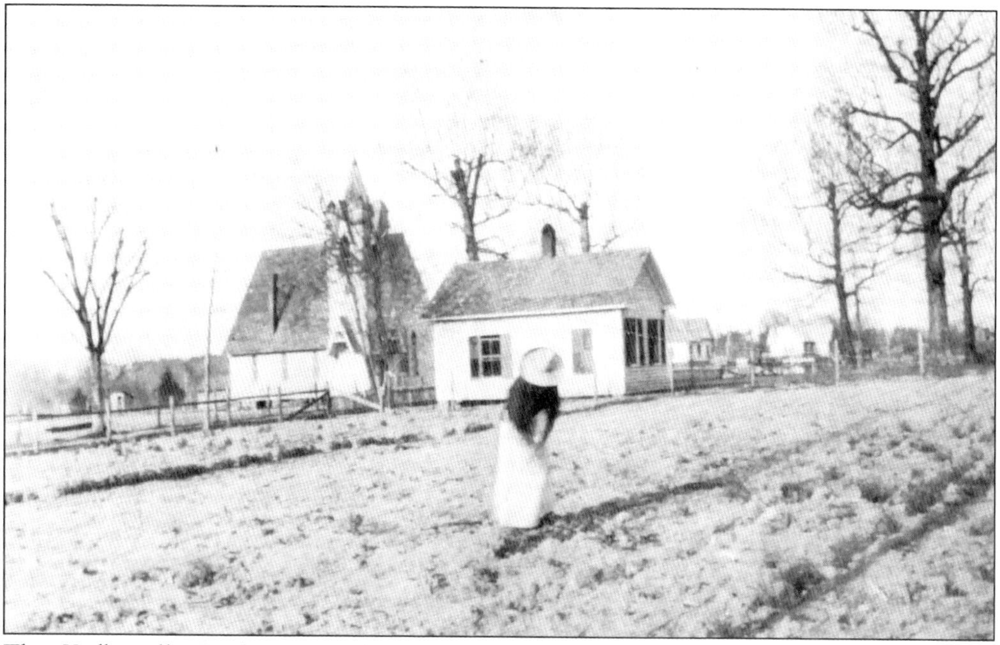

The Yadkinville Presbyterian Church, established in 1901, is shown here about 1910. Dr. Marler's dental office is on the right. An unidentified woman is hoeing her garden in the foreground. (MC)

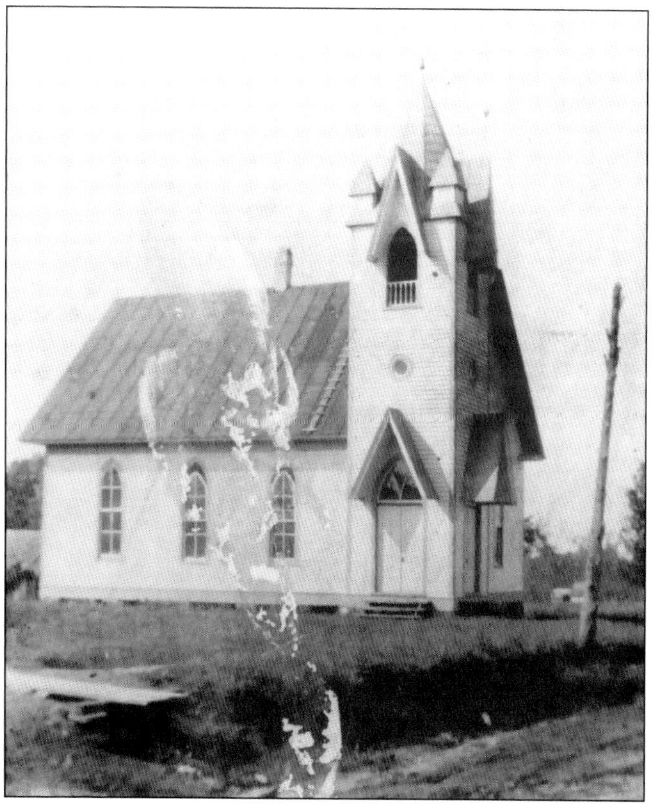

The Yadkinville Baptist Church, which was located on Highway 601 where the present First Union Bank stands, was built about 1902 at a cost of $1,700. It was used until 1950, when a new church was built. It is almost identical to the Presbyterian church, except for the chimneys, which are in different locations. (HHM)

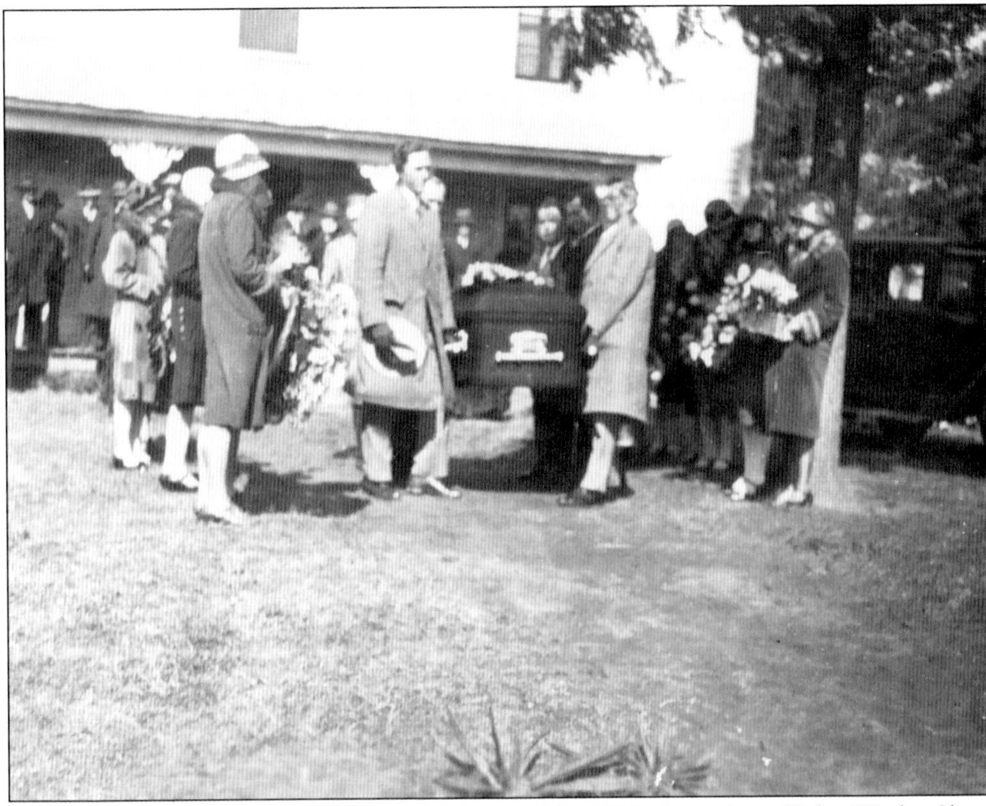

Wakes used to be held in the home of the deceased. In 1928, the casket of John Wesley Shore was carried from his home to the church for a funeral service and then to Deep Creek Friends cemetery. (NH)

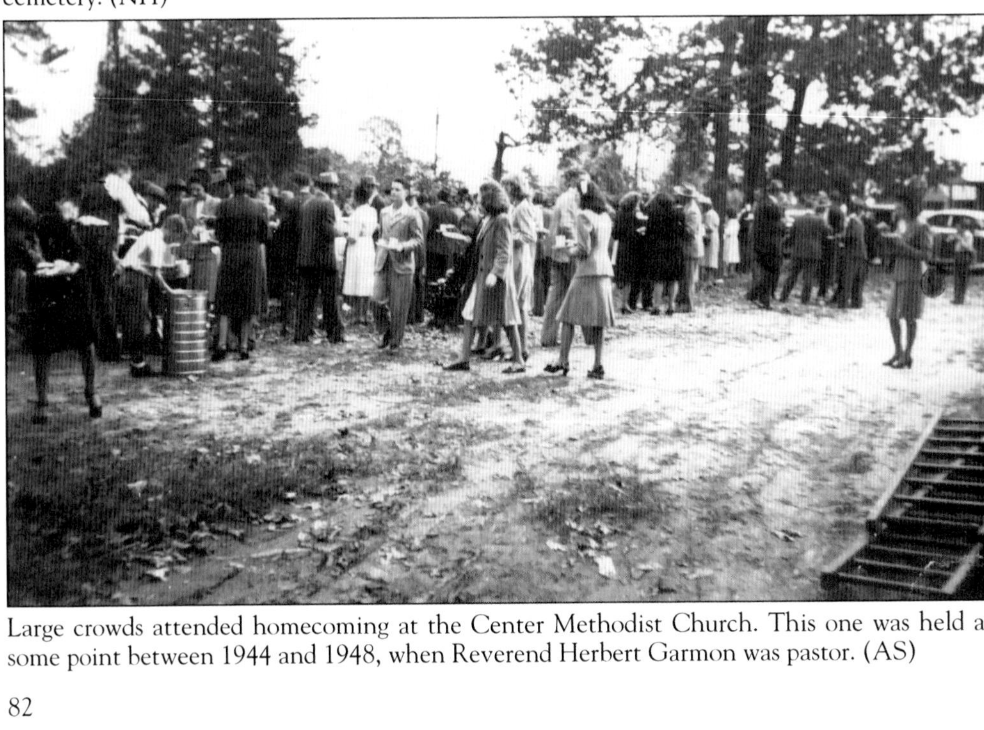

Large crowds attended homecoming at the Center Methodist Church. This one was held at some point between 1944 and 1948, when Reverend Herbert Garmon was pastor. (AS)

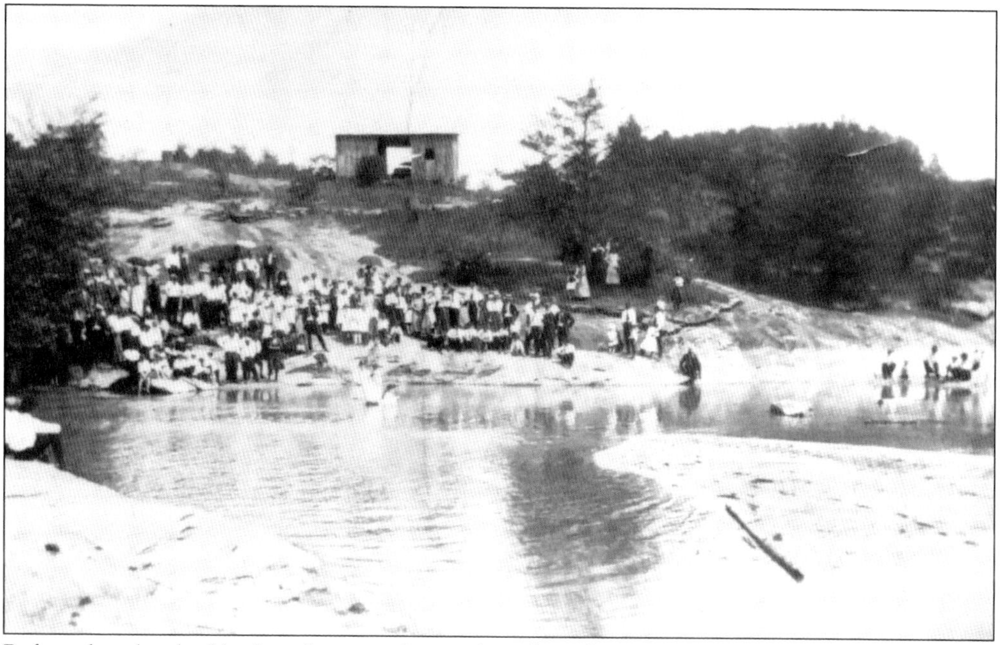

Before churches had built-in baptismals, ponds and creeks were used to baptize members. Here, a baptism is being conducted in South Deep Creek near Vestal's (Potts') Mill. (AS)

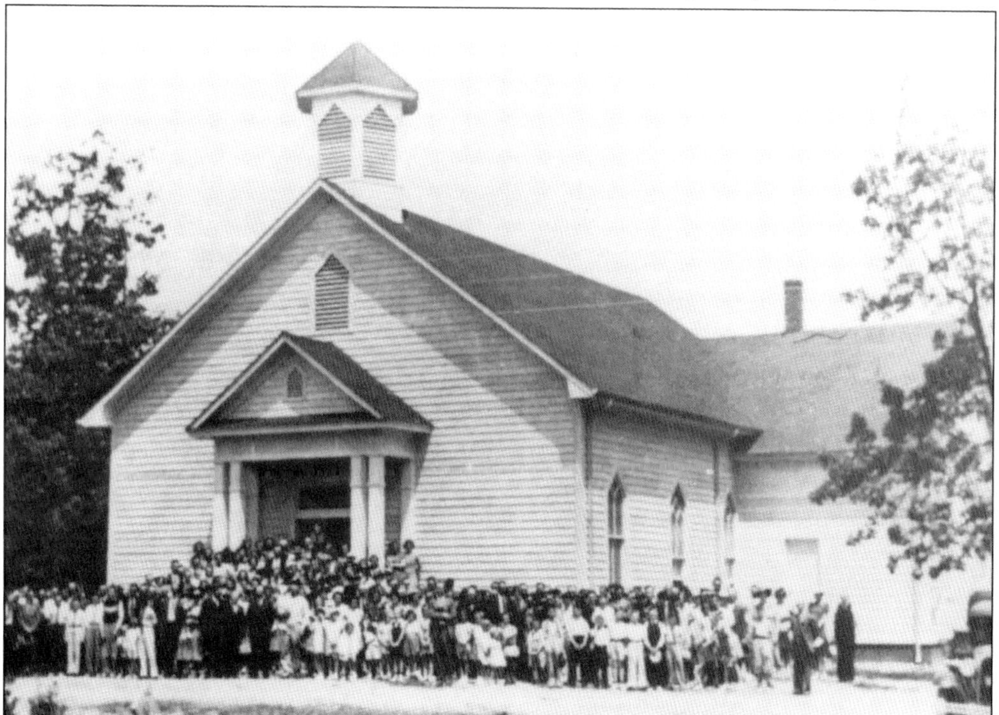

The North Oak Ridge Baptist Church was first organized on July 9, 1904, at Brown's School House, with eleven members. J.W. Bryant was the first pastor. The first building was dedicated in 1911. It was torn down and this church, shown here with the congregation, was completed in 1939. (KC)

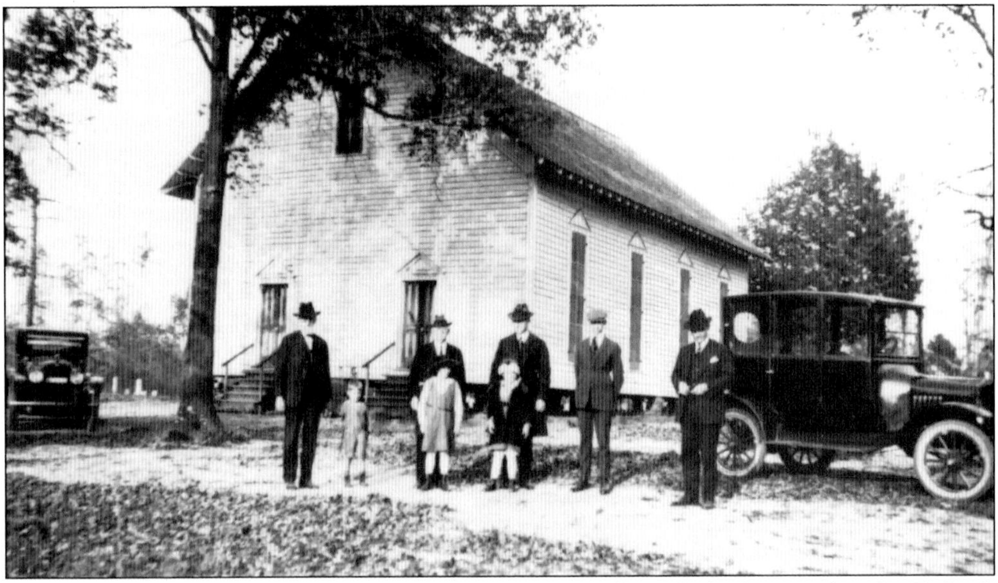

The first car to transport mail from Winston-Salem to Yadkinville had stopped at the Forbush Baptist Church on old Highway 421 when this photograph was taken in 1916. Arvil Speer is believed to be in this picture. (AS)

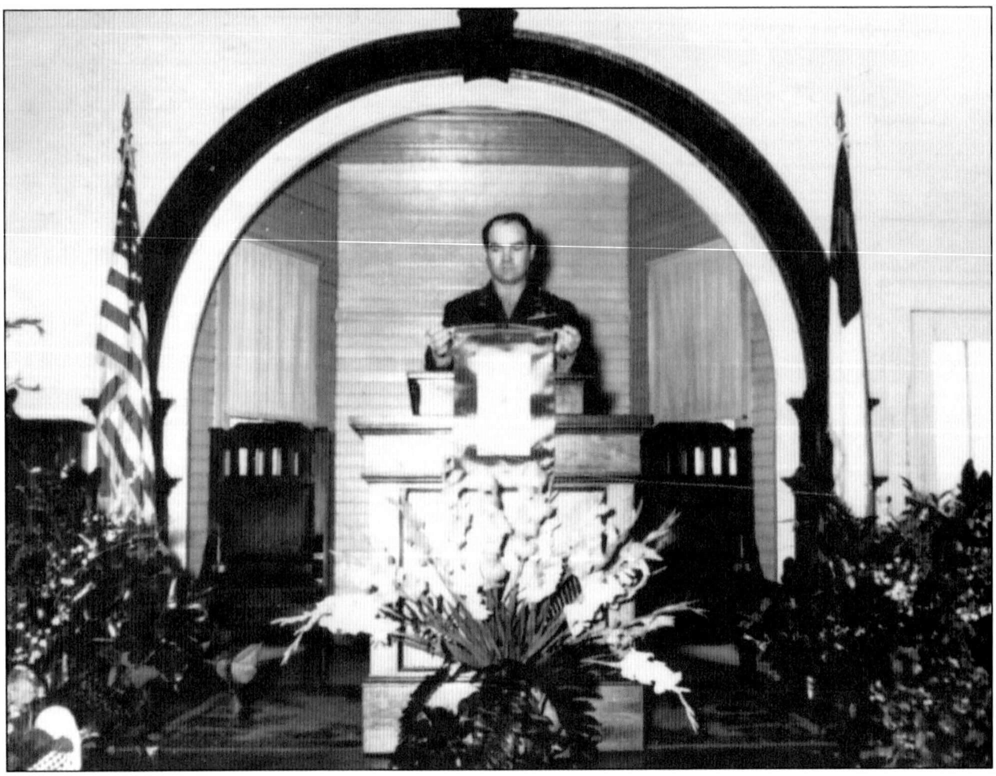

The interior and pulpit of the Forbush Baptist Church. (JL)

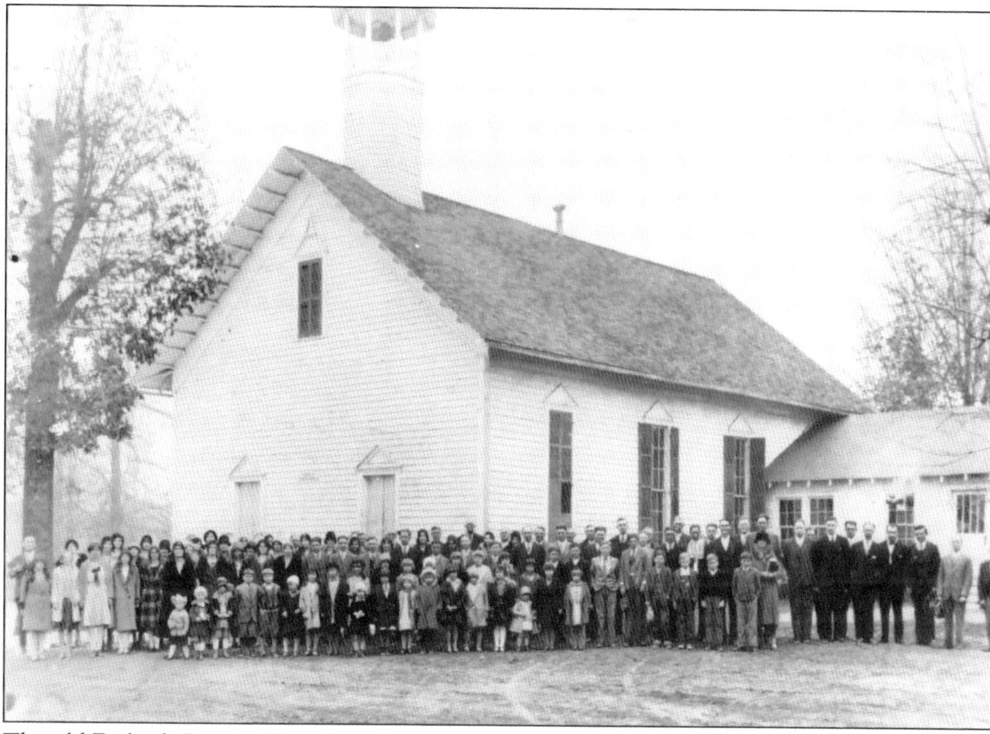

The old Forbush Baptist Church and its congregation as they appeared in January 1931. (JL)

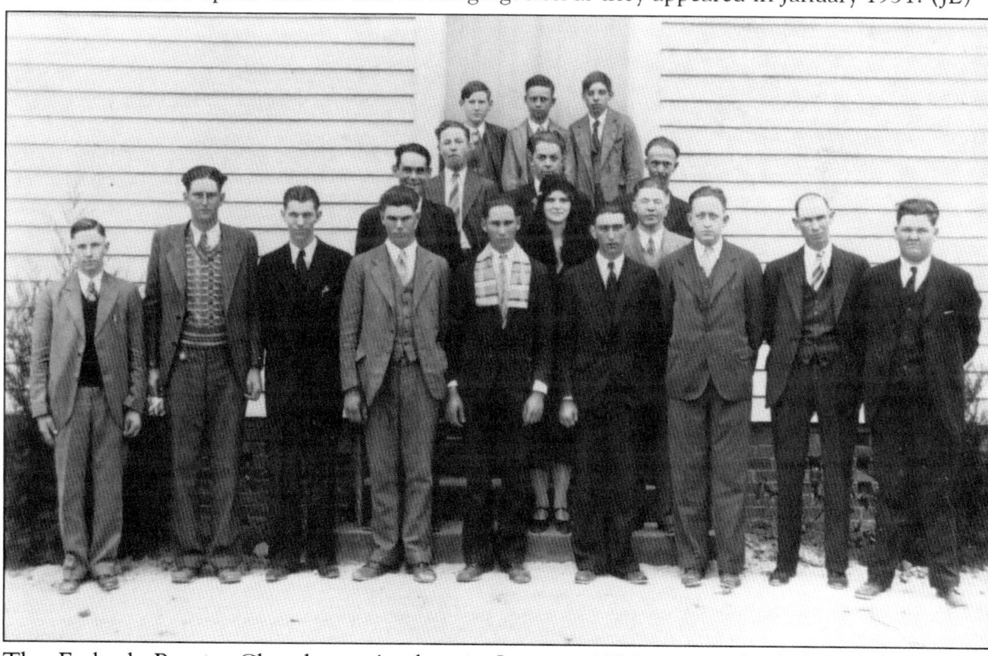

The Forbush Baptist Church men's class in January 1931 consisted of, from left to right: (front row) Paul Groce, Grady Eddleman, Benbow Phillips, Jasper Hobson, Robert Eddleman, unknown, Alie Dinkins, Albert Groce, and Gwyn Shermer Jr.; (second row) Willis Dixon, Della (Hobson) Carter (the teacher), and Ernest Groce; (third row) Ralph Groce, Astor Hobson, and Joe Eaton; (back row) John Hayes Eddleman, Cedric Hutchens, and Willie Phillips. (JL)

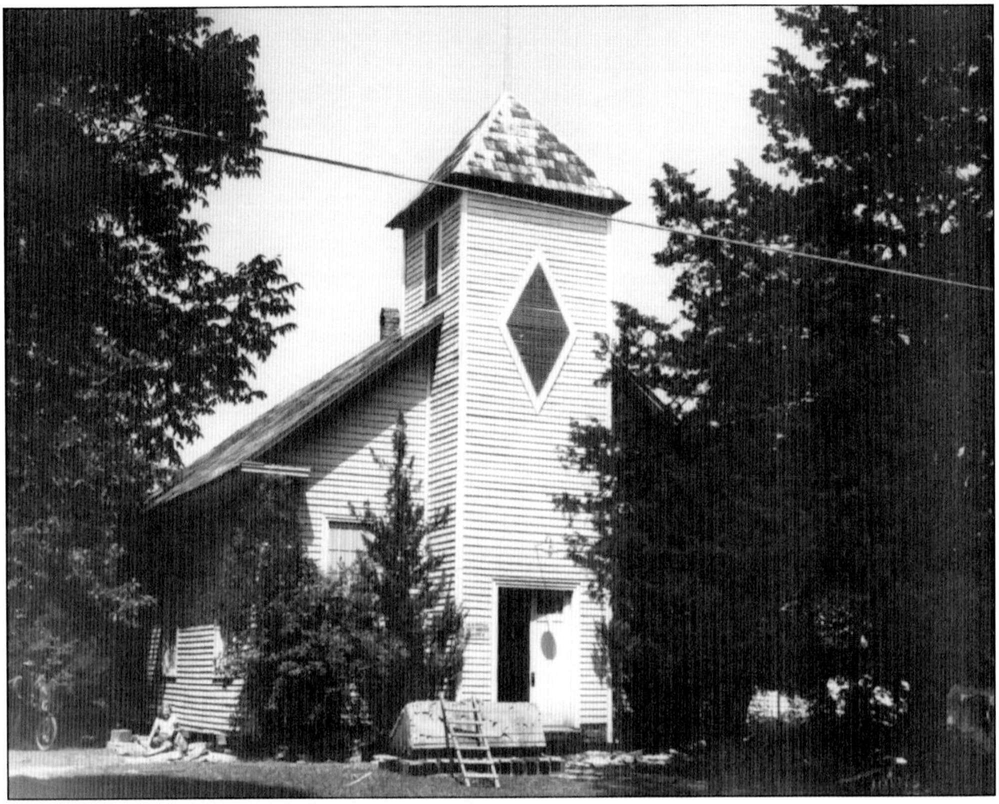

The Yadkinville Methodist Church in the process of being moved. Built in 1879, it was located on the present site of Dr. Frank Walker's office. It stood there until 1948, when it was moved one block west to the J.G. Marler lot. (DMcL)

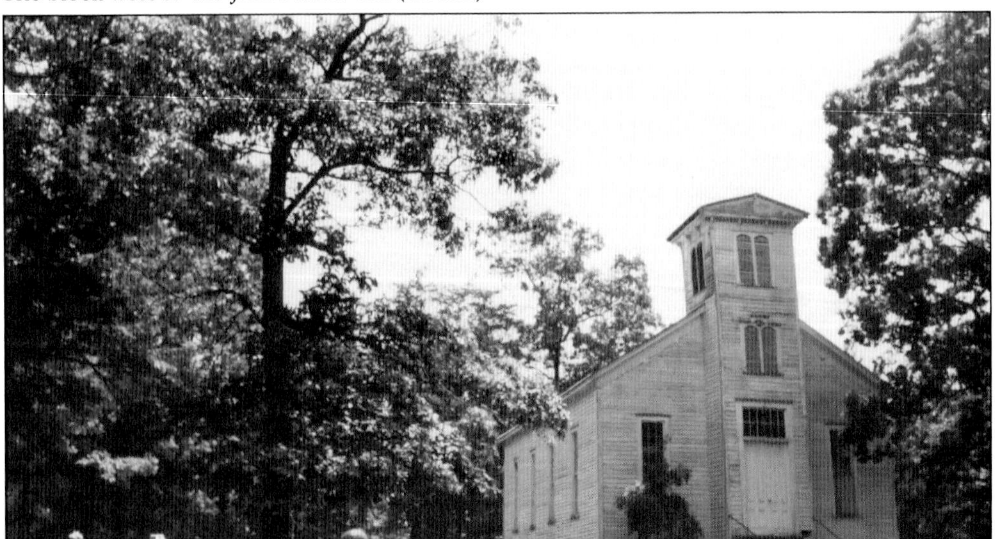

The Huntsville Methodist Episcopal Church South was built in 1888. It replaced the Mount Sinai Church, which was begun in 1808 or earlier. This church is very similar to the Farmington Methodist Church. (FHC)

Reverend Franklin Warden (1849–1929), the son of Eli and Rachel Warden, was pastor at the Deep Creek Friends Church. He may be standing in front of his store, which was near Brendle's Store in the Deep Creek community. (RW)

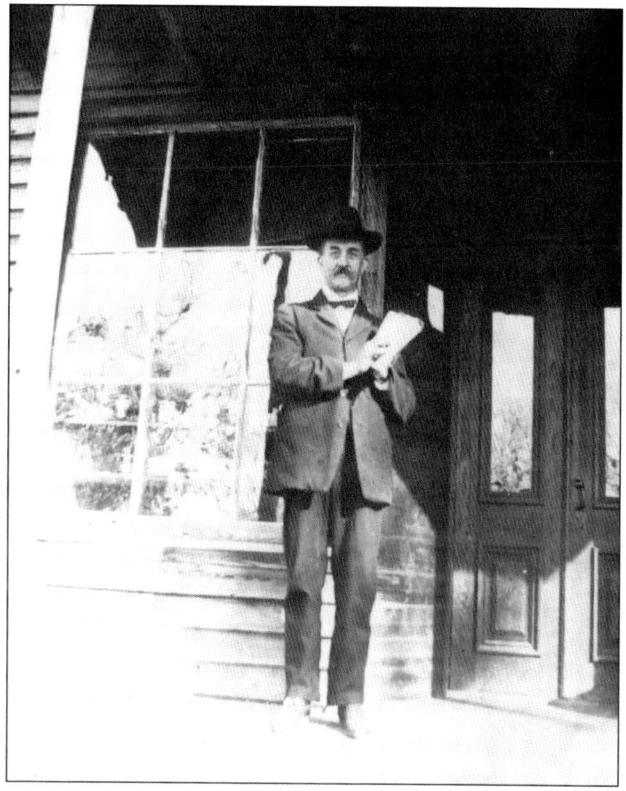

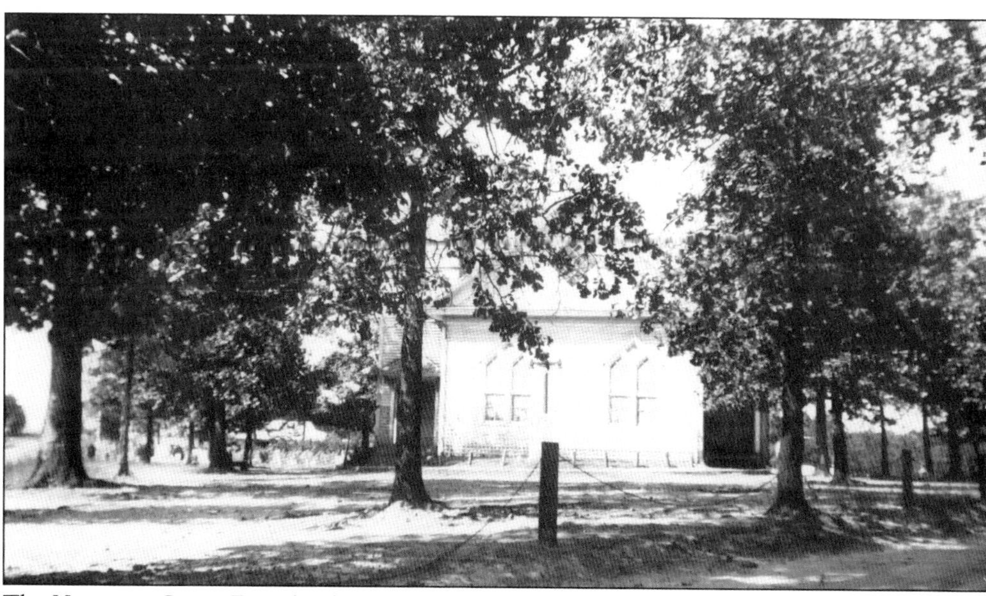

The Harmony Grove Friends Church, west of Yadkinville, as it looked in 1939. (AS)

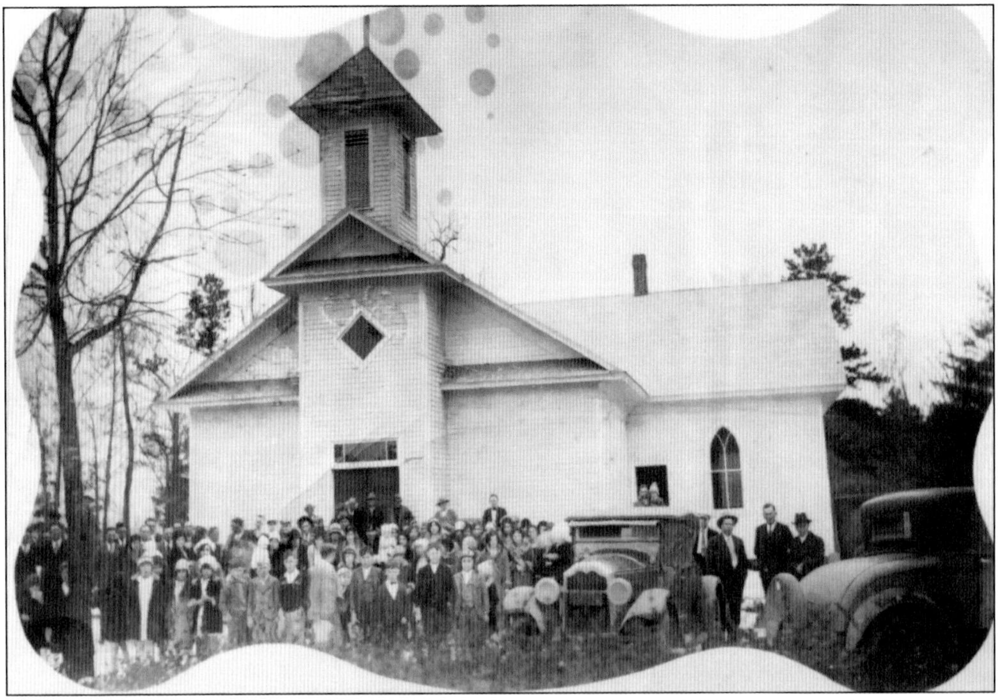

The Mitchell's Chapel Methodist Church on Center Road, in a 1930s photograph. (SO)

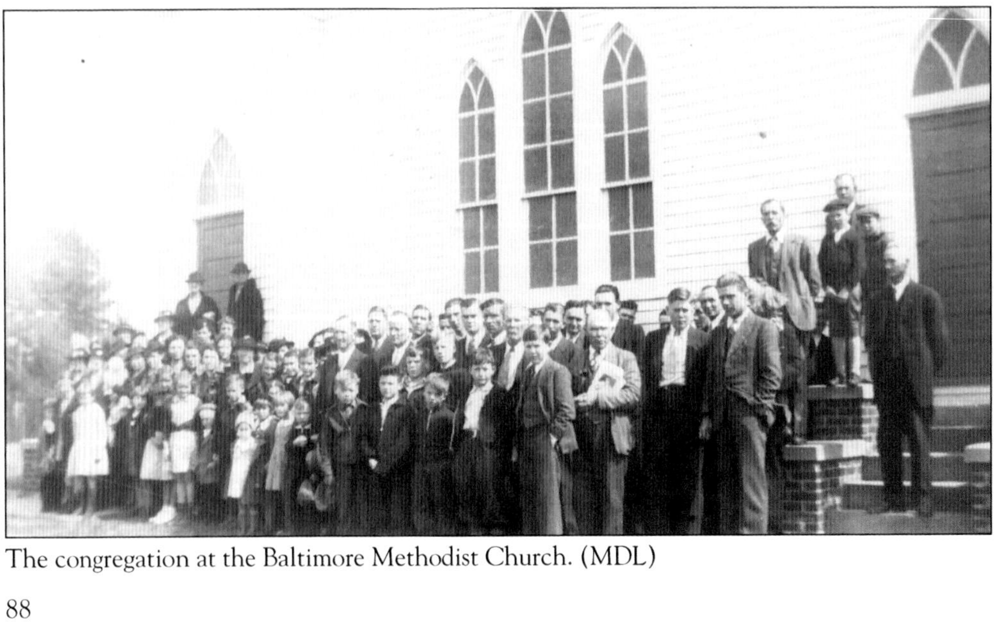

The congregation at the Baltimore Methodist Church. (MDL)

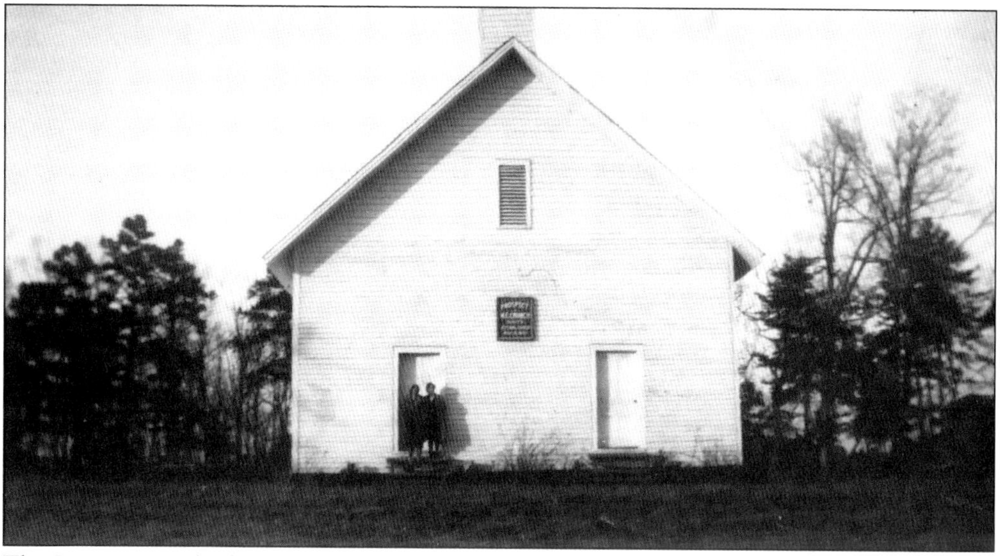

The Prospect Methodist Church in Smithtown. Note the two front doors, a feature typical of many early churches. (IMR)

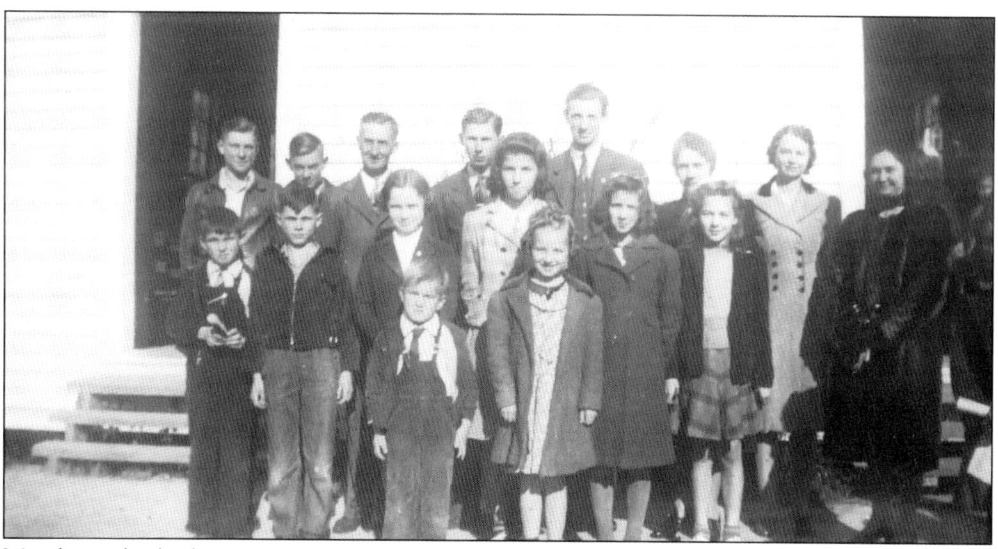

Members who had perfect attendance at Prospect Methodist Church. (IMR)

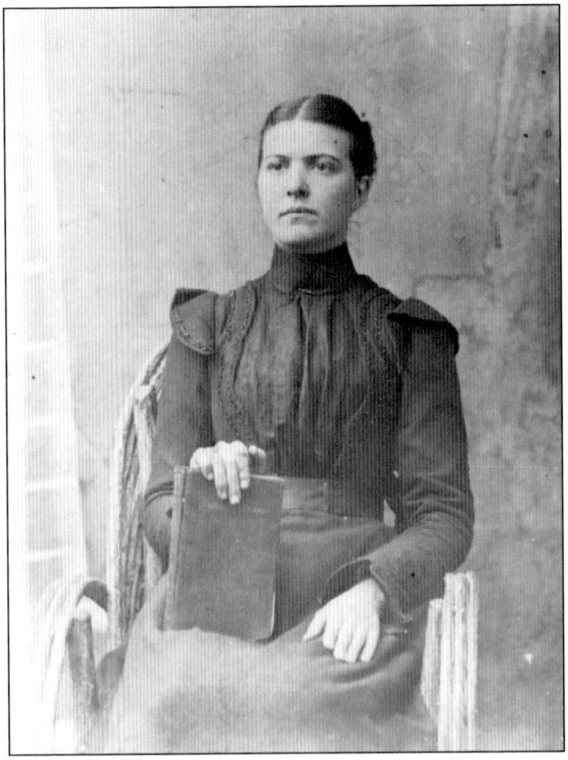

Nancy Elizabeth Gentry Long, the wife of Julian Long, holding a Bible, symbolizes the deep religious commitment of many Yadkin women. (MMS)

The Willing Workers Club was a community-based family service group. The group in this photograph includes, from left to right: (front row) Alma Hauser Russell, Florence Hauser Carter, Nettie Long McCrae, Betty Carter Russell (the president), and Callie Hauser Hauser; (back row) Velma Hauser, Helen Carter, Willie Mae White Lynch, Malene Williams Carter, Clara Carter, Odessa Williams Long, Maggie Dobson Boles, Kate Russell, Gertrude Carter Allison, and Beatrice Lynch. (JD)

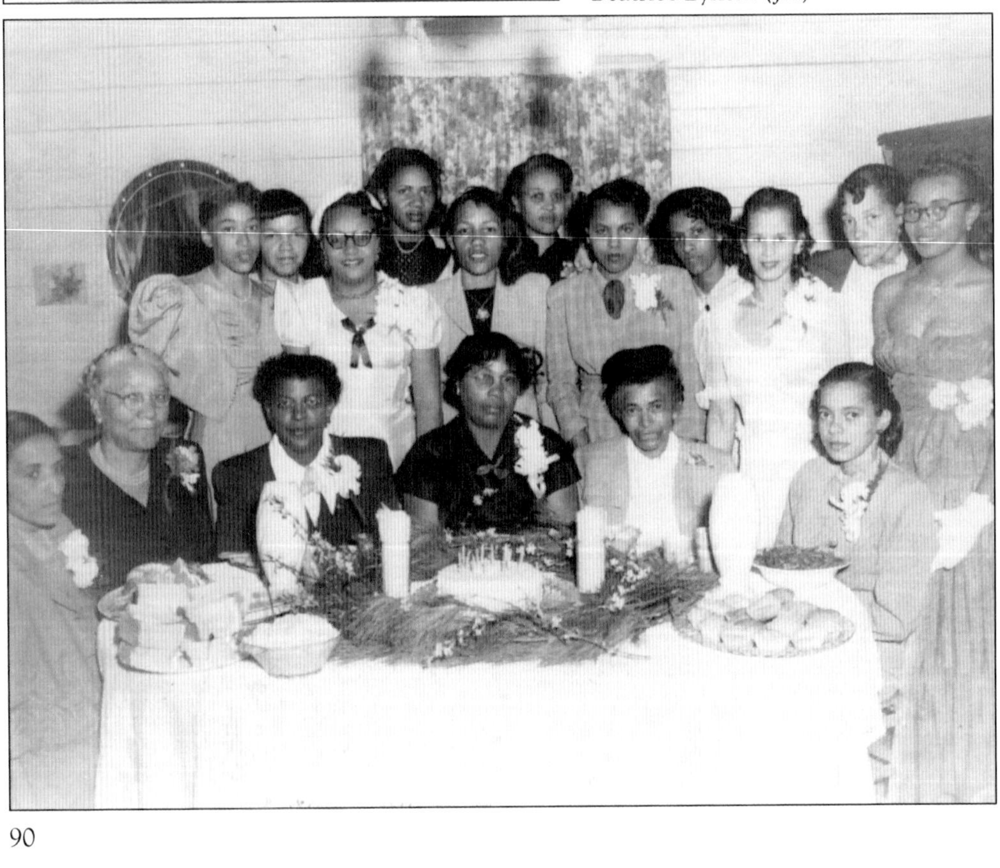

Eight

Spare the Rod

Education

The first schools in Yadkin County were affiliated with the Deep Creek Friends and Flat Rock Baptist churches as early as the 1790s. By the mid-1800s there were subscription schools in every community, but they only operated a few months each year. These schools were usually one-room log buildings, with one teacher, who taught on the elementary level.

Before the advent of school buses in the 1920s, students often walked many miles to attend. Those who wanted further education entered a high school-level school called an "academy" which also provided college preparation. In the 1930s the many small elementary schools were consolidated into six high schools.

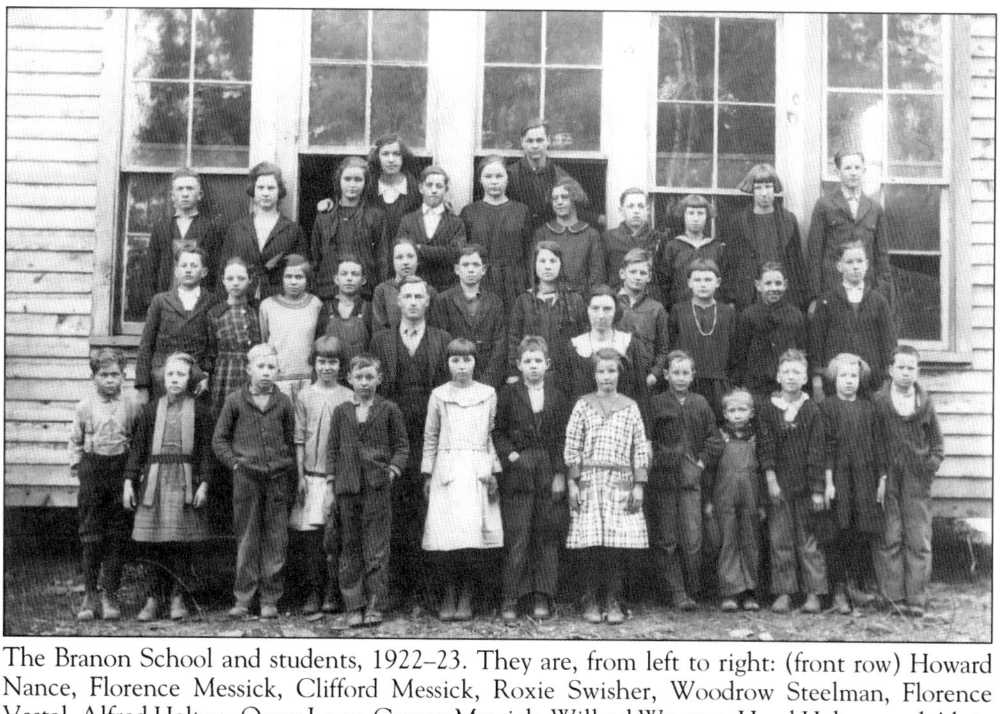

The Branon School and students, 1922–23. They are, from left to right: (front row) Howard Nance, Florence Messick, Clifford Messick, Roxie Swisher, Woodrow Steelman, Florence Vestal, Alfred Helton, Oscar Long, George Messick, Willard Wooten, Hazel Helton, and Alvin Swisher; (middle row) Lee Long, Mabel Vestal, Ethel Johnson, unknown, Hattie Wooten, Jess Swisher, Ruby Ireland, Herman Steelman, Beulah Hinson, Bill Helton, and Harry Helton; (back row) Gladys Messick Maggie Swisher, Leona Hinson, Herbert Vestal, Inez Hinson, Ruth Long, Willie Vestal, Nettie Ireland, Hattie Helton, and Sam Long. The students in the window are Ina Helton and Willie Nance. The teachers are Bruce Holcomb and Carlie Parks. (MMS)

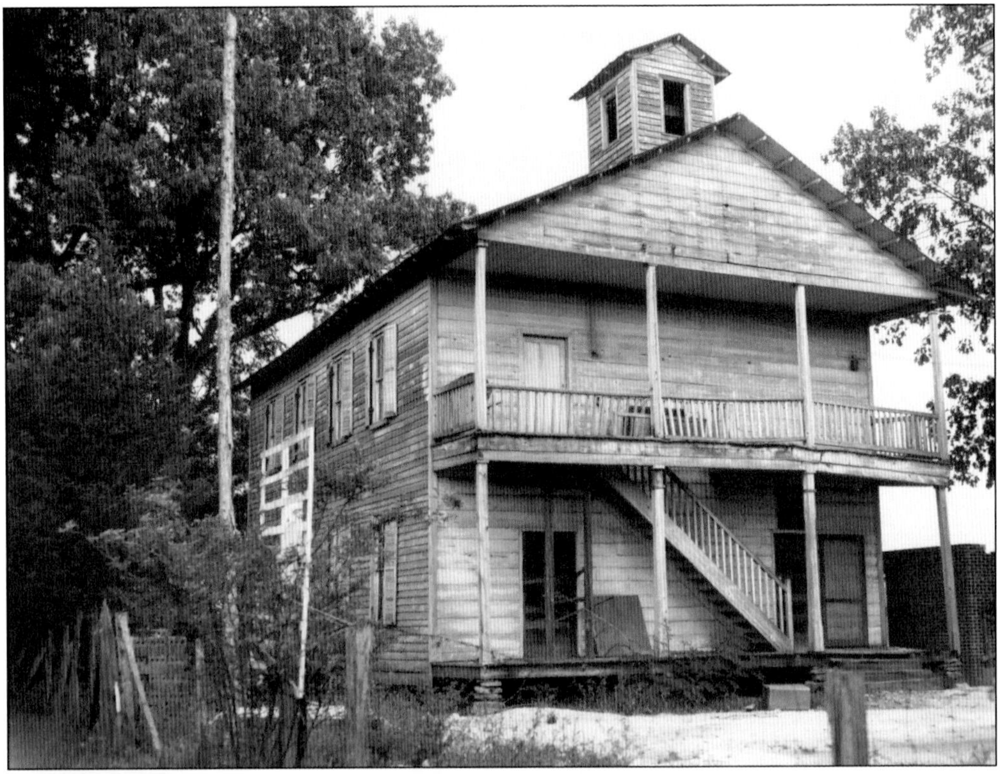

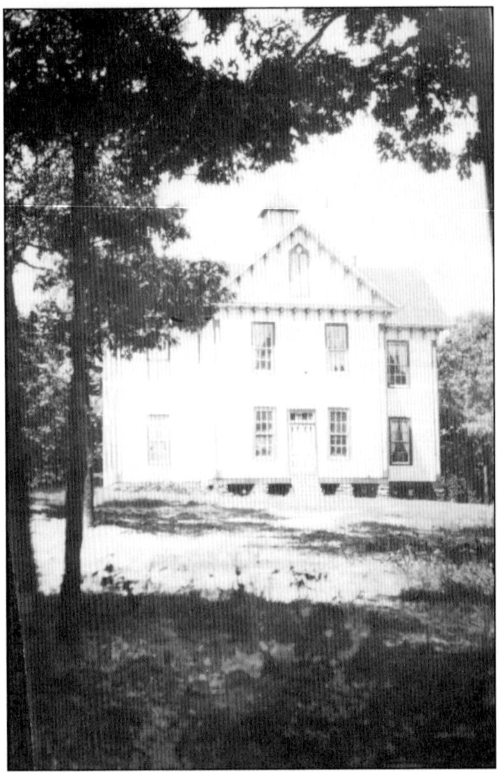

The old Academy building stood on the present Senior Citizens Center site. Its original purpose is unknown, but it probably was used in 1891 temporarily by Professor Zeno Dixon, who started the Yadkinville Normal School that year. After a new school building was constructed (see below), the upstairs portion was used by the Masonic Lodge, and the downstairs by the Women's Club. The Yadkin County Public Library was also on the ground floor for a time. (SO)

Built between 1891 and 1896, the Yadkinville Normal School was located on the present Yadkinville Elementary School grounds. The principal's home was nearby. Yadkinville High School began here in 1917, and this building was demolished in 1923 when a new brick school was completed. (MC)

Professor Zeno Dixon with his wife, Mary A. Dixon. Professor Dixon, a graduate of Vanderbilt University, founded the Yadkinville Normal School. Under his tutelage, students were prepared to enter college. There were also seven primary grades for those not planning to attend college. In 1913, Dixon became principal of the school at Elkin, and later of the school at Jonesville. (DMcL)

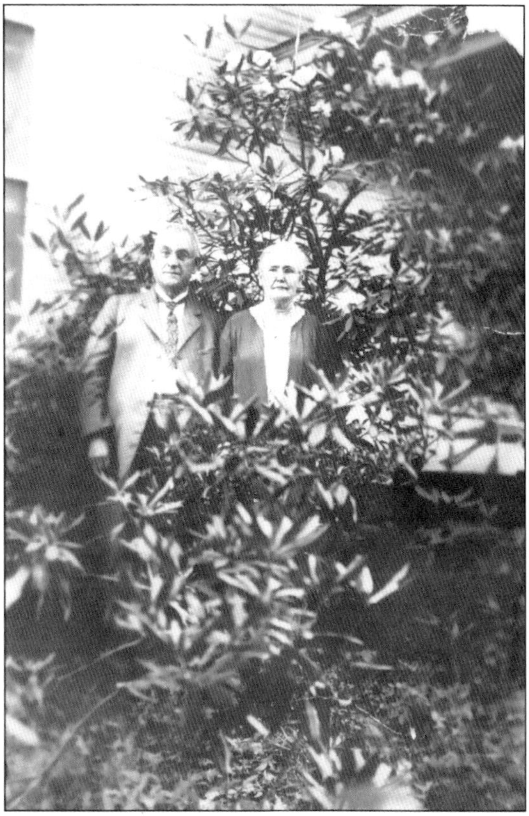

The residence of the principal (Professor Dixon) of the Yadkinville Normal School was near the school on the site of the present Yadkinville Elementary School. This photograph was taken from a 1911 postcard: on the back of the postcard was a note from Professor Dixon to a student giving the date that school would open. (RW)

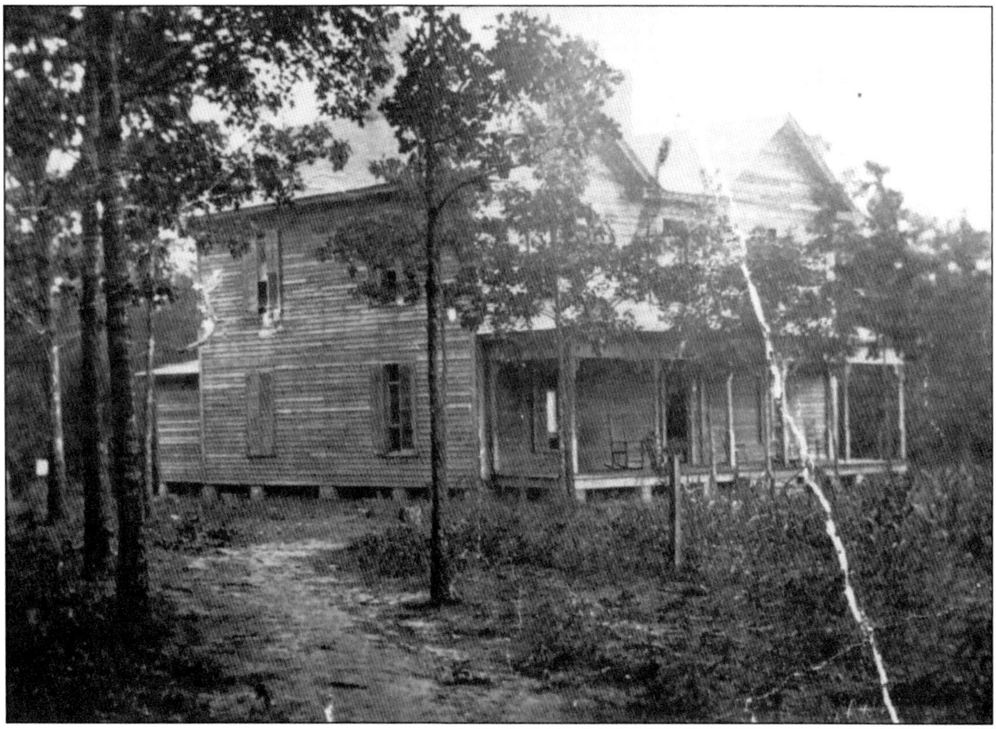

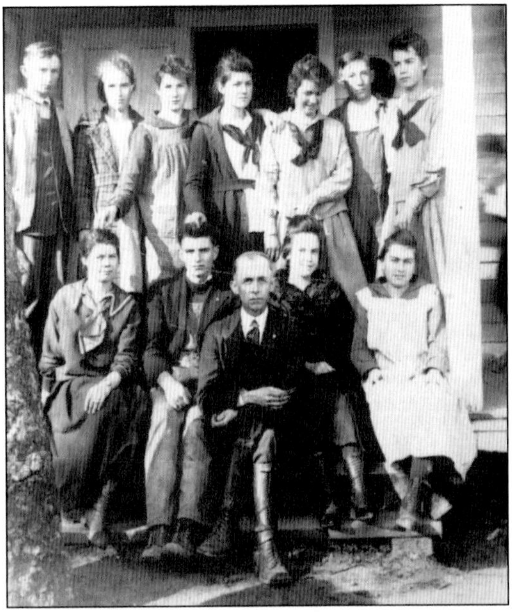

The Union Cross School in Fall Creek Township began as a one-room school in 1903. Additional rooms and additional teachers were later added. In 1914 Pearl Vestal was one of the students, and T.S. Hobson was one of the teachers. (AS)

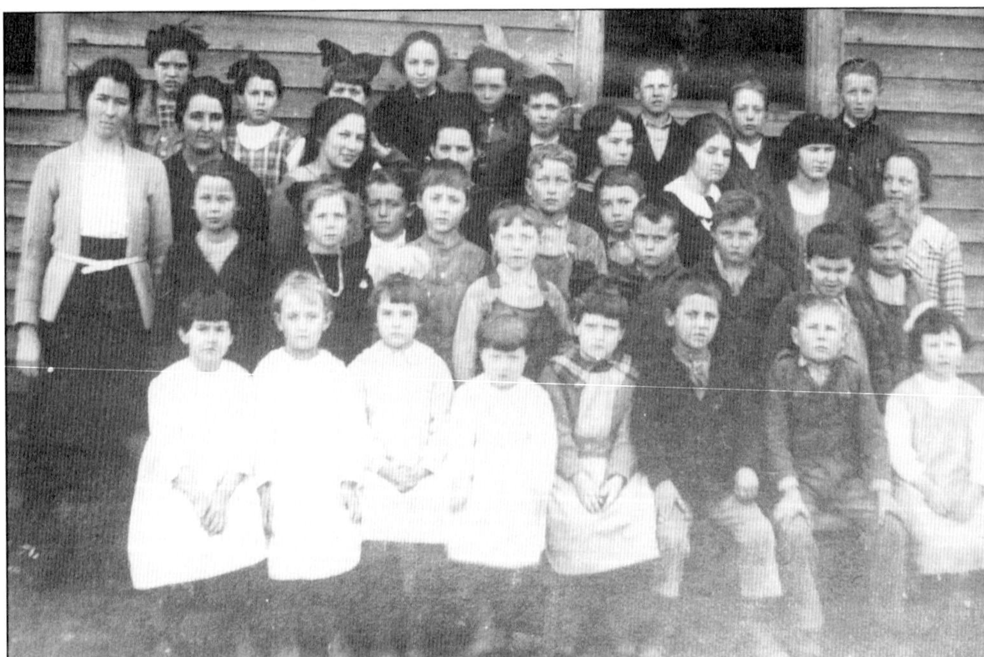

Baltimore School, originally a separate school, was later combined with the Enon and Forbush Schools. The students in this 1922 picture are, from left to right: (front row) Ruth Doub, Maude Carter, Johnsie Shore, Louella Doub, Martha Doub, ? Lakey, Wade Cornelius, Edna and Hutchens; (second row) Beulah Williams, Rachel Smitherman, Thomas Wesley Doub, ? Lakey, Willie Smitherman, Jasper Phillips, Howard Doub, Tom "Pete" Smitherman, Ellis Phillips, and Abram Phillips; (third row) Fannie Saylor, Elsie Carter, Ella Cornelius, Ora Phillips, Harold Williams, Ada Smitherman, Ethel Carter, Kate Cornelius, and Grace Williams; (back row) Mamie Phillips, Irene Doub, Inez Doub, Clark Shore, ? Lakey, Aldene Doub, Paul Cornelius, Paul Pilcher, and John Henry Doub.

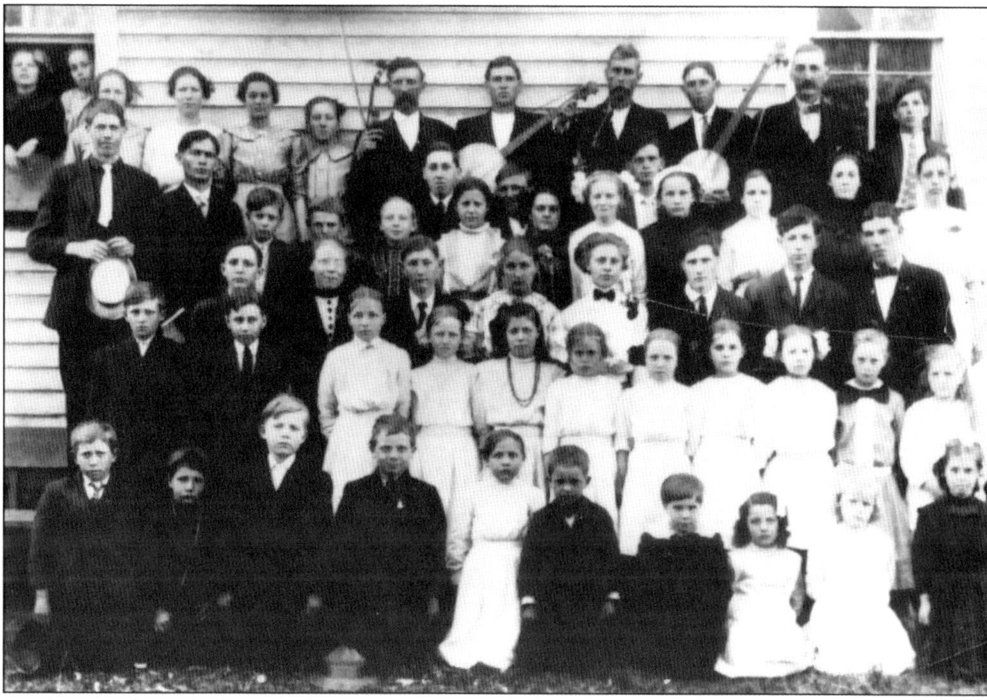

Students at the Cranberry School on Center Road about 1914. Note the band in the back row, which is composed of two banjos, a fiddle, and an instrument that looks like a guitar. (IMR)

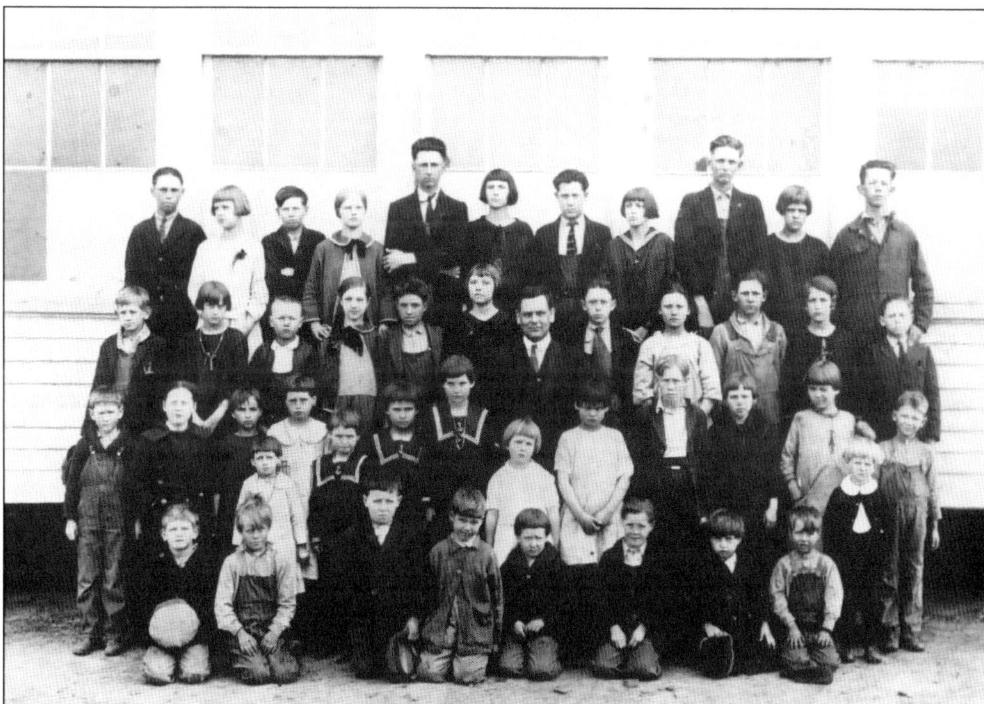

Students at the Star Peak School in the 1920s, with teacher Nereus P. Bryant in the center. Dick Bray is the last boy on the right in the back row. (EM)

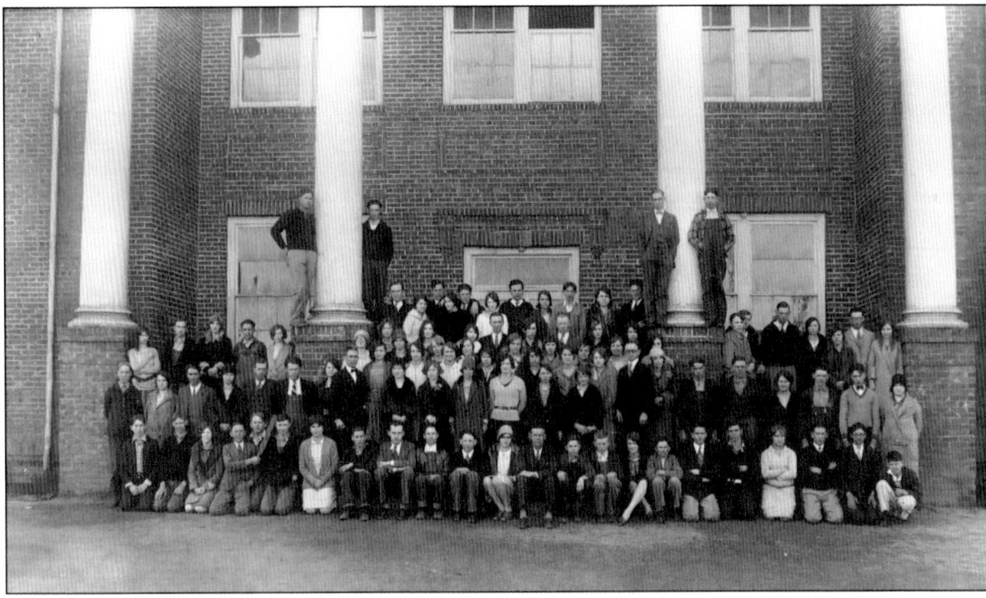

The entire student body of Boonville High School in 1930. (EM)

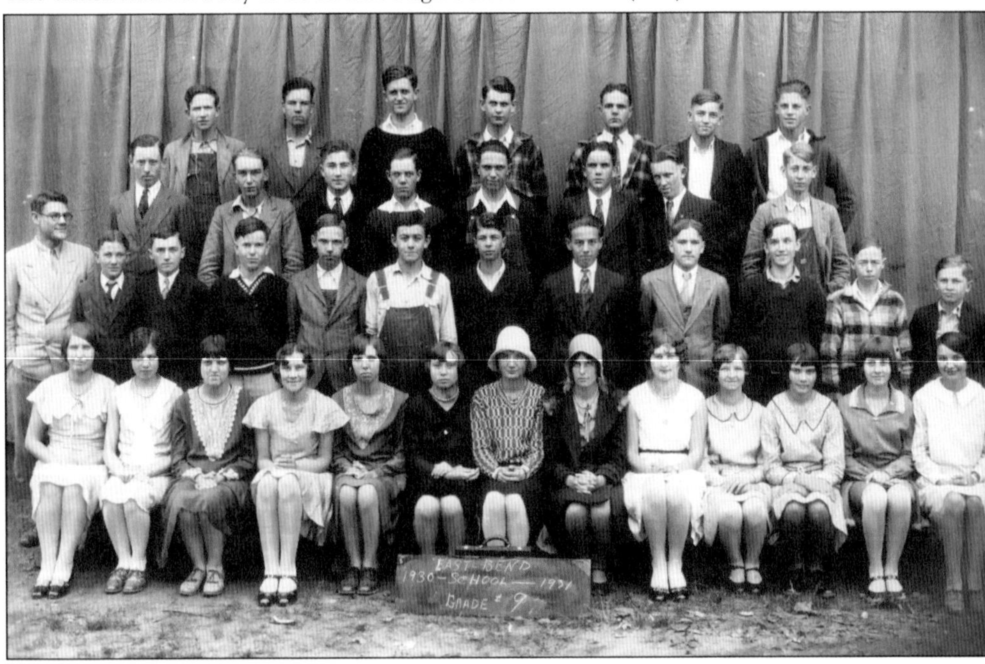

The students in this photograph of the ninth grade at the East Bend School in 1930–31 are, from left to right: (front row) unknown, Fern Wilhelm, Martha Doub, Clara Hill, Katharin Welch, Mabel Smitherman, Lucy Bell Smitherman, Jessie Smitherman, unknown, Sadie Davis, Hazel Matthews, Ruth Smitherman, Lois Adams, and unknown; (second row) Mr. Lassiter (the teacher), unknown, Folger Matthews, ? Poindexter, ? Davis, Norman Marler, Grady Ammons, Clarence Hill, Ernest Kirkman, Woodrow Poindexter, and Gilbert Hobson; (third row) ? Smitherman, unknown, Charles B. Huff Jr.,? Norman, Aldene Doub, Richard Benbow, Thomas Sanford Griffin, and Charlie North; (back row) Frank Miller, unknown, George Davis, Charles Burchett, Sherril Wooten, Troy Matthews, and unknown. (MDL)

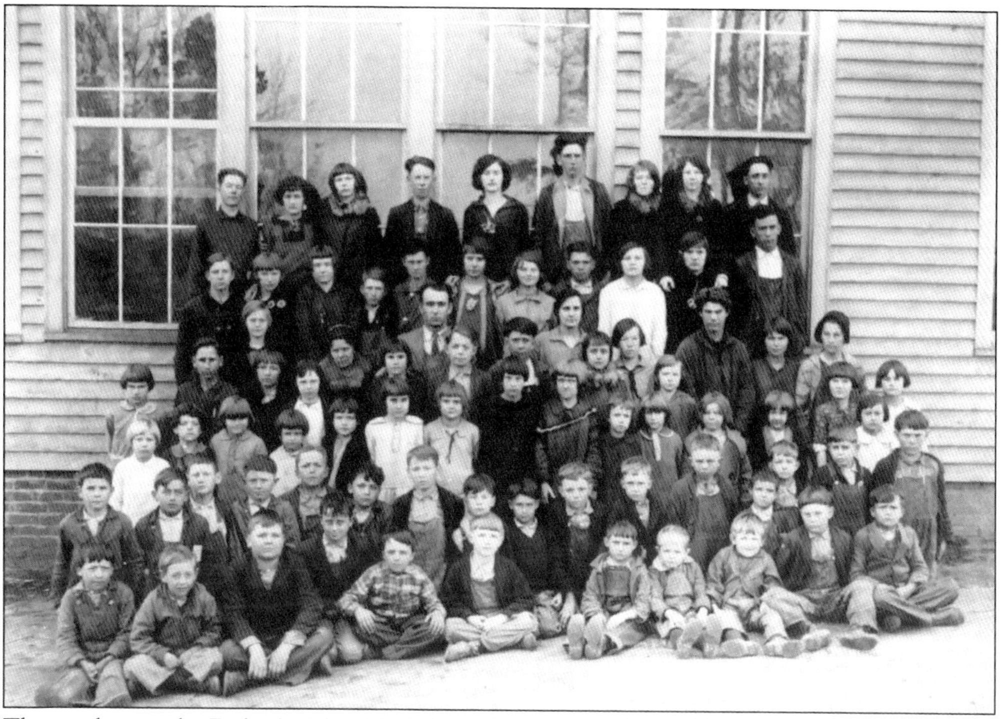

The teachers at the Forbush School in 1926–27 were Jasper Long, Blanch Williams, and Minnie Mackie. (JL)

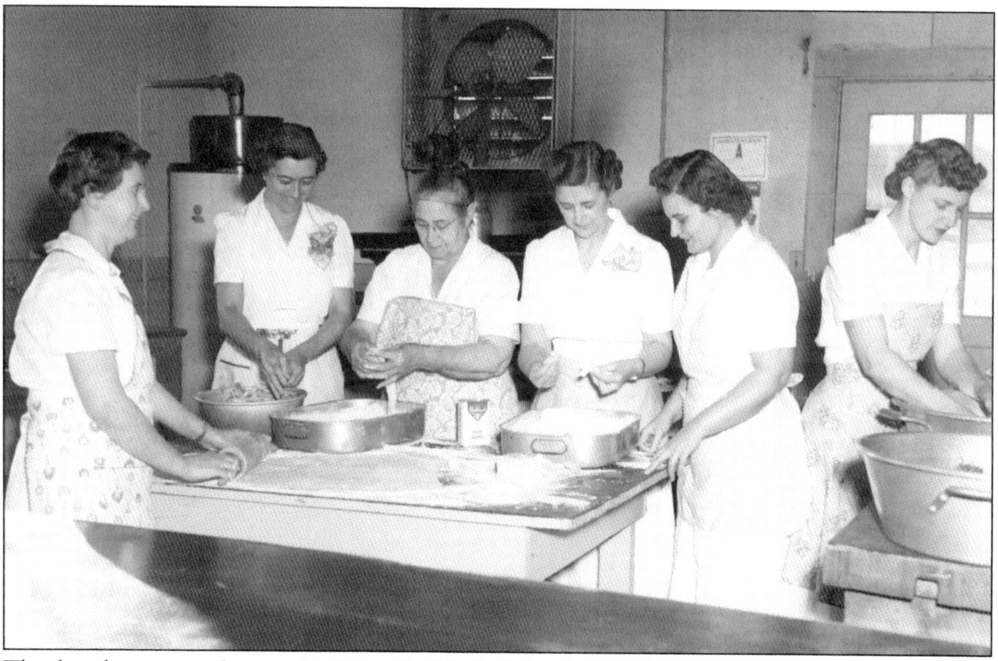

The lunchroom workers at Yadkinville High School served a hot, nourishing lunch to the students in a building that was erected on the site of the old gymnasium. Pictured here are, from left to right: Laura Kiger Brannon, Helen Reavis, Lola Phillips Garner, Veigh Long, Marguerite Goins Trivette, and Frances Royall. (EGS)

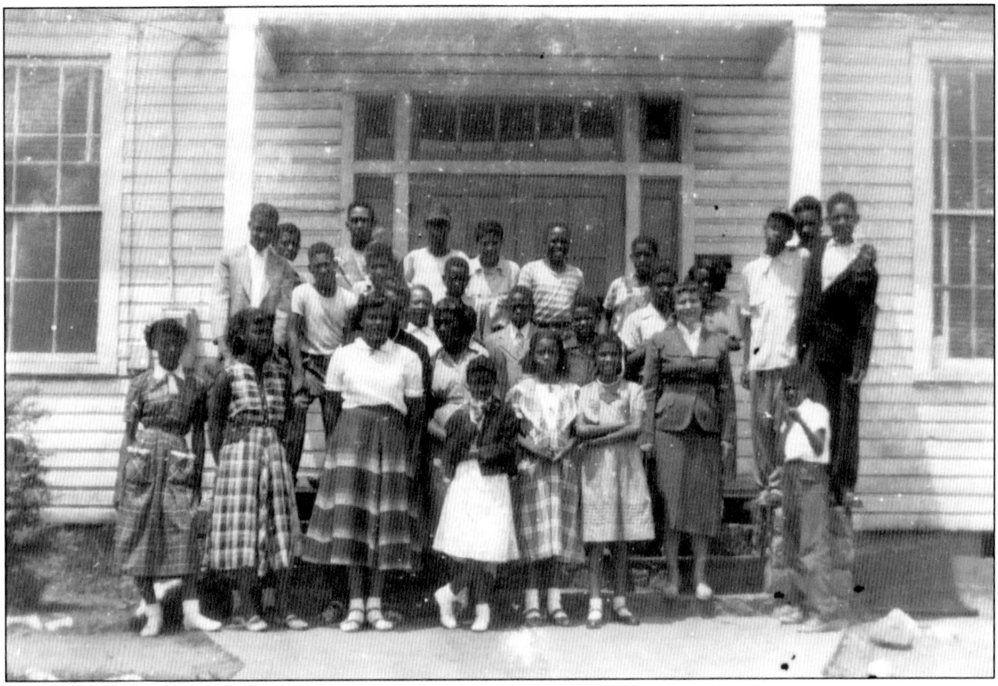

The students of Yadkin High School, at Boonville, pictured with teacher Ann Blackburn. (AB)

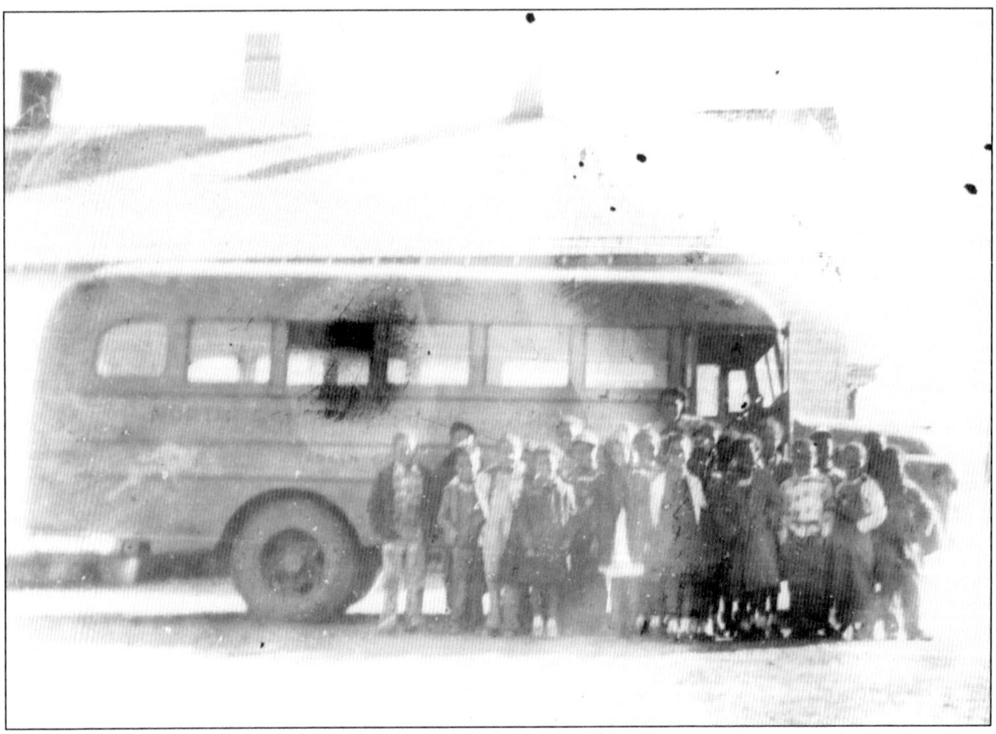

Before desegregation, the students of Yadkin High School had to travel many miles by bus from all over the county to attend a consolidated school located at Boonville. (AB)

Nine

An Ounce of Prevention
Home and Health

Before the 1950s, few families had indoor plumbing, electricity, or telephones. Homes were heated by fireplaces or wood stoves. Even cooking was done over an open fireplace or on a wood stove. Women kept their milk and butter cool by placing them in a spring of cool water or by lowering them into a "dry well." Drinking water was obtained from a nearby spring or a well dug near the house. Meat was preserved by smoke- or salt-curing. Bathing was usually done on Saturday in an old tin tub or in the creek and most families had an outhouse.

There was no hospital in the county until 1952, although Dr. Locksley S. Hall Sr. did have a private clinic in Yadkinville. Doctors made visits on horseback, and were often paid in eggs and other produce for their services. Midwives delivered babies. Folk medicine and home cures were widely practiced. Even minor diseases, easily cured today by antibiotics, were often fatal.

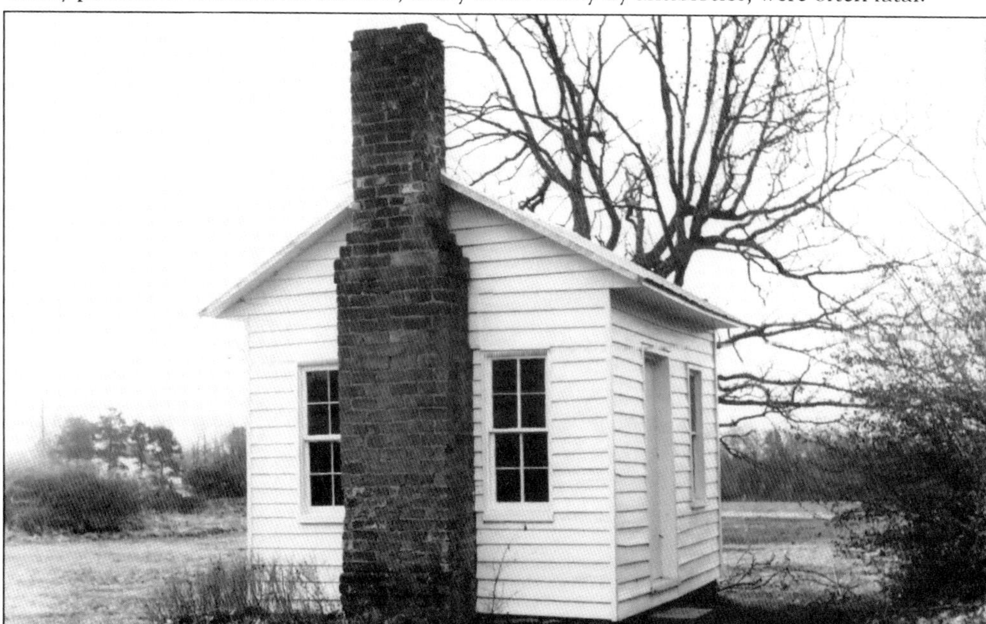

The office of Dr. Calvin Holcomb (1841–1918) still stands beside his former home on Center Road. Holcomb, a Civil War veteran, made medicines from herbs planted near the office. (LW)

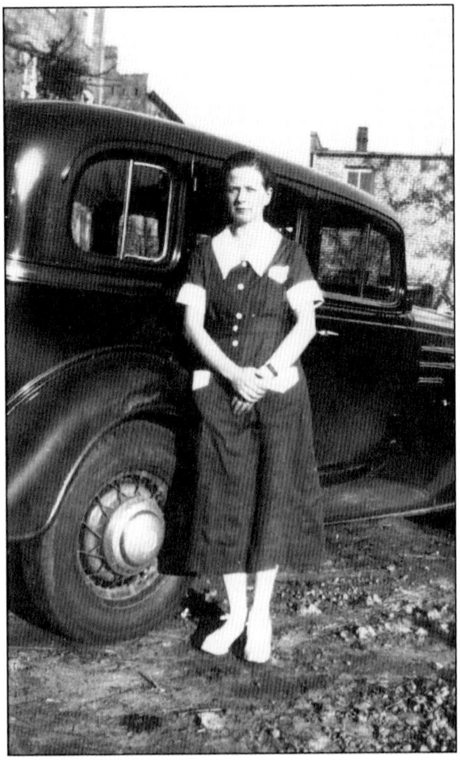

After its establishment, the Health Department provided inoculations for smallpox and typhoid fever, and employed a county health nurse who visited families throughout the county. Laura (Bowman) Harding was the first public health nurse in the county, serving from 1931 to 1935. (FHC)

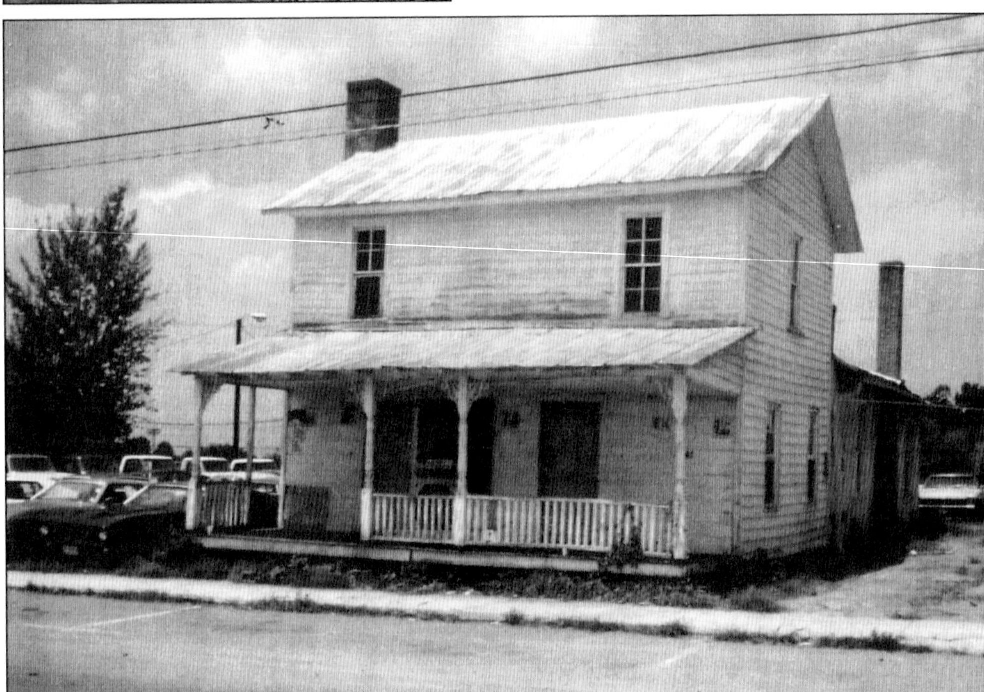

The Thomasson house housed the Yadkin County Health Department and the Welfare Department. The house, on West Main Street, was built in the 1850s and demolished about 1965. The property is now used as a lot for new cars by Dan Beck Ford. (LW)

For many years, Mrs. Julia Steelman Burcham (1883–1963) used her own special remedy to treat cancerous growths. She continued until 1955, when she was indicted for practicing medicine without a license. Mrs. Burcham, a native of Wilkes County, reportedly obtained the recipe from her first husband, Jesse Burcham (d. 1905), who learned how to prepare the ointment while a Confederate prisoner in a northern prison. Defense lawyers Marion Allen and Smith Williams won an acquittal by arguing that "old women using home remedies in assisting the sick" were not violating the Holy Bible or state law. (KMcE)

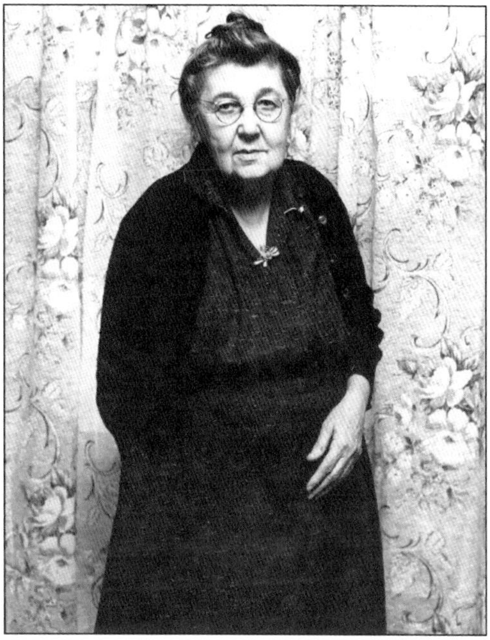

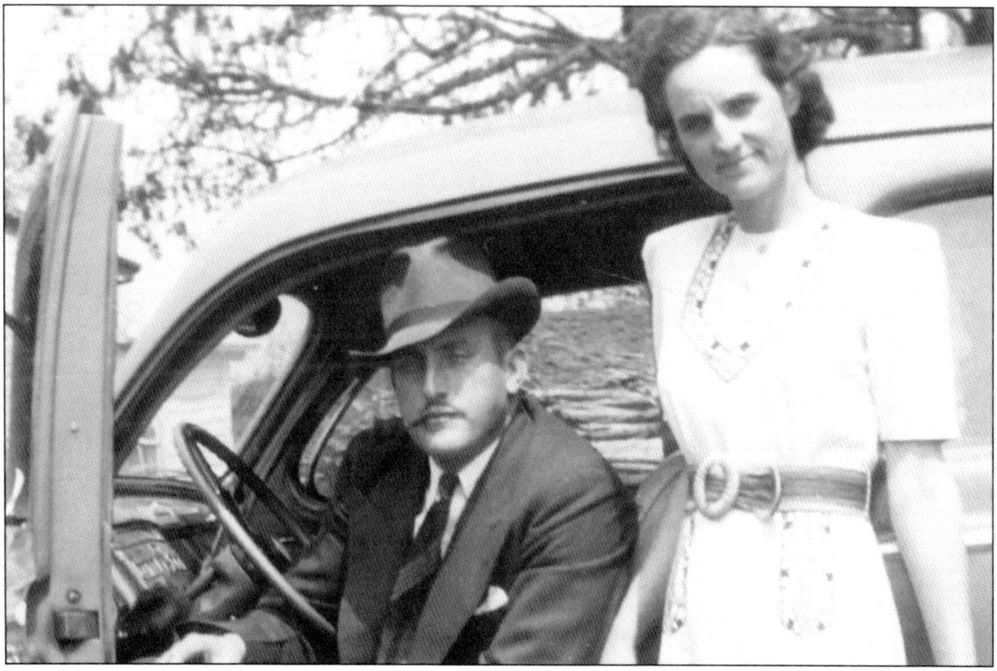

Health professionals Dr. Benjamin Hackett Harding and his sister, Joseline Graves Harding, shared their training with Yadkin County residents. Miss Harding, who graduated from Women's College in Greensboro and attended graduate school at UNC Chapel Hill, was the first Yadkin County superintendent of public welfare. She served in that capacity from 1937 to 1942. Dr. Harding, a graduate of the University of North Carolina, received his MD from the Medical College of Virginia. He began his practice at Brooks' Cross Roads in 1934, and continued there until he was commissioned a captain in the Medical Corps during World War II. After the war, he moved his practice to Elkin. (FHC)

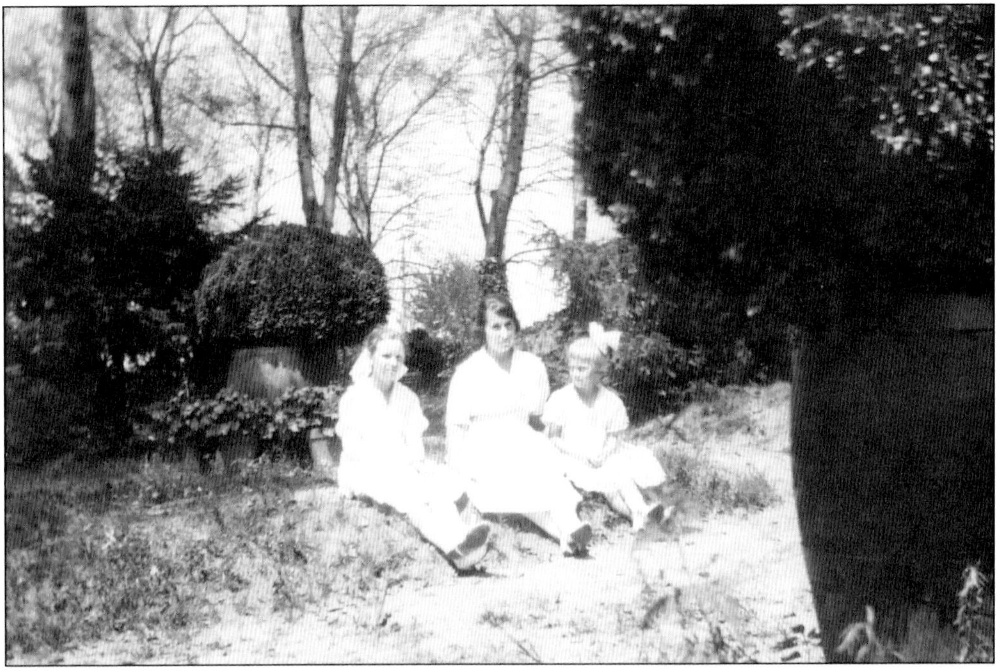

Locke Sears (in the center) and friends sit in the garden behind the Yadkin Valley Hotel. Locke was a dental assistant to Dr. Rosebud Morse Garriott. Dr. Garriott graduated from the Atlanta Dental College in 1916, and practiced in East Bend from 1916 until her death. Her sister, Italy, graduated from the Atlanta Dental College and practiced in East Bend for a year, and her brother, Duke Morse, also practiced dentistry in East Bend for some time. (JN)

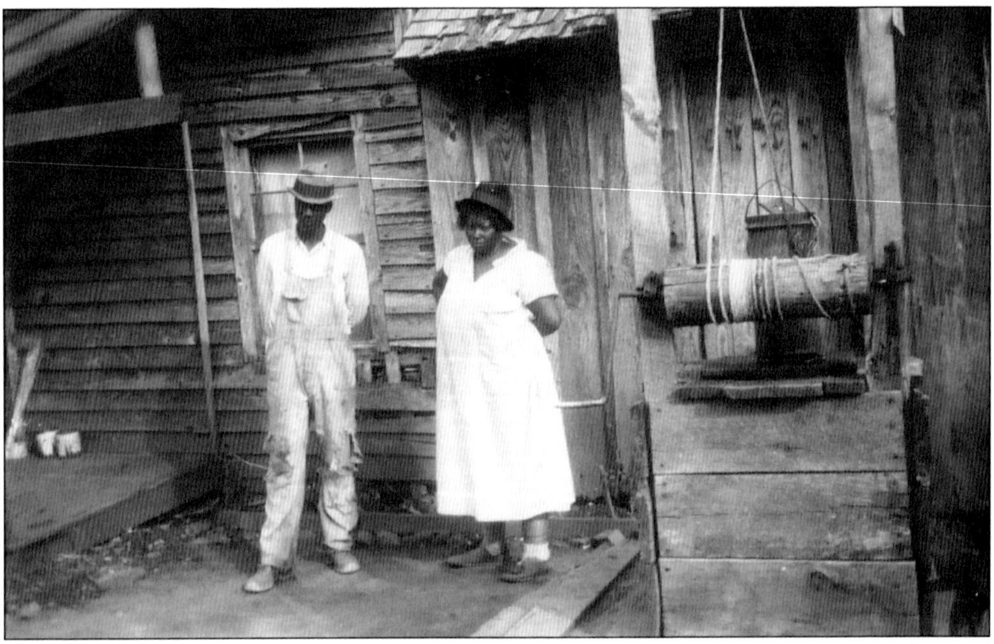

Indoor plumbing was a longtime coming to Yadkin County. Here, an unidentified couple stand beside the well outside their home. The cool, pure water had to be drawn up in a bucket, usually made of oak wood, by a windlass and a rope. (FHC)

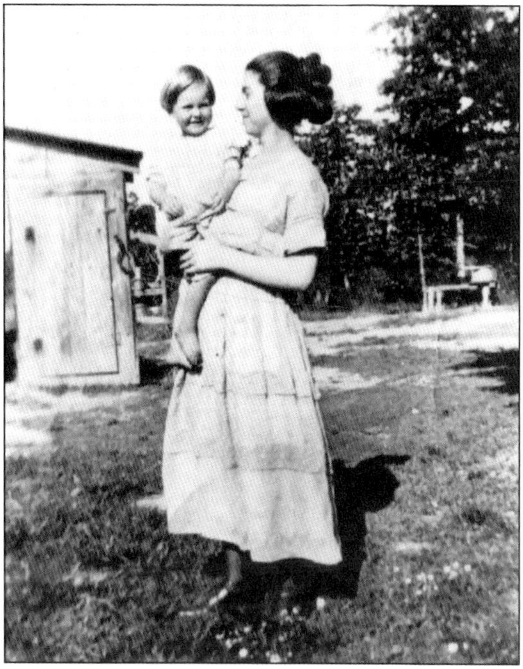

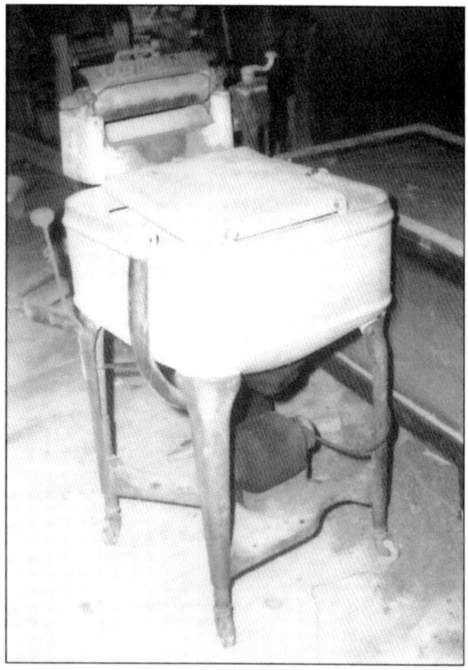

Left: "Milk" wells, like the one shown here in the background, were essential in the days before refrigeration. Milk, butter and, perhaps, lemonade, were lowered into a dry well to keep them cool. This 1921 photograph was taken at the Mozelle (Mackie) Hutchens home on Shacktown Road. In the foreground is Laura (Shermer) Martin holding young Mildred Mackie. (MM)
Right: Before electricity and automatic washing machines, some families did their laundry using a washing machine with a gas-powered motor attached, like this 1930s Maytag. Beside the washing machine is a hand-crafted crib covered with screen wire. The crib was made in 1933 by Roscoe Campbell for the children of "Dalt" Casstevens. (CDC)

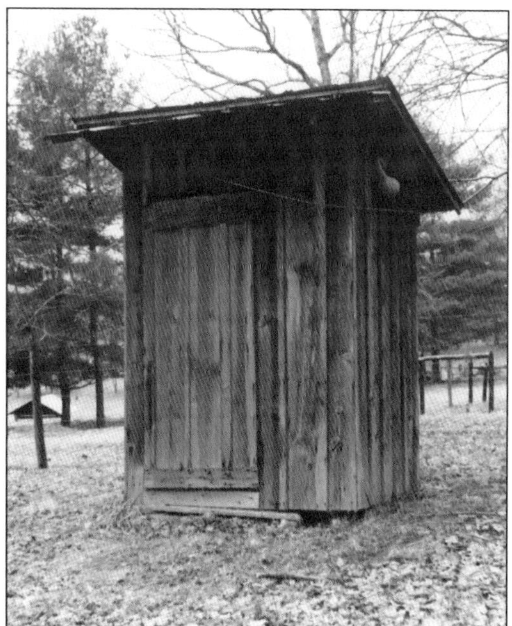

The outhouse in back of the family home, such as this one at the Lee Allgood place, served families for many years, until the advent of indoor plumbing and septic tanks. (LW)

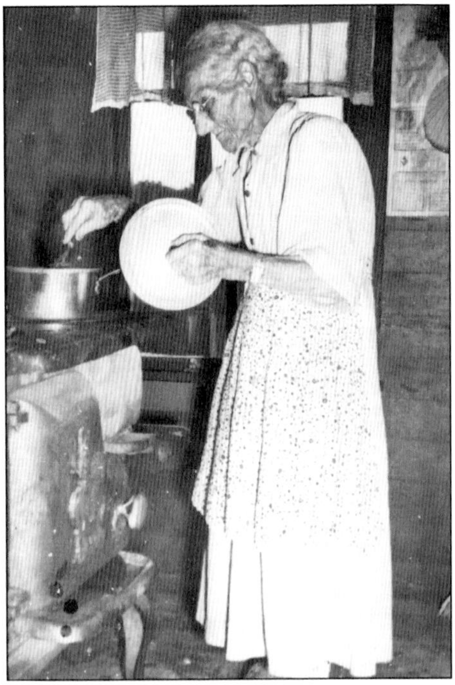

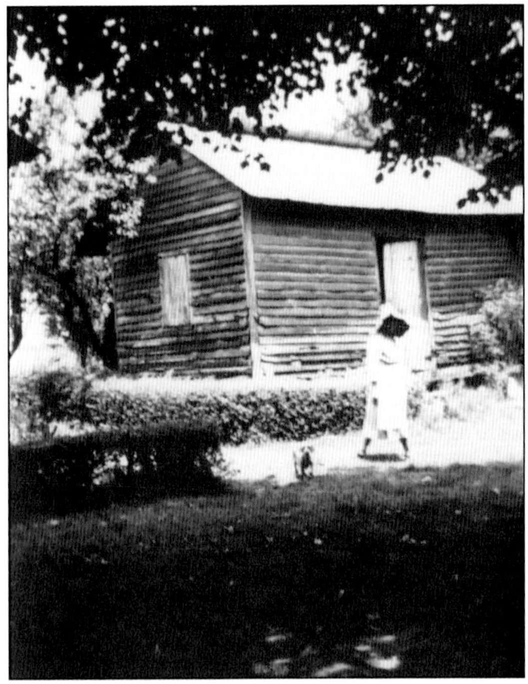

Left: Mrs. Jane (Sprouse) Robertson, of the Longtown community, married Lee B. Robertson in 1883. Until the 1950s, most women did their cooking on a wood stove. Even after homes were wired for electricity, many older women preferred food cooked on the wood stove. (IMR) Right: Kitchens were originally detached from houses, to prevent the entire house burning in the event of a fire. Mrs. Maggie (Holcomb) Hinshaw is shown here outside her kitchen. (MLH)

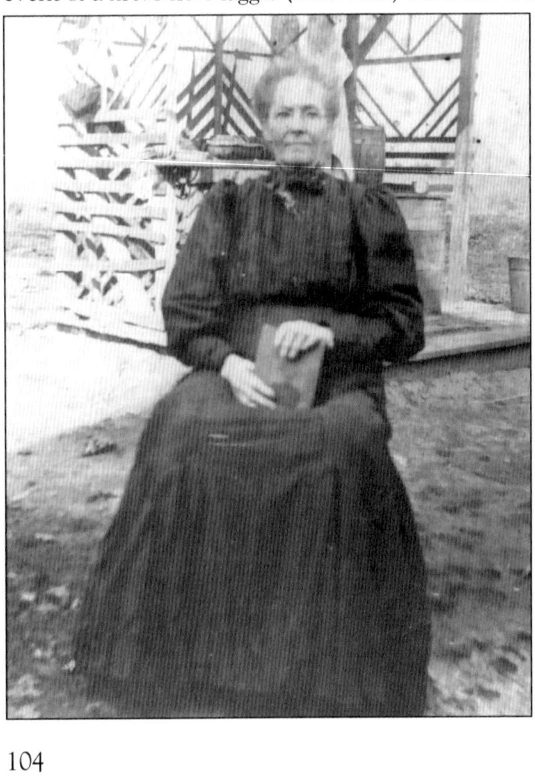

Wells were usually covered over and sometimes decorated with lattice work. In this photograph, Mrs. Ollie L. Carter (1849–1929) is sitting in the shade near her well, holding what appears to be a picture in her lap. (RW)

Ten

Strike One
Sports and Recreation

Yadkin County people have always worked hard and played just as hard. People created their own fun with ice cream suppers, picnics, swimming, fishing, and hunting. They sang, danced, and played musical instruments, and turned work, such as corn huskings, into social events.

Children played football and baseball in any open field. They amused themselves by jumping rope, or by playing hop-scotch or hide-and-seek. They rode tricycles and bicycles and skated on the sidewalks around the old courthouse. Together, families listened to the Grand Old Opry on the radio or came to town on Saturday night to see Westerns at the movie theater.

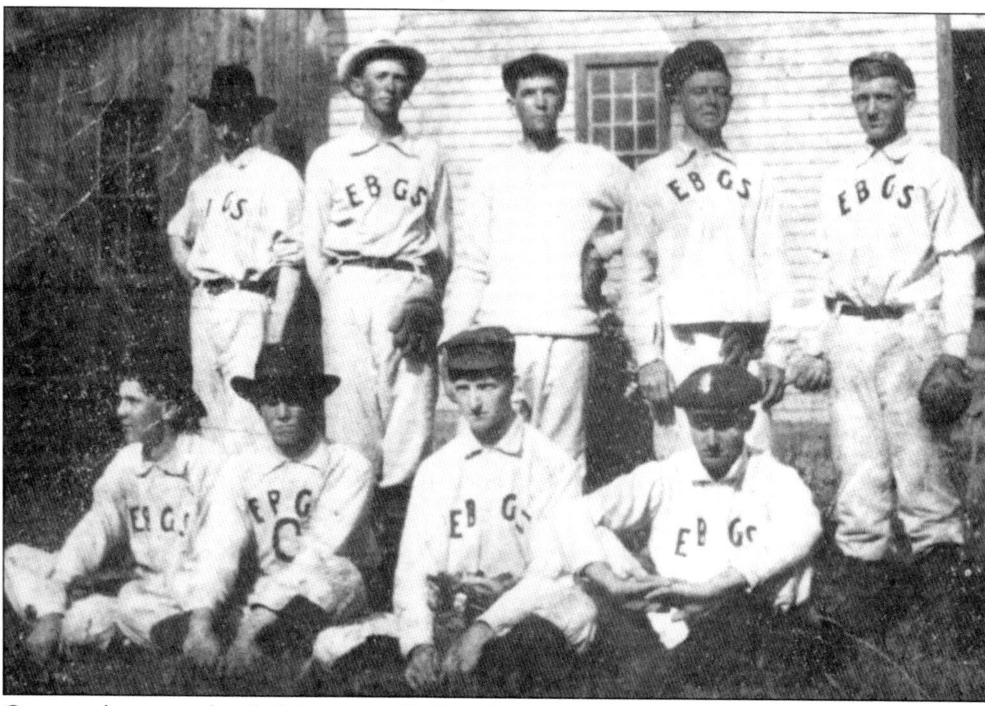

Organized amateur baseball began in Yadkin County about 1890. The most famous of several teams was the Red Strings team, which played throughout the area between 1896 and 1902. This photograph of some of the former Red Strings players was taken on the day they were going to assist the East Bend team in a 1907 commencement game against Boonville. Unfortunately the game was rained out. The players are, from left to right: (seated) Ernie Shore, J. Thad Reece, David Lee Pardue, Oscar D. Casstevens; (standing) Marvin Holcomb, Thomas H. Mackie, Charlie Frank Benbow, William R. Royall, and Evan Poindexter. (AS)

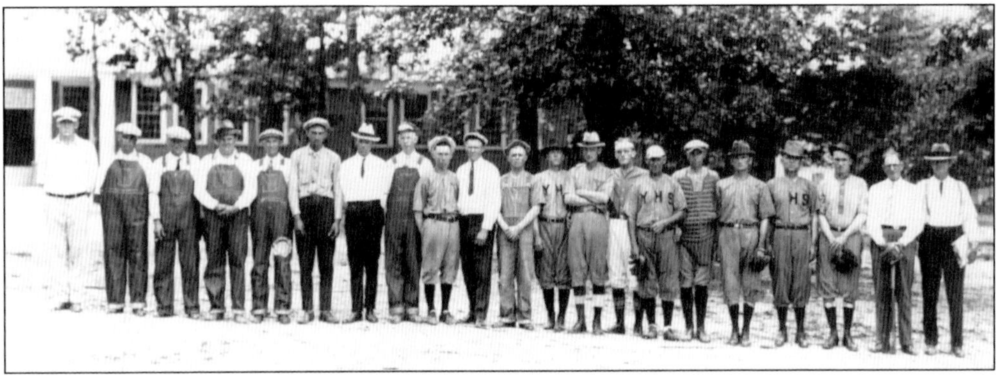

Baseball games were popular at graduation events and Fourth of July celebrations. Jesse Lee Mackie's team included, from left to right: unknown, ? A. Dickerson, unknown, unknown, unknown, Walter Southard, Marvin Mackie (or Cranfill), Bill Sheek, unknown, ? Royall, Arthur Warden, John H. Hauser, unknown, Harry Fox, Walt Hinshaw, Walter Carter, Everette Joyce, Cling Driver, J.L. Mackie (the manager), and Joe Bill Goslen. (JGM)

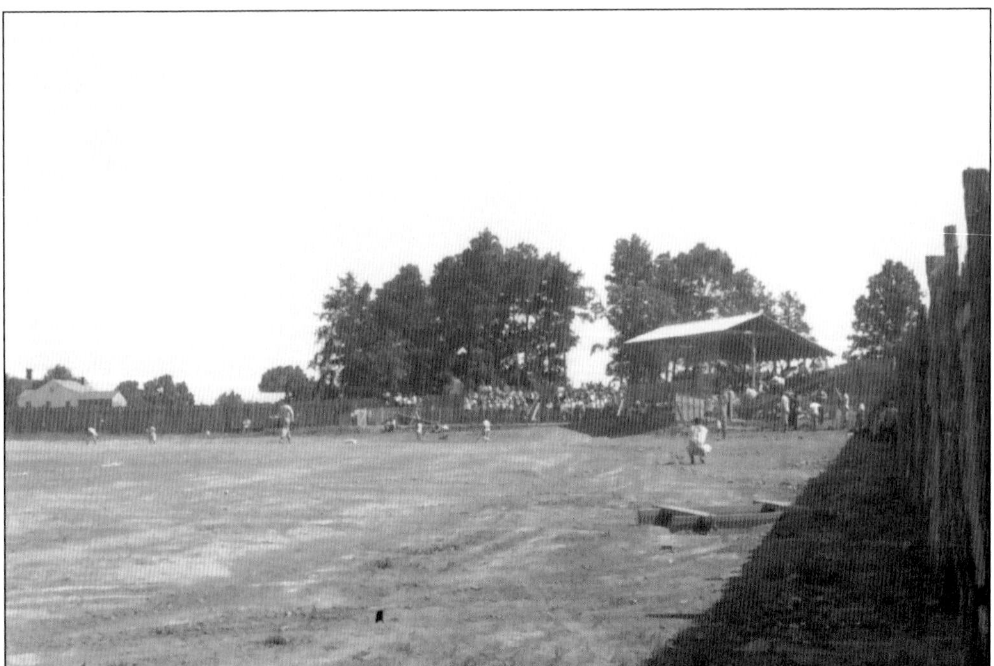

Many baseball games were played in the ballpark in Yadkinville. A housing development now stands on the old ballpark site. (SO)

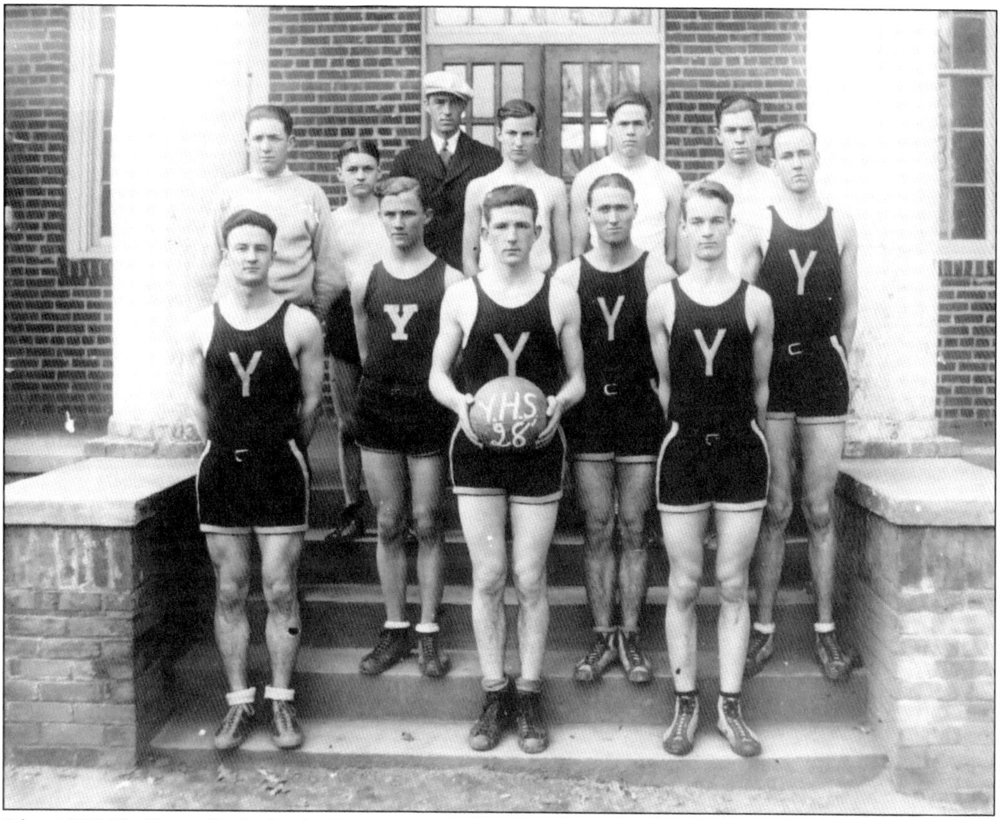

The 1928 Yadkinville basketball team. The players are, from left to right: (front row) Paul Brandon, Clarence "Tat" Davis, John Crater, Gus Nicks, Joe Martin, and Weldon Brown; (back row) Grady Royall, Charlie Gough, Newton Kelly, George Williams, and Fred Hinshaw. The coach, at the back, was Henry Allen Brandon. (MLH)

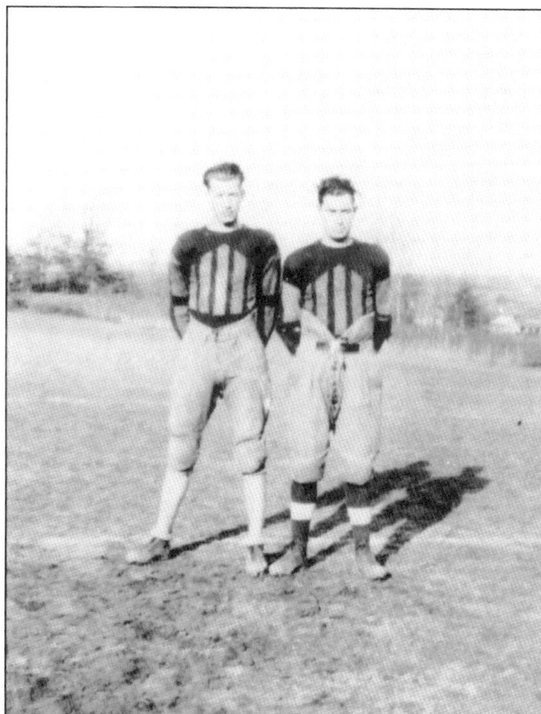

The Yadkinville High School football team was first organized in 1929, with Hackett Harding as coach. Shown here are two of the members of that team. The one on the right is Fred Hinshaw. (MLH)

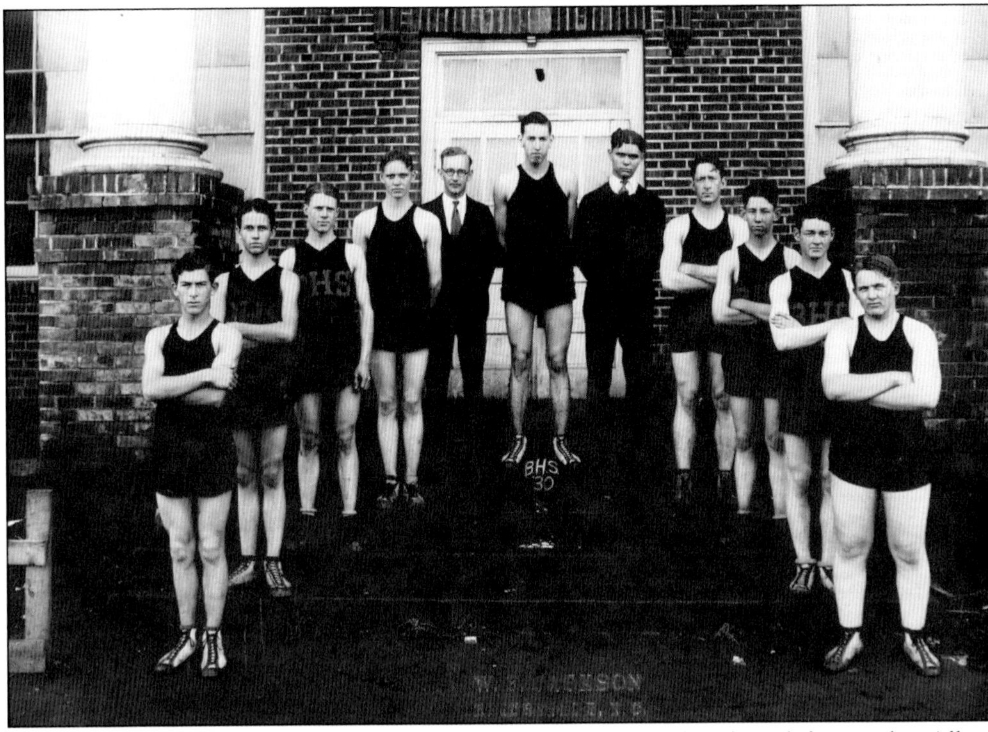

This photograph of the 1930 Boonville basketball team includes, from left to right: Albert Woodruff, John L. Amburn, James Reece, Delma Brown, Coach Walker, Miles Reavis, Wade Williams, Odell Groce, Wayne Spencer, Eli Mosteller, and Jack Jones. (EM)

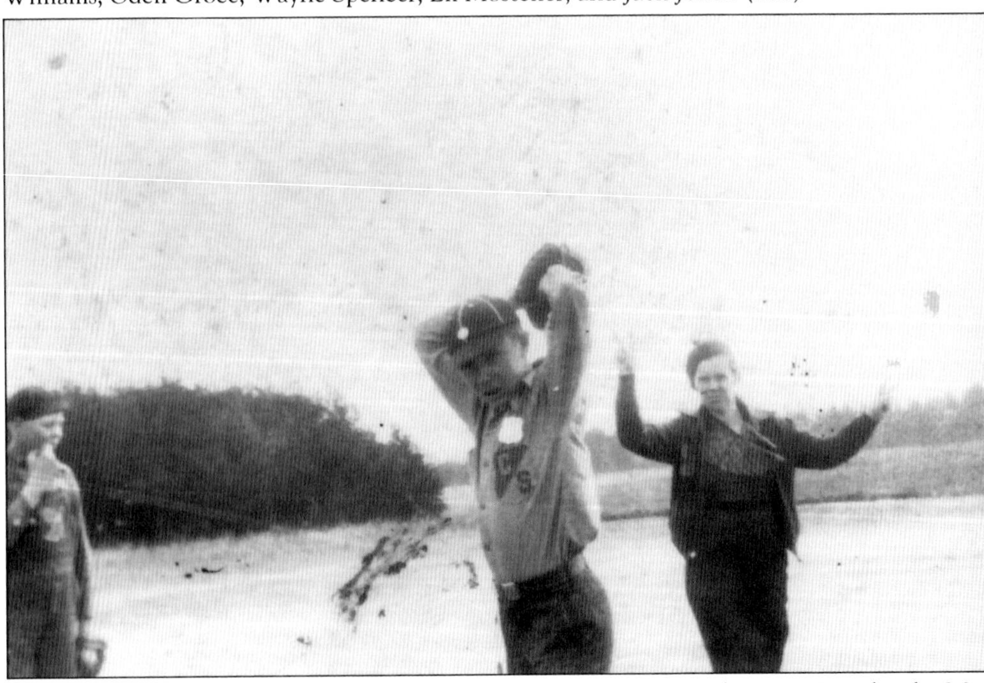

Boys playing ball at the Cranberry School on Center Road in March 1930. Can that be Miss Irma Matthews calling the strikes? Miss Irma taught at the Cranberry School in 1934. (IMR)

Girls were not to be outdone and they had some fine basketball teams. Shown here is the 1935 Courtney High School team. The players are, from left to right: (kneeling) Leona Belle Joyner, Myrtle Lynch, and Lottie Renegar; (standing) Pearl Miller, Joyce Shermer, Pauline Reavis, Sally Virginia Miller, Myrtle Reavis, and Pearl Melton. (VS)

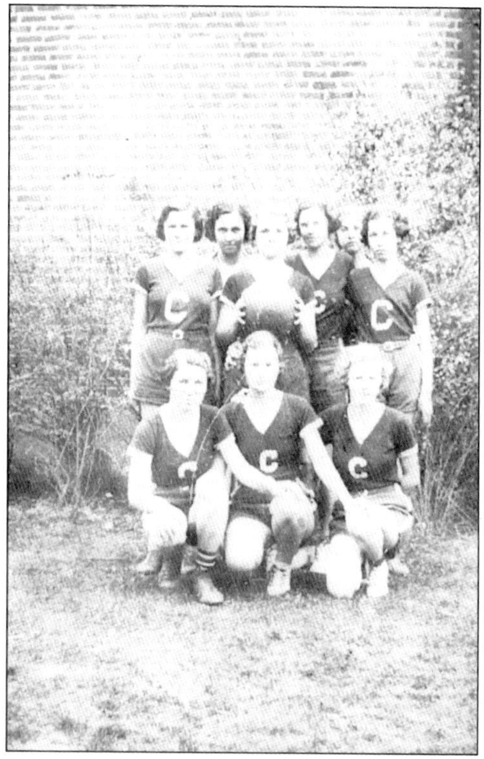

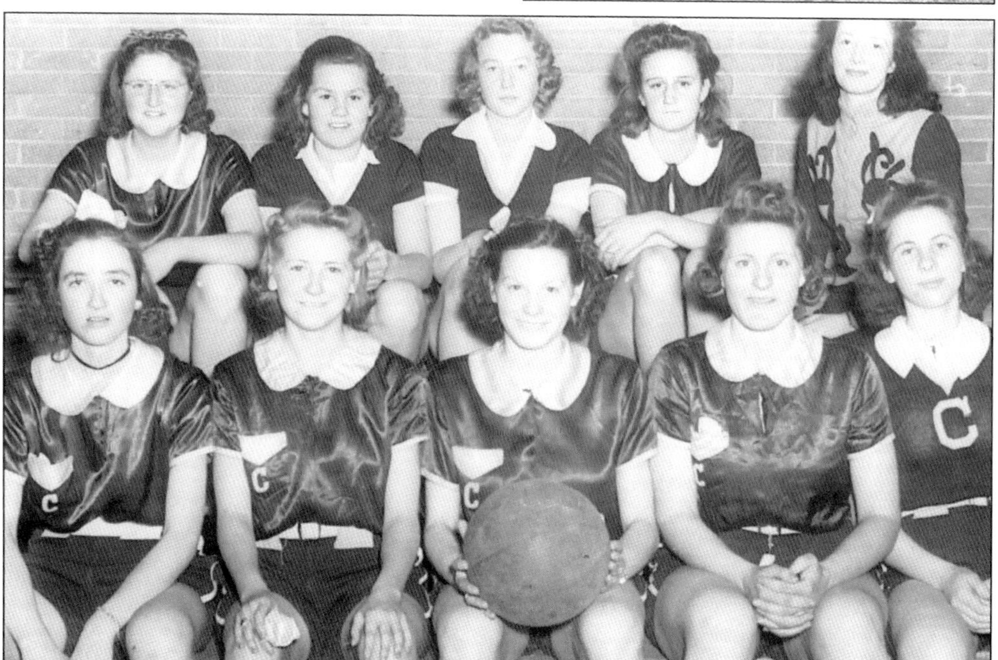

The girls of the 1941 Courtney High School girls' basketball team were county champions. Shown here are, from left to right: (front row) Nellie Reavis, Avonell Hobson, Bertha Lee Miller, Ruth Brandon, and Stella Mae Rutledge; (back row) Jessie Hauser, Nancy Brandon, Audrey Sofley, and Jewel Steelman. The coach, at the top right, is Miss Aiery. (VS)

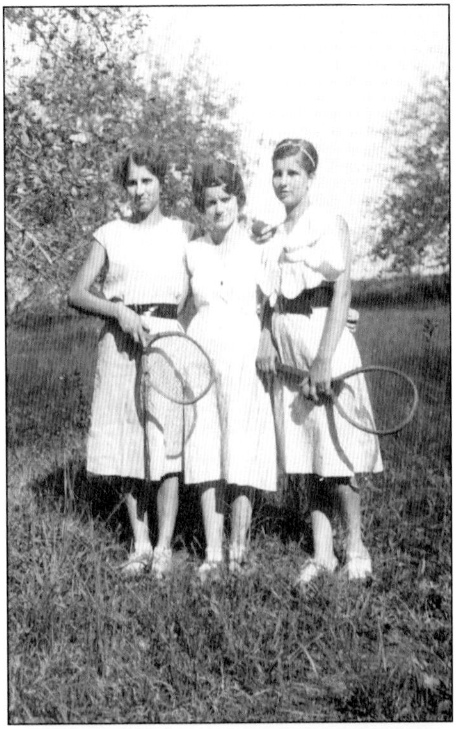

Tennis was a popular sport in the 1930s. Phyllis Dianne Brendle (left), Mary Speer (middle), and Lucy Brendle were about to begin a game at the home of Aaron Speer near Boonville when this photograph was taken in the summer of 1935. (LBH)

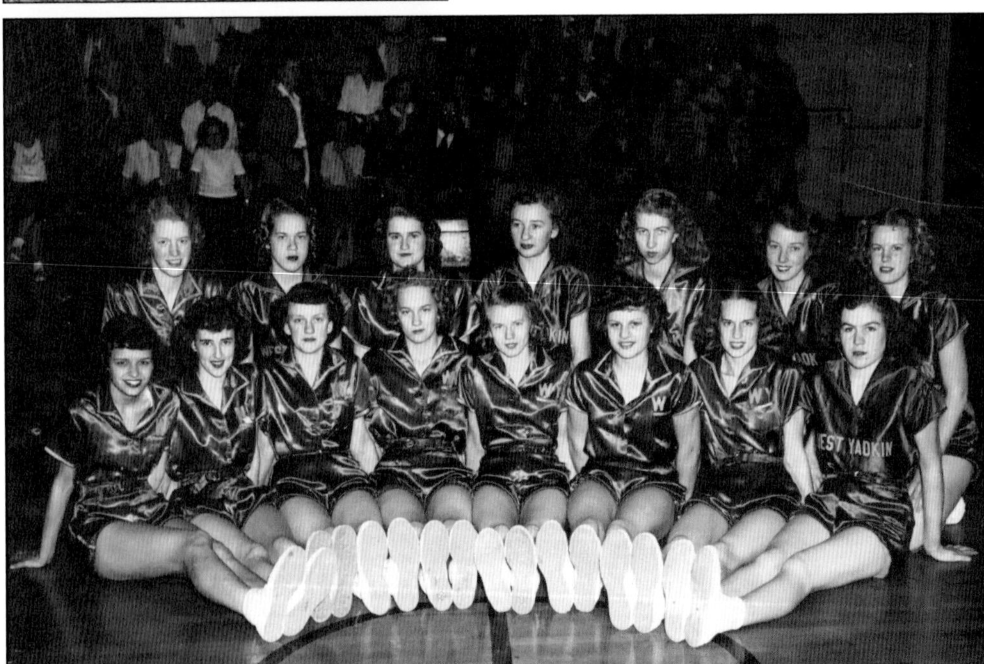

Members of the 1949 West Yadkin girls' basketball team pose in a gym filled with spectators. The girls on the team are, from left to right: (front row) June Wallace, Barbara Ireland, Annie Vee Wishon, Freda Mitchell, Pat Weatherman, Betsy Johnson, Mina Wagoner, and Maxine Cheek; (back row) June Wood, Ollie Mae Groce, Mary Lou King, Betty Lou Shore, Joan VanHoy, and Dot Wagoner. (BJM)

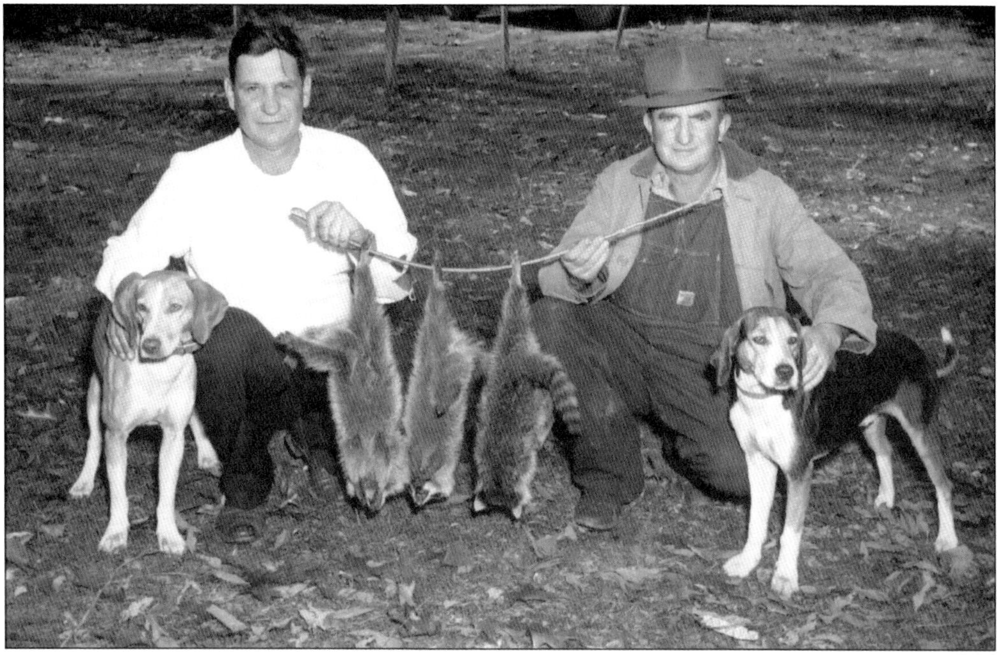

Raccoon hunting could be both fun and profitable. Shown here are expert hunters Cliff Carter (left) and Jim Bray with the night's catch of three 'coons. (SO)

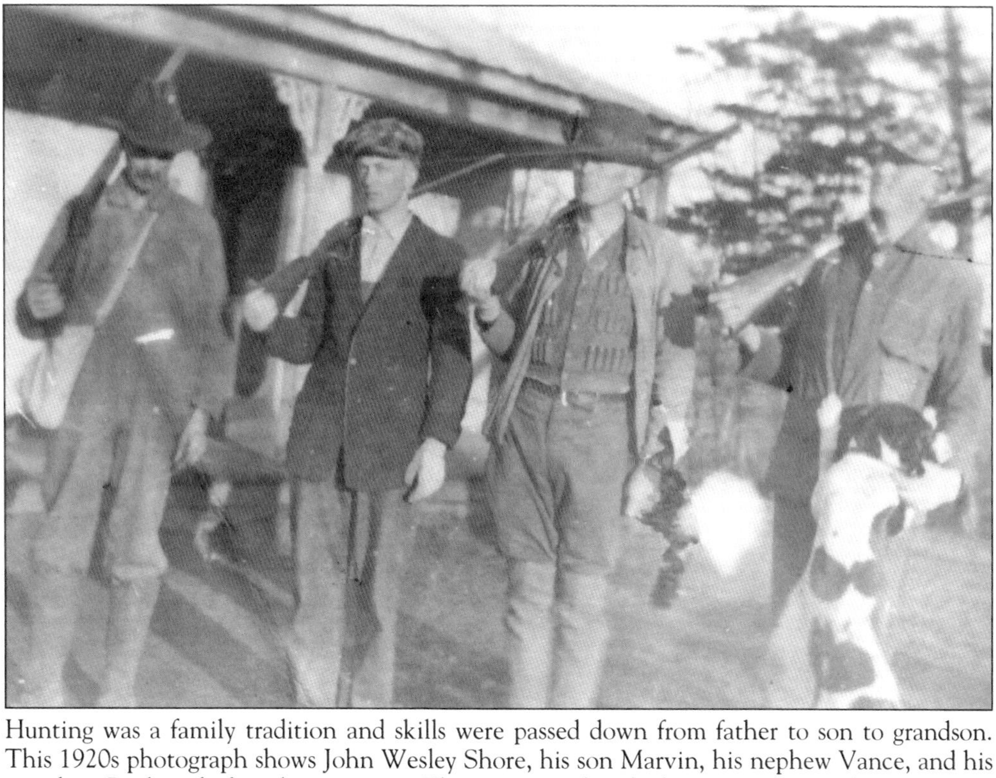

Hunting was a family tradition and skills were passed down from father to son to grandson. This 1920s photograph shows John Wesley Shore, his son Marvin, his nephew Vance, and his grandson Paul ready for a hunting trip. They are armed with shotguns, plenty of ammunition, and a dog. (NH)

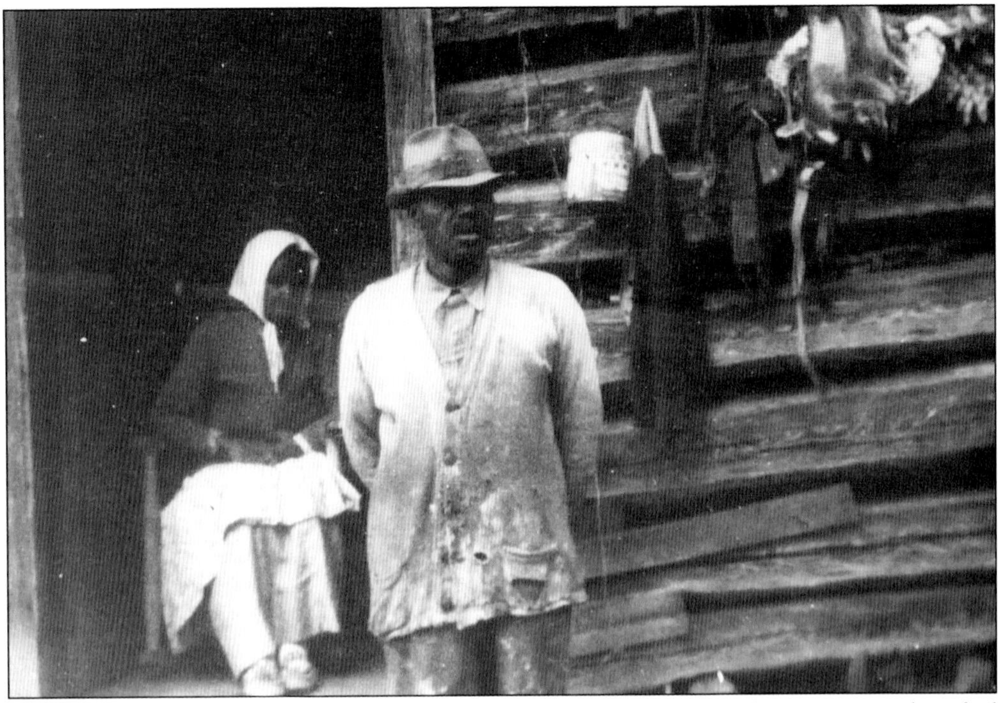

The results of the hunt were nailed to the wall before they were skinned. Here, an unidentified man poses beside a pair of rabbits and a quail, which will shortly become the main course at supper. (FHC)

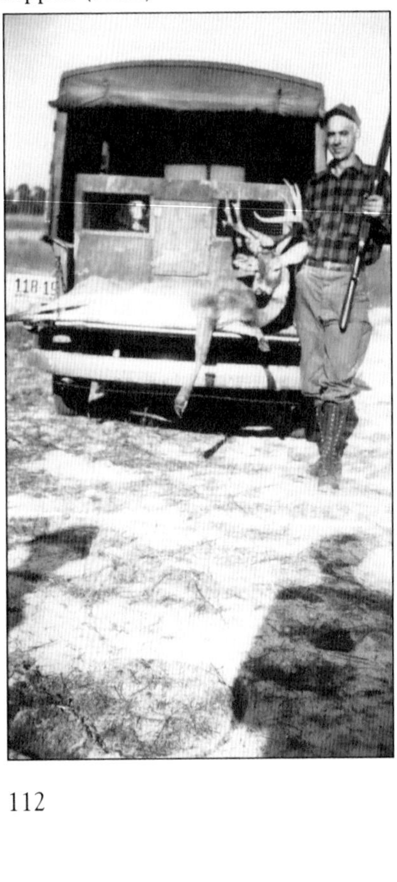

Men delighted in showing off the prize deer they killed. Herman Matthews displays the large buck he has just bagged. (IMR)

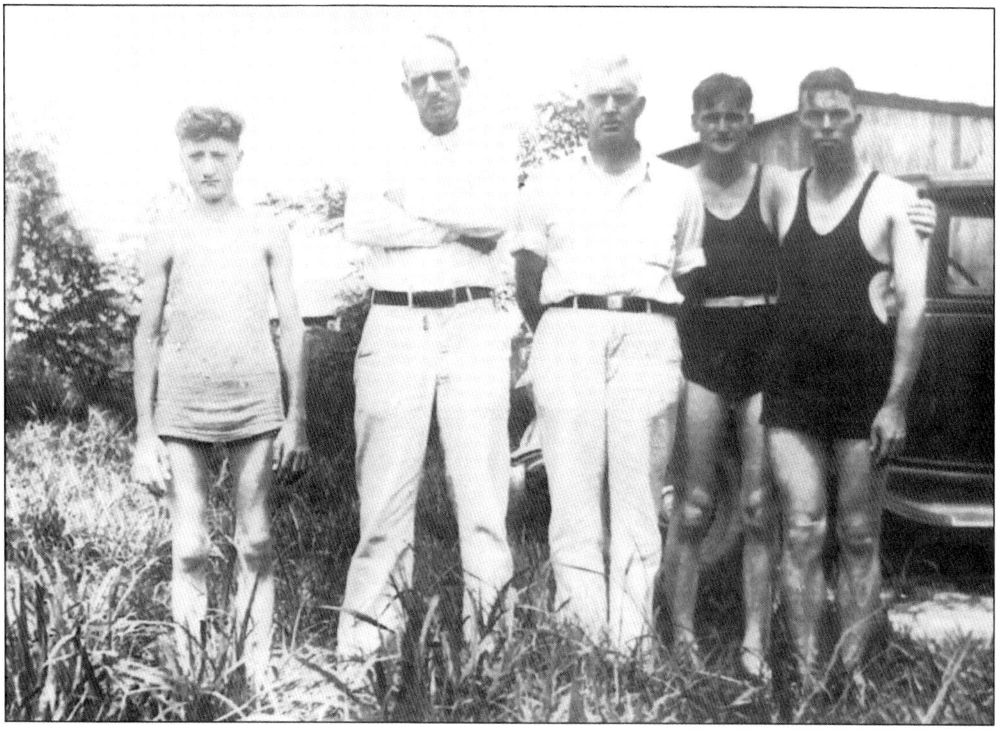

Local boys model the latest in swimwear for 1932 before they take off on a fishing trip. From left to right are: Thomas C. Hauser, John Henry Hauser Jr., Reverend Marshall Reavis, Labon Hauser, and Bynum Reavis. (VS)

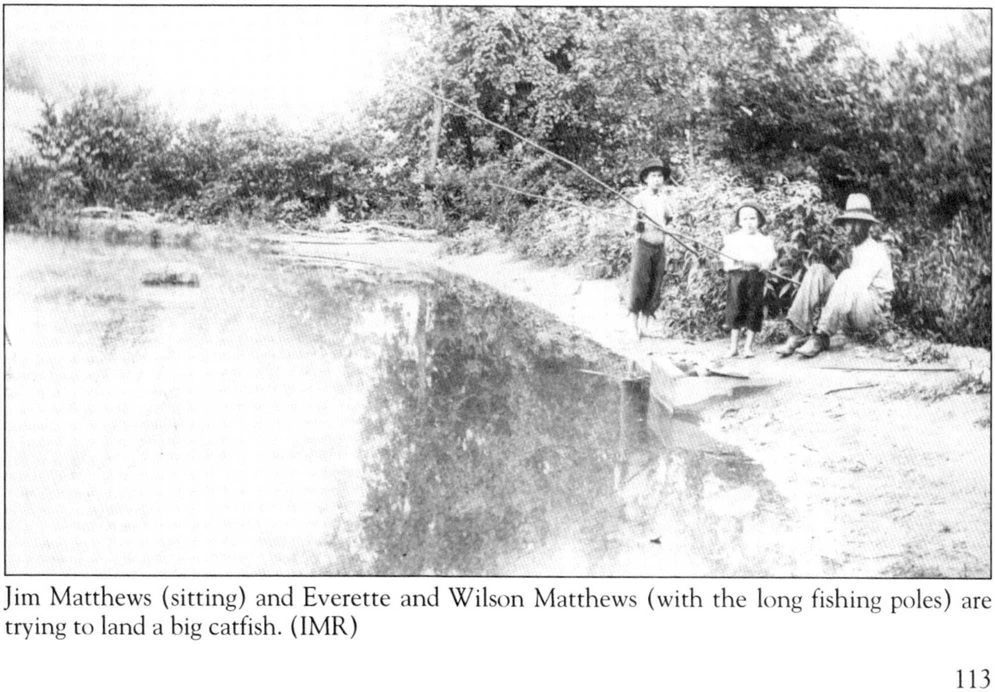

Jim Matthews (sitting) and Everette and Wilson Matthews (with the long fishing poles) are trying to land a big catfish. (IMR)

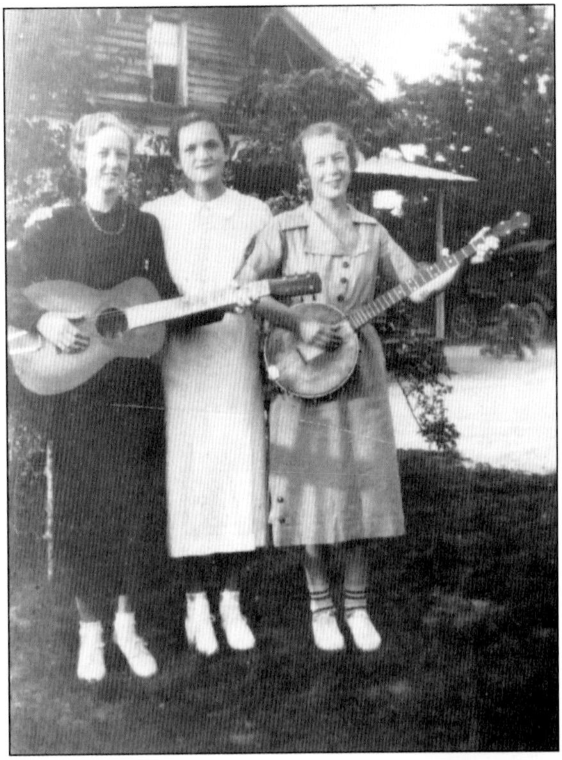

Women expressed their talent and creativity through music and song. Arizona Brown (with the guitar) and her sister, Minnie Ruth Brown (holding the banjo), flank their cousin, Minnie Mae Carter. The three were fifteen or sixteen years old when this photograph was taken c. 1936. (WC)

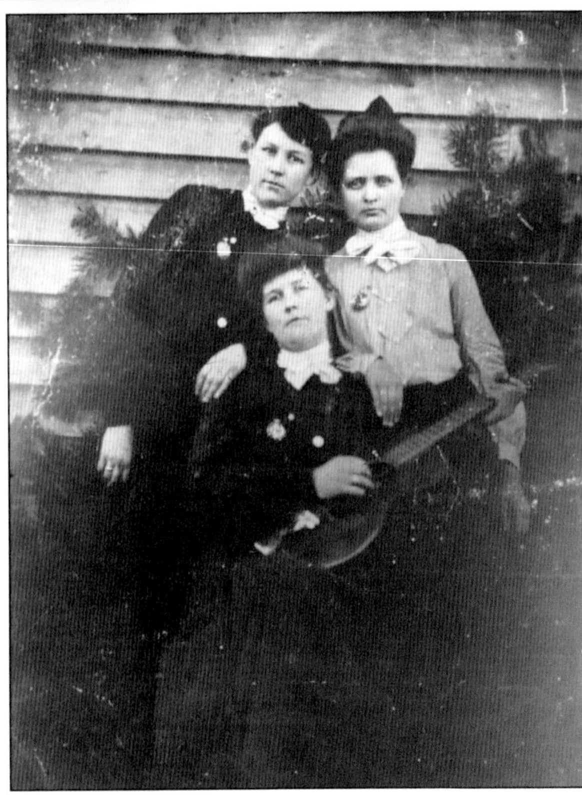

This old daguerreotype (tintype), probably made between 1860 and 1880, has no identification on it. The girl in the middle appears to be holding a guitar. (RW)

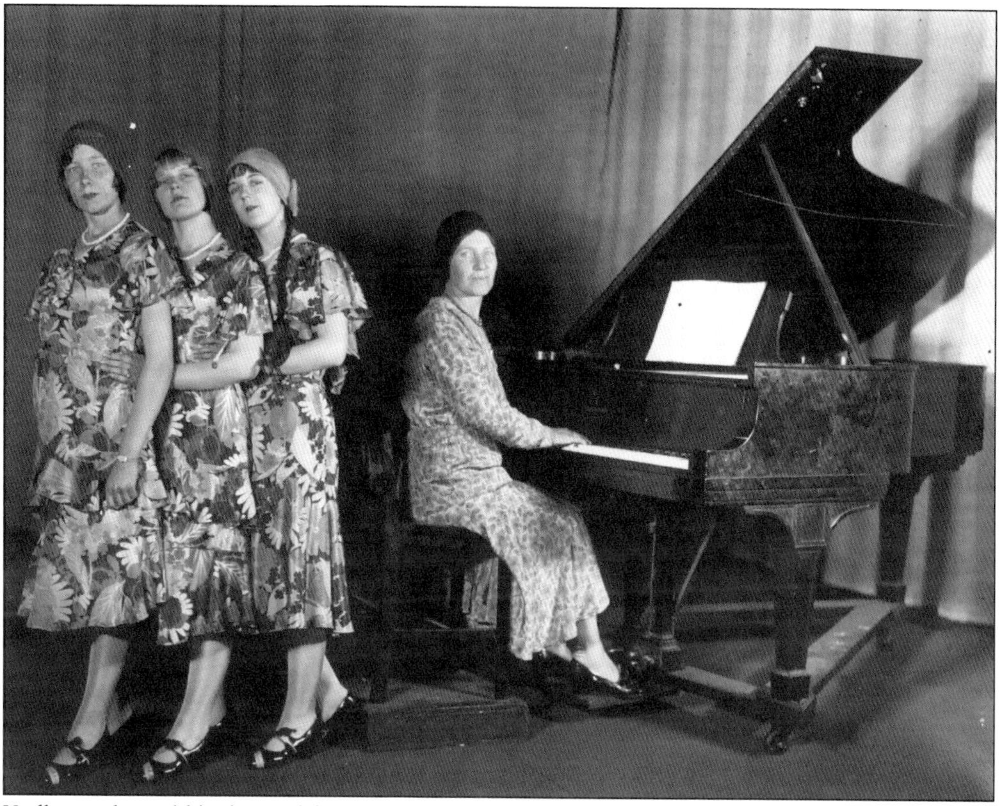

Yadkin girls could be beautiful, talented, and ambitious. This photograph shows Helen (Nance) Church, Valena (Jolly) Mosteller, and her sister, Rita Jolly, singing for a 1931 or 1932 New York City radio show. They are accompanied on the piano by Mealie (Brown) Church, Helen's mother. Billed as the "Nance Singers," the girls also recorded some songs in New York City. Helen Church is perhaps better known as a piano teacher and a conductor of shaped-note singing schools. (EM)

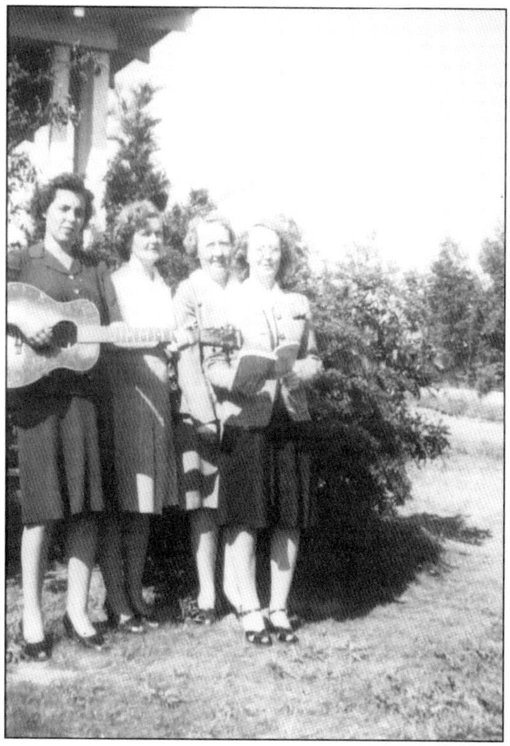

The Happy 4 Quartet was composed of Yadkin girls who sang gospel music and performed over area radio stations. Pictured here in the late 1930s or early 1940s, the girls are, from left to right: Ina (Rose) Bryant, Valena (Jolly) Mosteller, Gladys (Chappel) Newman, and her sister, Beulah (Chappel) Brown. (EM)

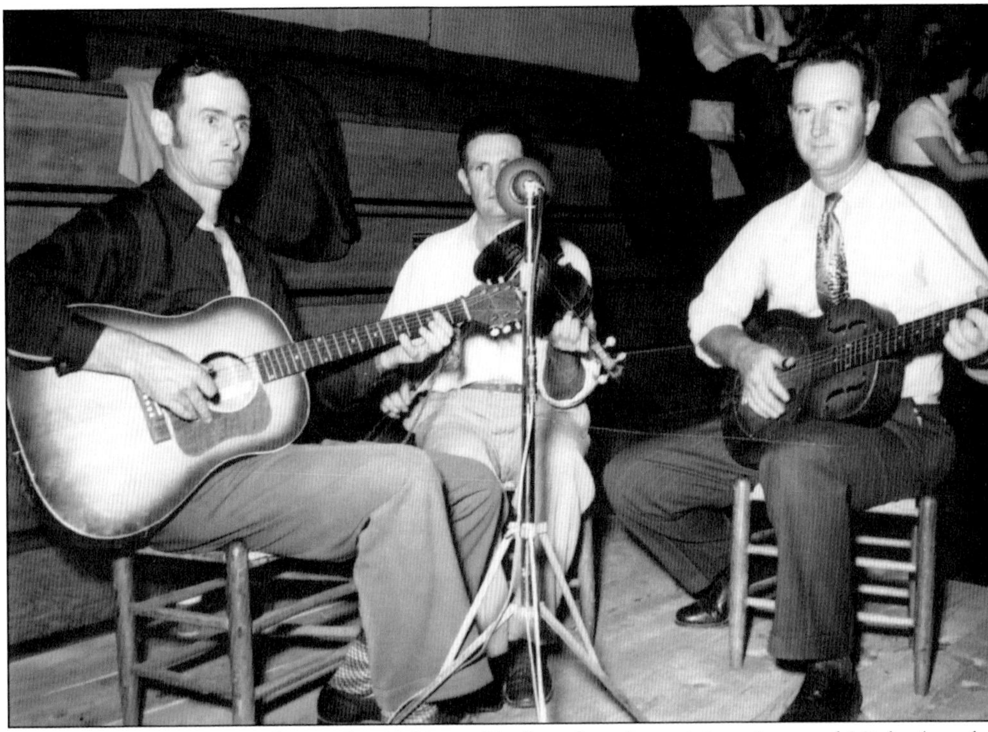

Square dancing was popular in the 1950s and before. Local musicians Leonard Hicks (on the guitar), Buford Jester (on the fiddle), and Carl Cranfill (on the dobro) are shown here playing in the Yadkinville High School gym for a square dance that was held as part of the 1950 Yadkin County Centennial Celebration. (SO)

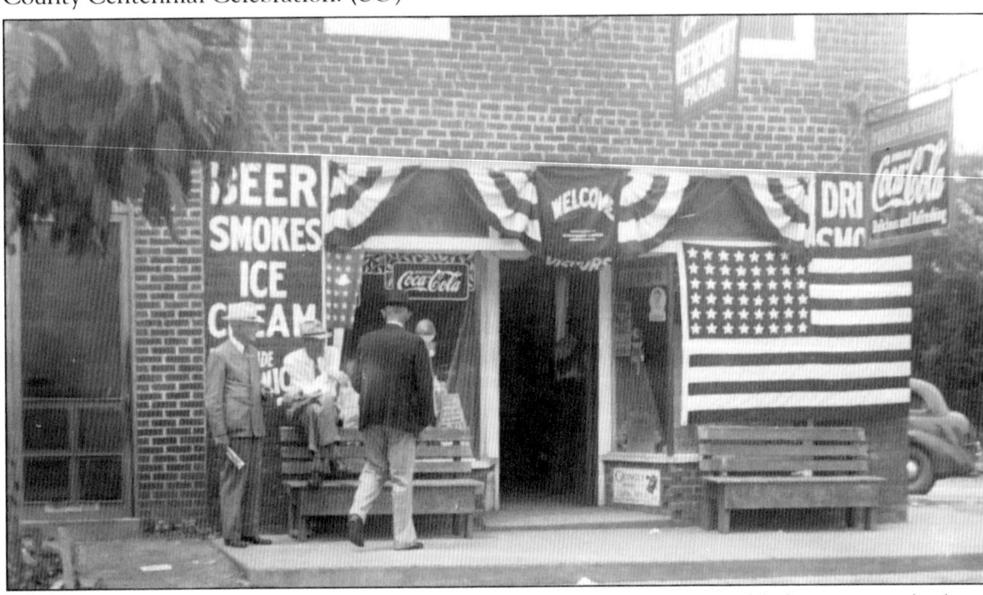

When there was nothing else to do on a hot summer afternoon, one could always go to the local refreshment parlor for a milk shake, a Coke float, or an ice cream cone, and catch up on the latest news and gossip at the same time. Standing on the left is Clerk of Court Lon H. West. Seated on the bench is Attorney Thad Reece. (FHC)

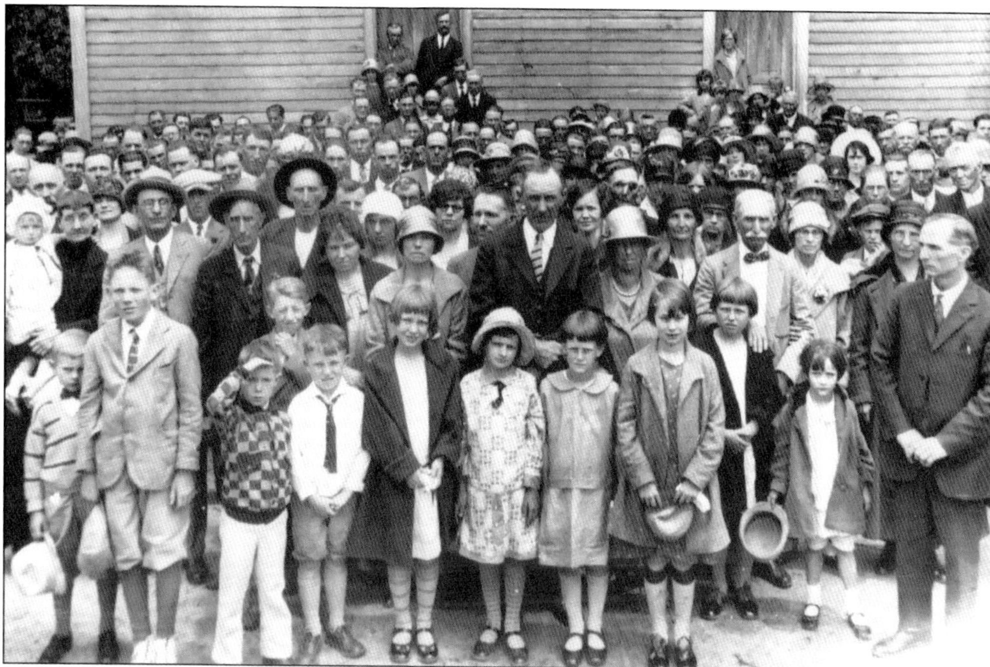

Sunday afternoon could be spent at a family reunion and picnic, such as this large gathering of the Vestal family at the Center Methodist Church in 1925. (AS)

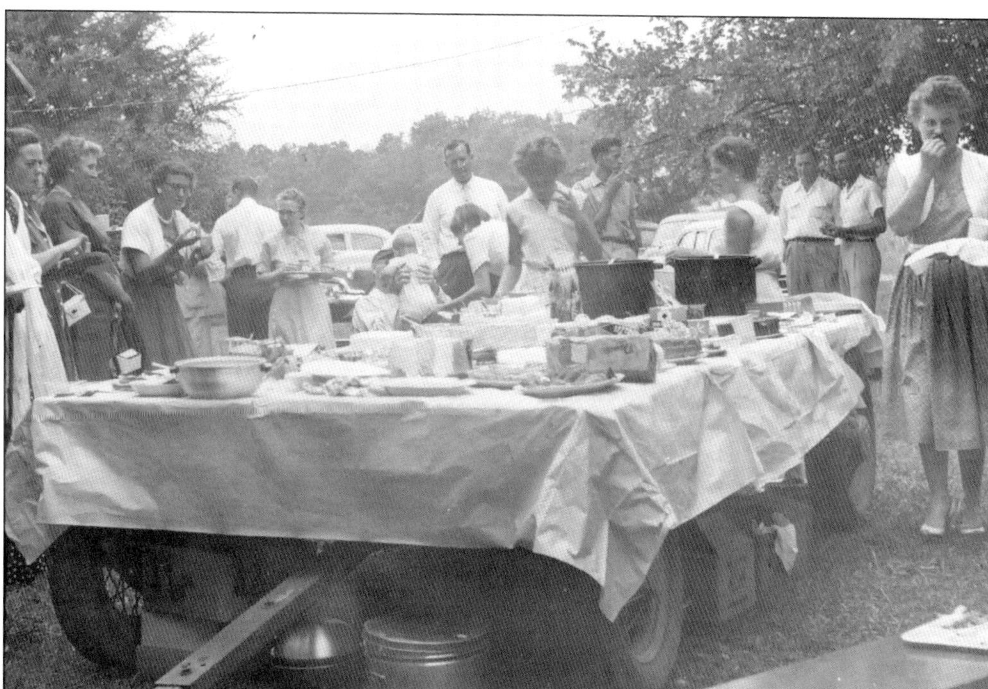

At the Phillips family reunion there was plenty of food for all. Favorites were fried chicken, ham biscuits, green beans, corn, and lots of home-made pies and cakes. (EGS)

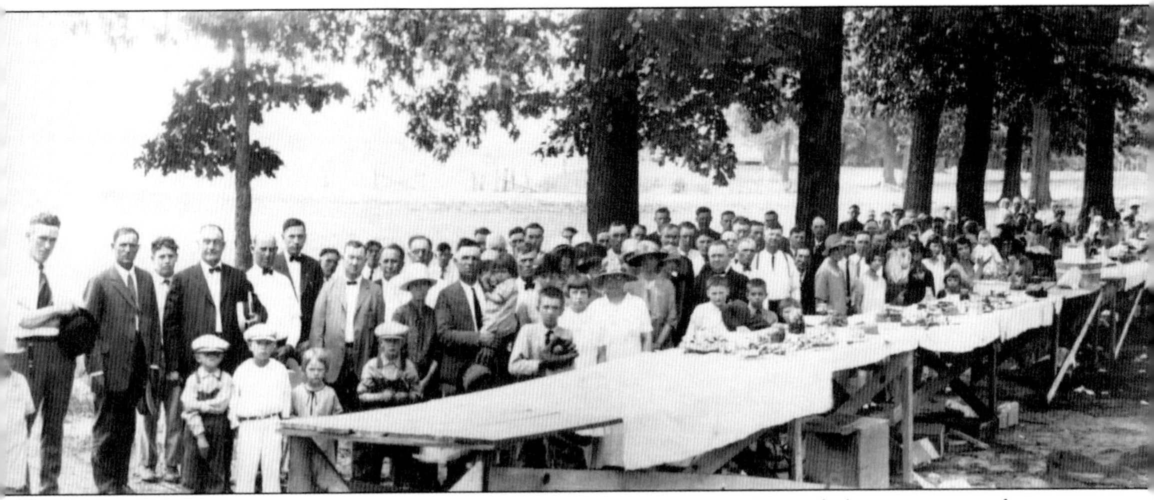

The big oak trees at Yadkinville School offered plenty of shade, and the spot was a favorite place to have a get-together and picnic. One such picnic, about 1925, was sponsored by the North Carolina State Highway Commission, of which Jesse Lee Mackie was the district supervisor. (Mr. Mackie is in the second row, the eleventh person from the left, wearing glasses, behind the woman with the white hat.) Typical of such gatherings, each family brought an item of food to share with others. The long table looks permanent, indicating frequent use by the community. The quality of attire indicates that the event may have occurred after church on Sunday. In the background is US Highway 601, then called Highway 80. Also in the background through the trees is the old Yadkinville Academy. Many family groups in this photograph have been identified, including members of the Carter, Dickerson, Driver, Edgerton, Fox, Goslen, Hauser, Hinshaw, Holcomb, Joyce, Mackie, Sheek, Speer, and Warder families. Three photographs of this picnic survive, including the one of the baseball team (p. 106). (JGM)

Swinging could be restful and fun, as shown by Margaret and Carl Shore, Jimmy Brown, and Martha Moxley in 1941. (MMS)

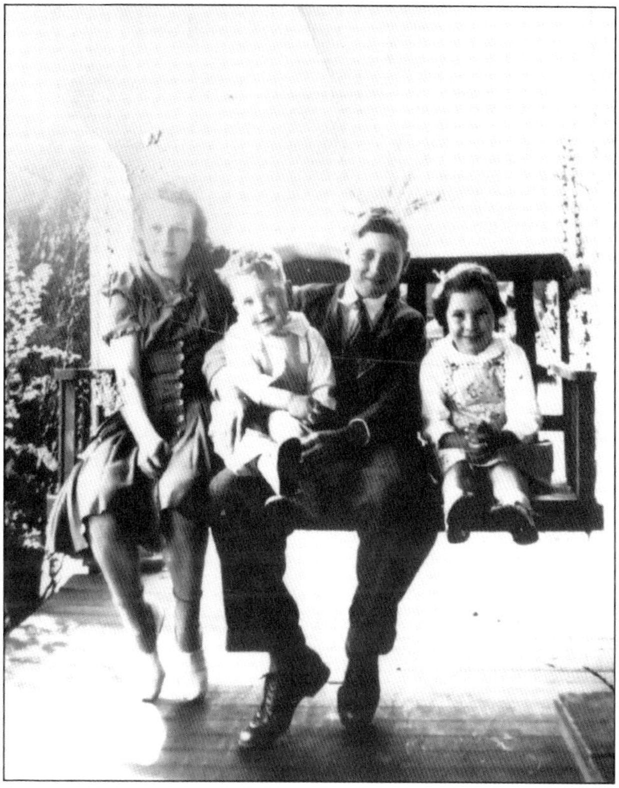

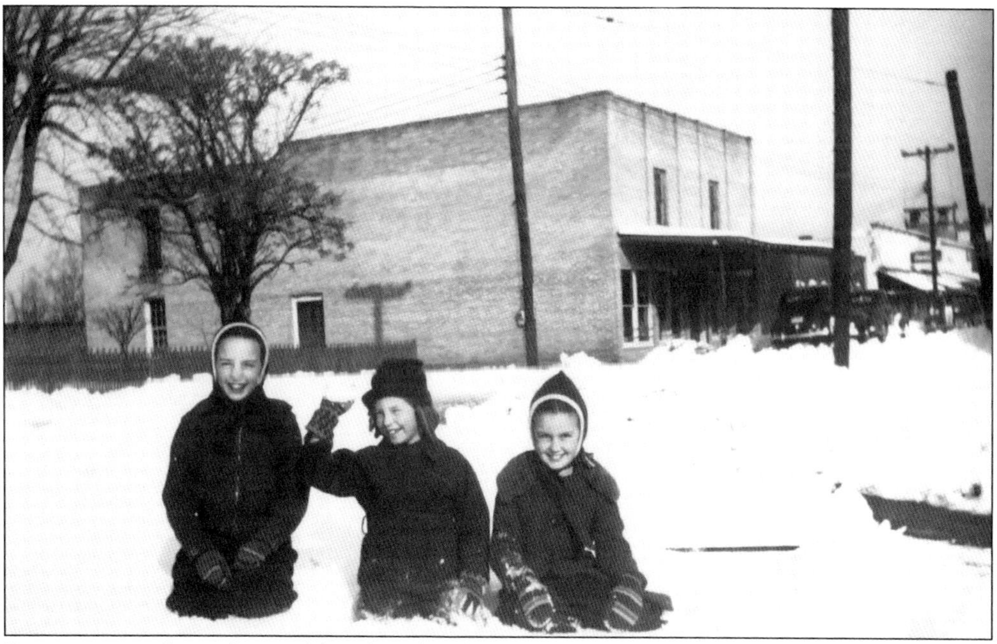

Snow presented new forms of fun, from building snowmen to throwing snowballs, as these little girls are doing in this 1939 Boonville snapshot. They are, from left to right: Cassie Williams, Ann Speas Martin, and Mary Ruth Williams. The T.L. Hayes store is in the background. (JN)

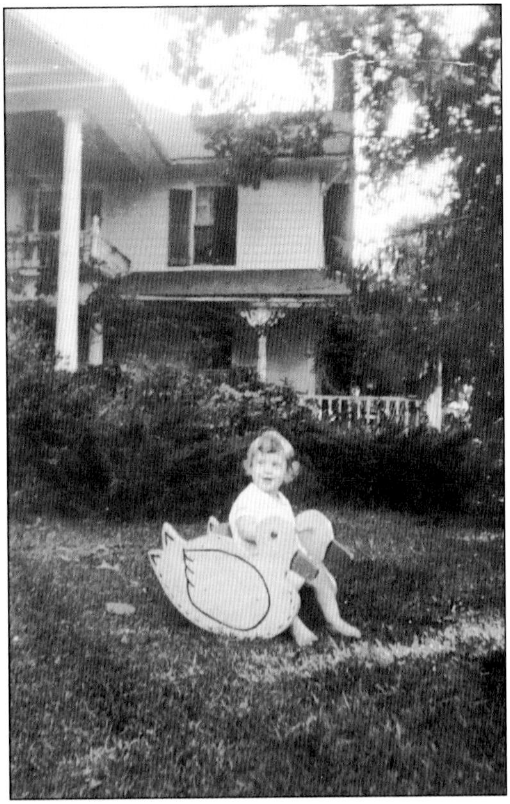

Young children amused themselves for hours with the simplest of toys. Pictured here is Charles Bruce Davis (1934–1973), the son of Paul Price Davis and Elma Farabow Davis, in a duck rocker when he was about two years old. (NMD)

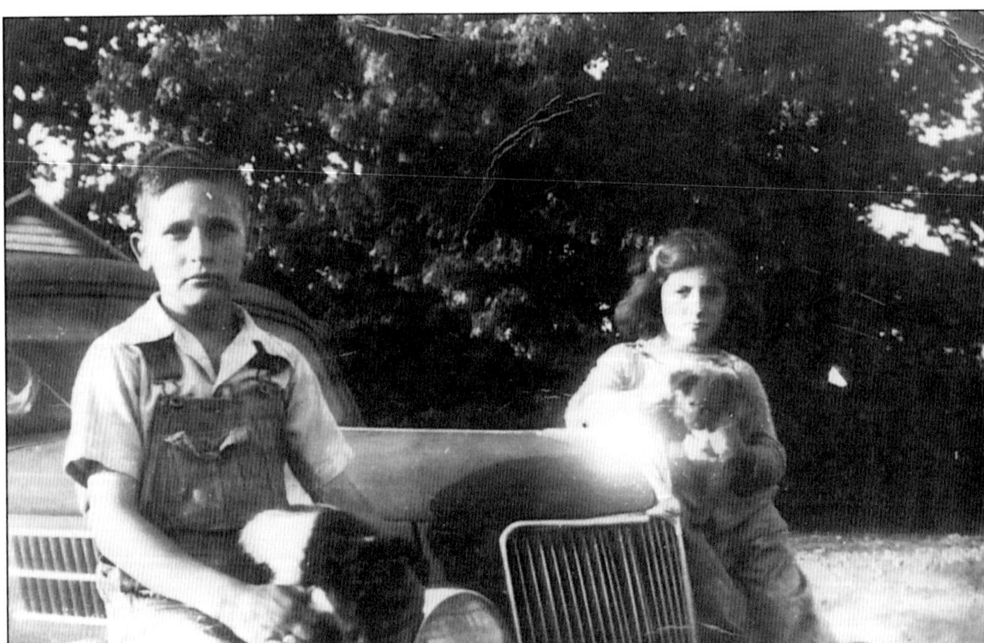

In 1946, when they were not working or playing ball, Bobby Hauser and his cousin, Wanda Hauser, sometimes played with their favorite dogs. (VS)

Eleven

Strike Up the Band

Celebrations

The two biggest celebrations ever held in Yadkin County were on the Fourth of July of 1919, and the Centennial Celebration Week in October 1950. The first event celebrated the founding of the country as well as the end of World War I.

The 1950 Centennial Celebration was a week-long event to commemorate the county's first one hundred years. Each night a pageant depicting the county's history was presented at the ball park in Yadkinville, which ended with fireworks. Other activities were a beard-growing contest, a square dance, a parade, and Youth Field Day. The celebration ended with the Centennial Queen's ball, complete with an orchestra. The event succeeded through the cooperation of every town and community in the county.

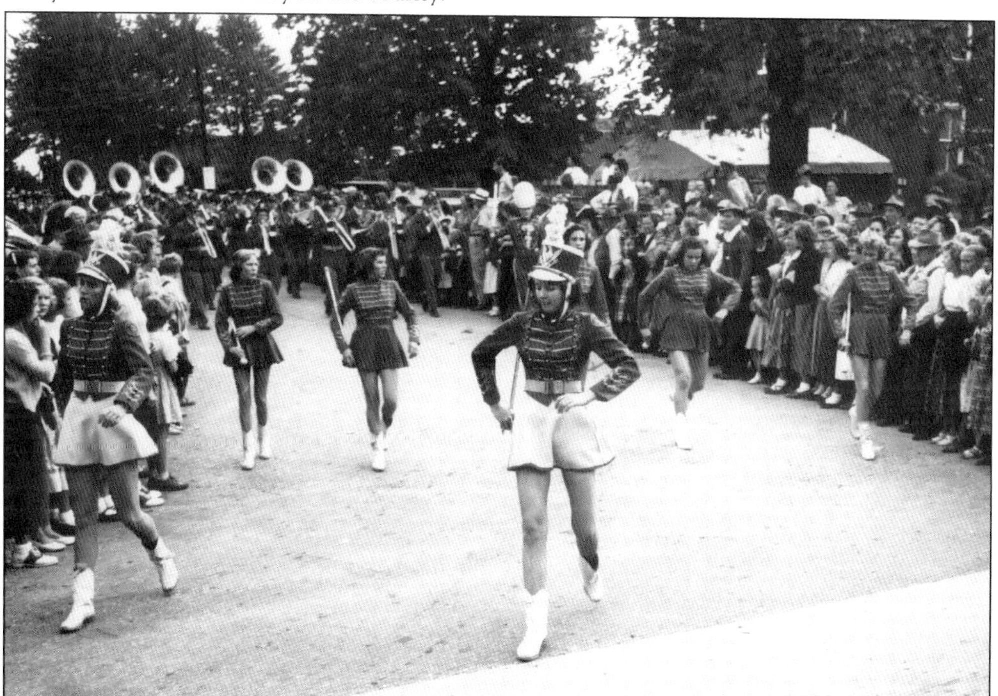

The 1950 Yadkin County Centennial Celebration drew large crowds. The parade through Yadkinville began at 4 p.m. on Monday, October 2. Since there were no high school bands in the county, the Elkin High School Band and Drum Majorettes substituted. (SO)

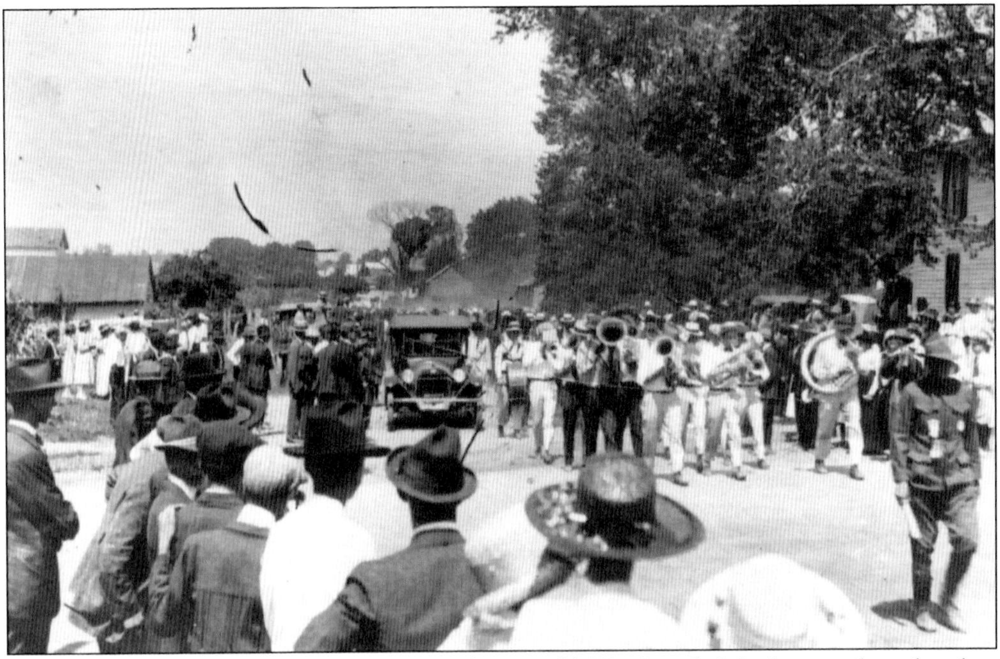

The July Fourth celebration in 1919, just after World War I ended, had a marching band to entertain the spectators. (AS)

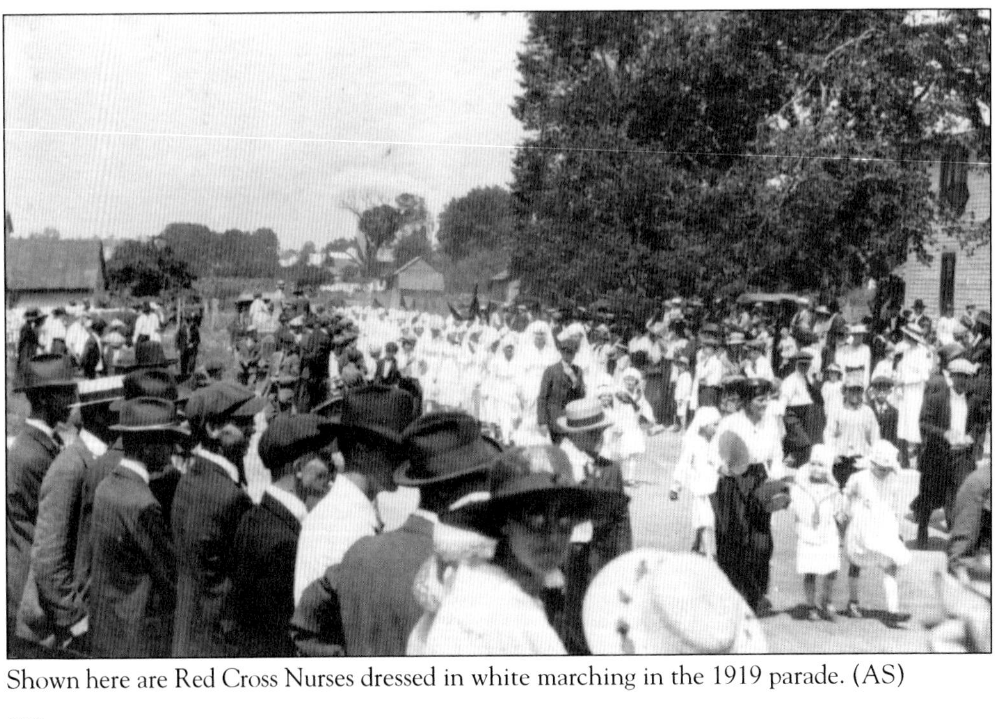

Shown here are Red Cross Nurses dressed in white marching in the 1919 parade. (AS)

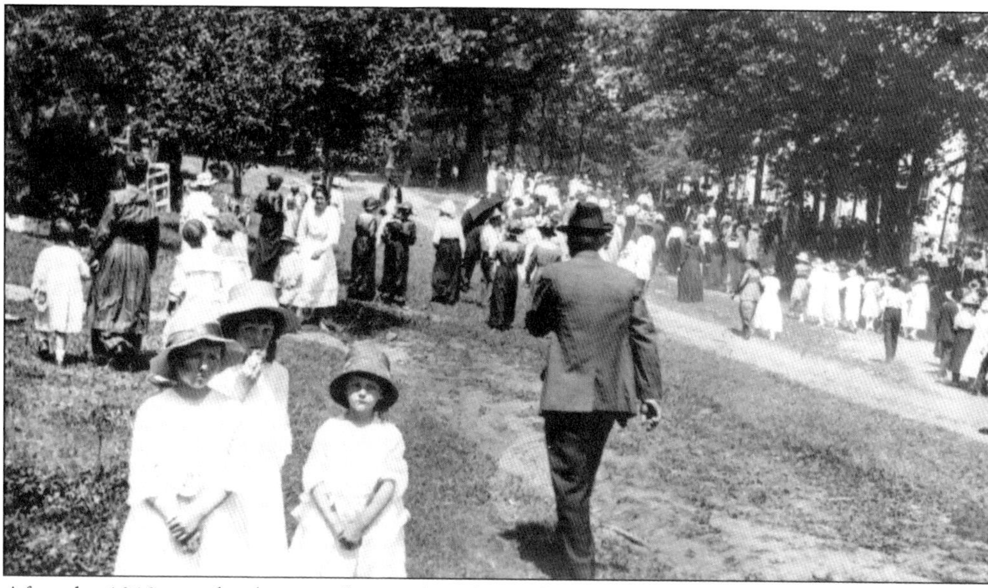

After the 1919 parade, the crowd moved to the Yadkinville School grounds for a picnic. (AS)

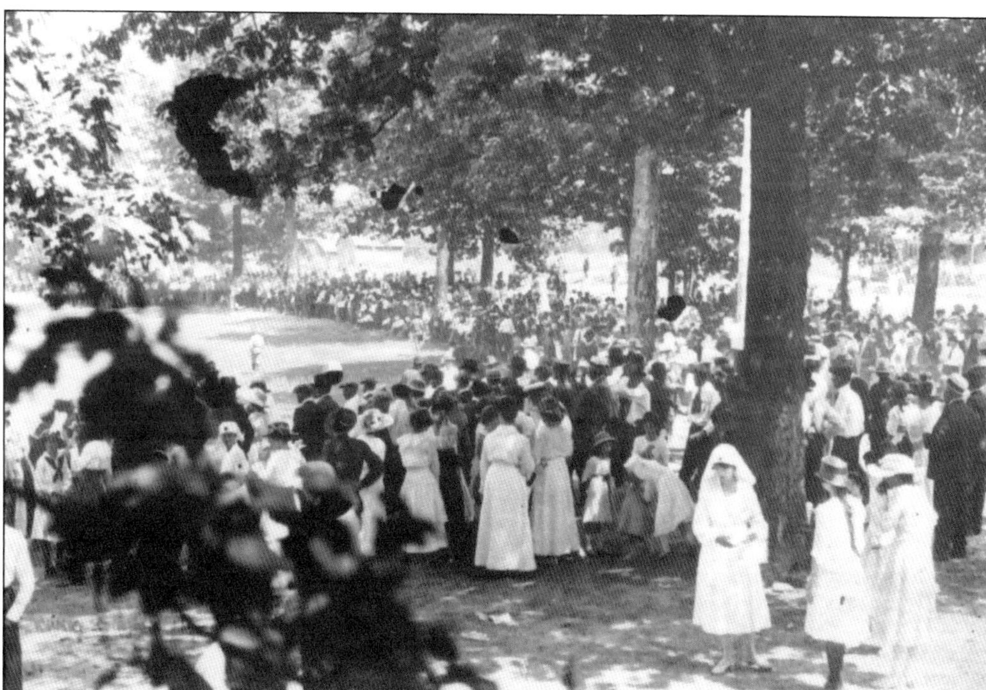

The crowd watching the Fourth of July ball game is enormous. (AS)

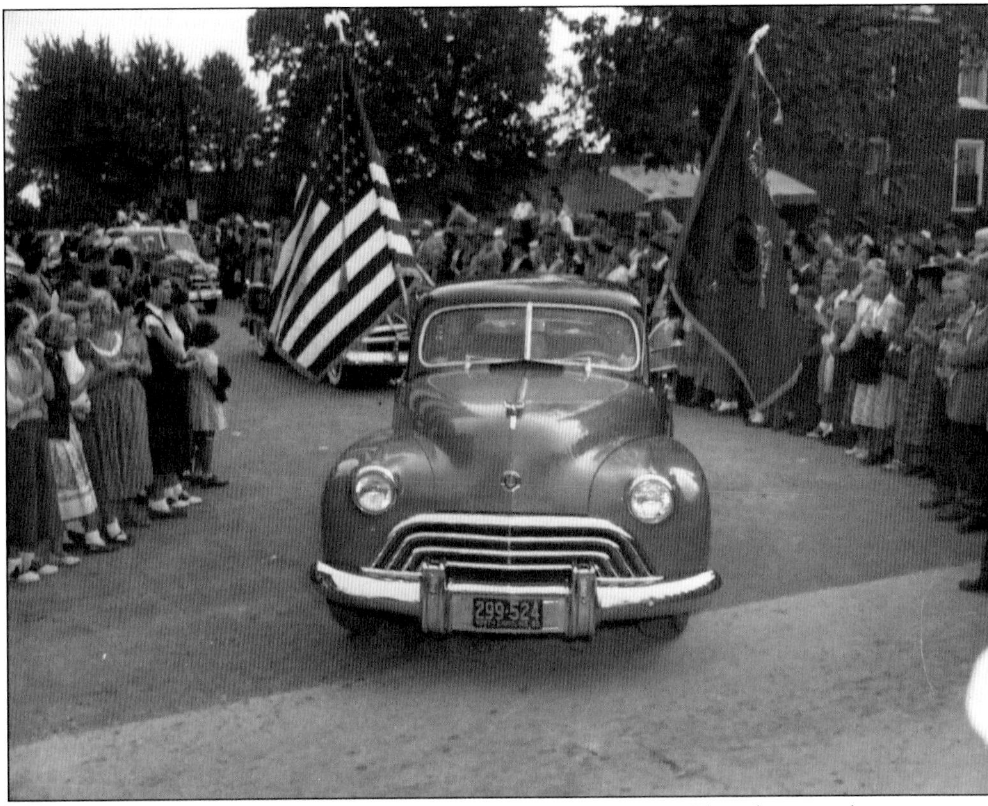

This photograph was taken as one of the lead automobiles in the 1950 Centennial Parade turned the corner from Jackson Street into Main Street. The old courthouse can be seen at the far right in the background. (SO)

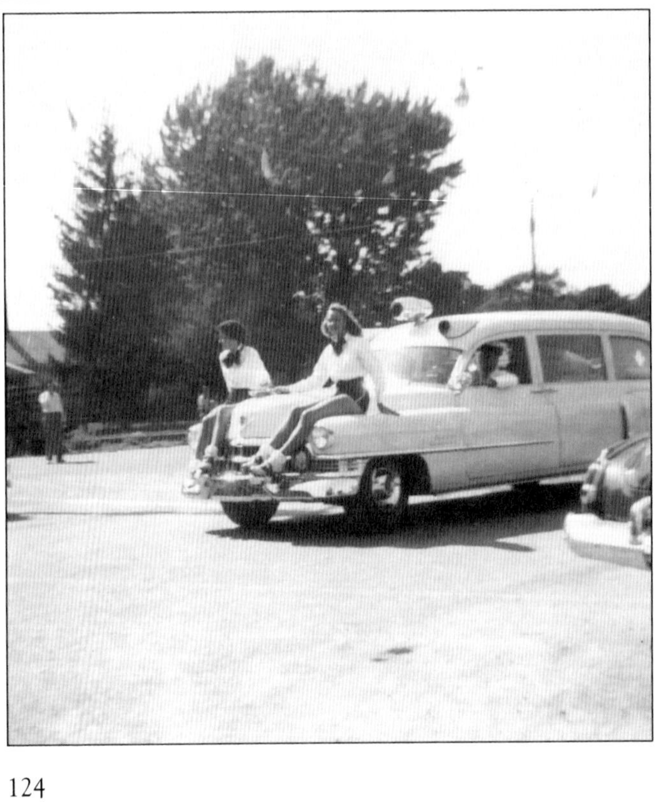

Cheerleaders Georgia Ann Cashion (left) and Adelaide Hinshaw rode on a Mackie-Hinshaw Funeral Home ambulance in the 1950 parade. (EGS)

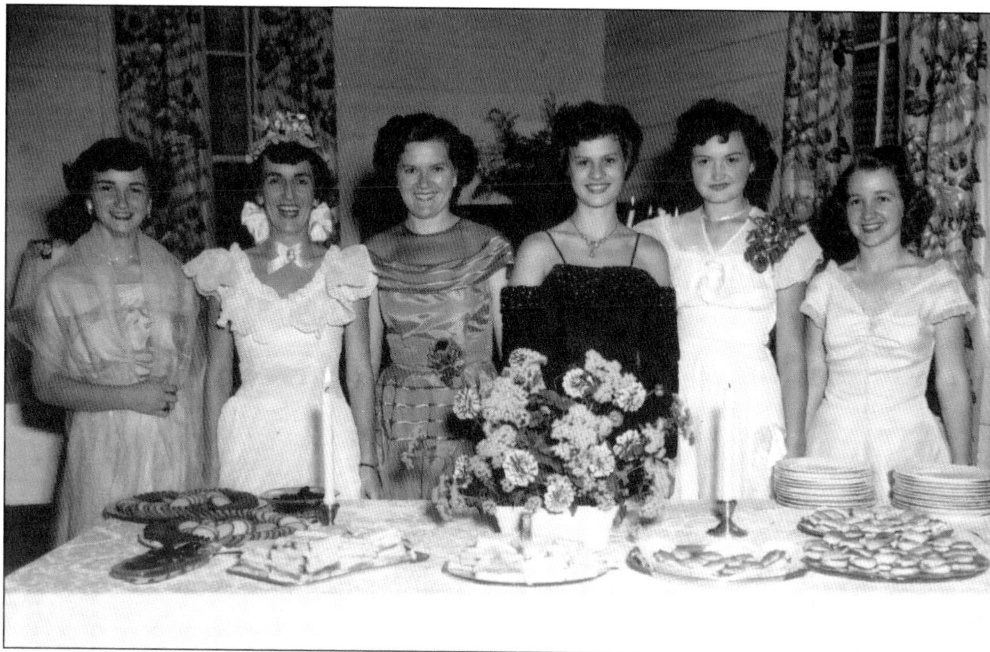

The 1950 Centennial Queen and the princesses of her court were honored at a tea held at the Woman's Club in the old Academy building. Congressman C.B. Deane attended, and he later crowned the queen at the first night of the pageant. The girls are, from left to right: Dorothy Brooks, Ruth Haire, Georgia Campbell, Betsy Johnson, Virginia Miller, and the Centennial Queen Ann Davis. (SO)

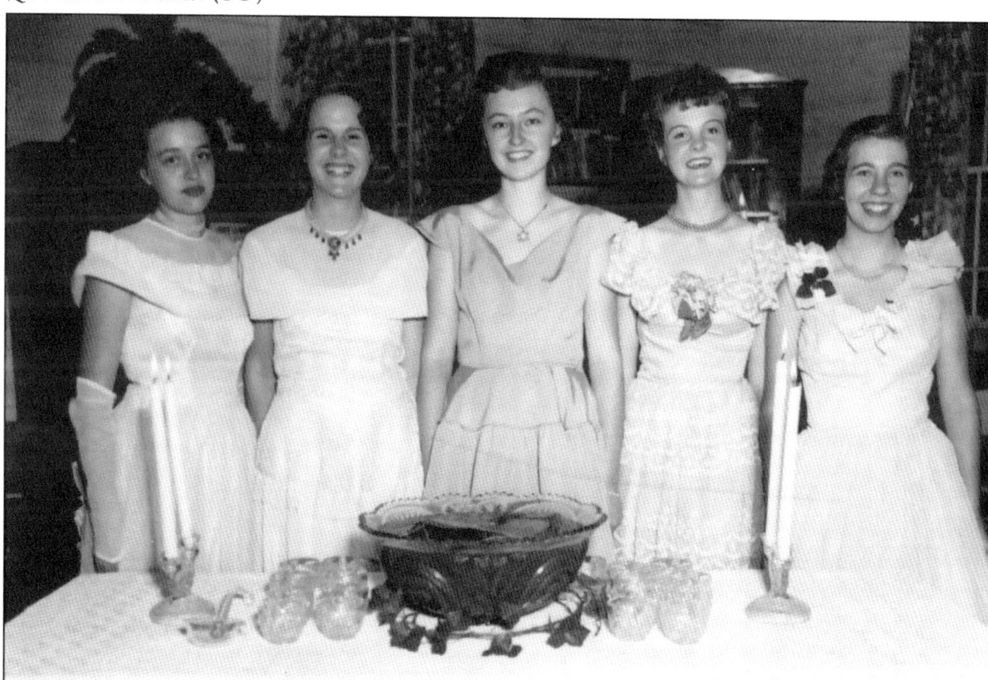

The other girls in the queen's court were, from left to right: Tina Brown, Emma Lou Carter, Rosemary Taylor, Sue Baity, and Shirley Ray Moore. (SO)

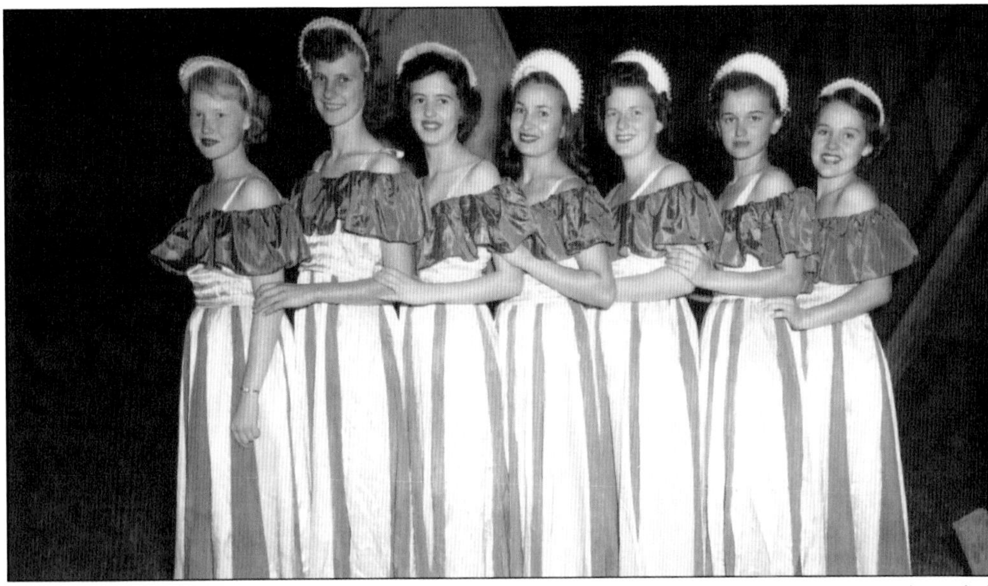

These girls from West Yadkin played a part in the centennial pageant. They are, from left to right: Frances Jean Davis, Doris Jean Wells, Betty Ann Steelman, Loretta Casey, Dorothy Dickerson, and Lutrelle Oliver. (SO)

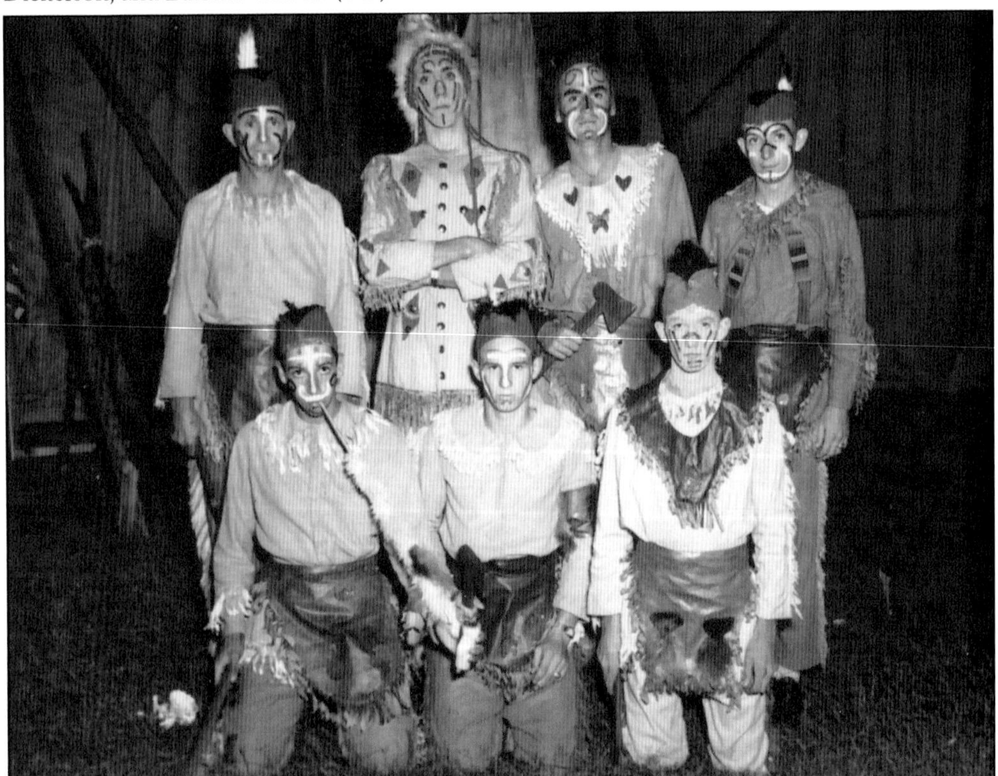

These West Yadkin boys were Indians in the pageant. They are, from left to right: (front row) Wendell Wood, Jimmy Crown, and unknown; (back row) Jack Turner, John Durham, Harold Brandon, and Hugh Welborn. (SO)

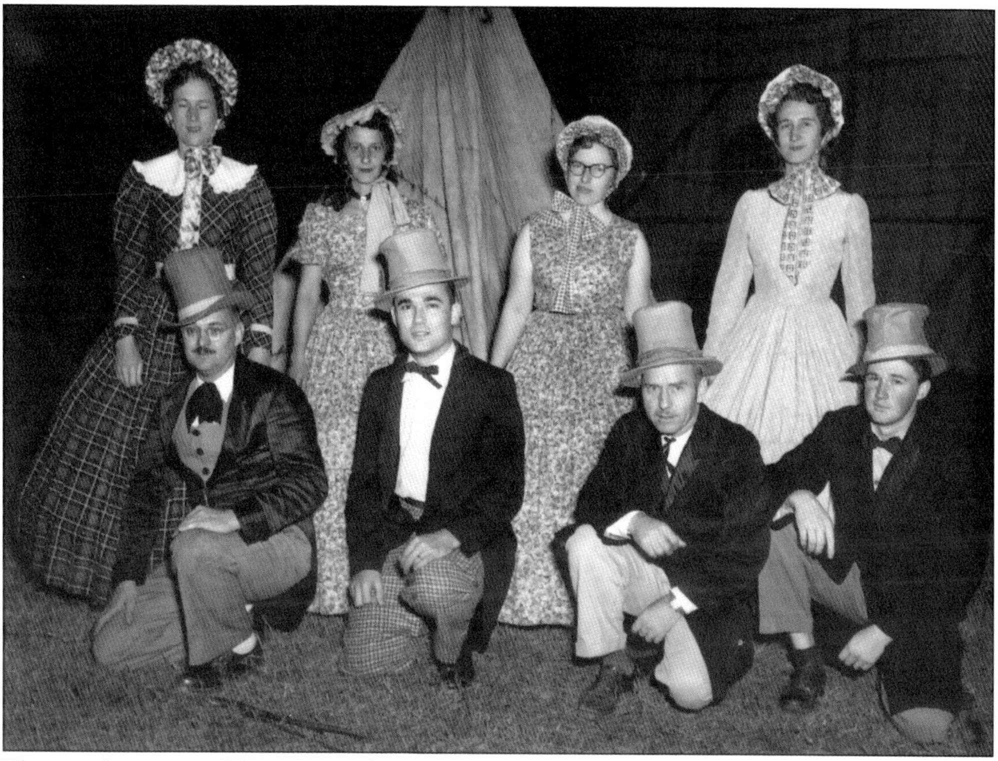

The couples pictured here were also in the pageant. The men are Coy Johnson, unknown, Clyde Wishon, and Frank Steelman. Their wives, standing behind them, are Lottie Clanton Johnson, unknown, Helen Sheek Wishon, and Susan Shore Steelman. (SO)

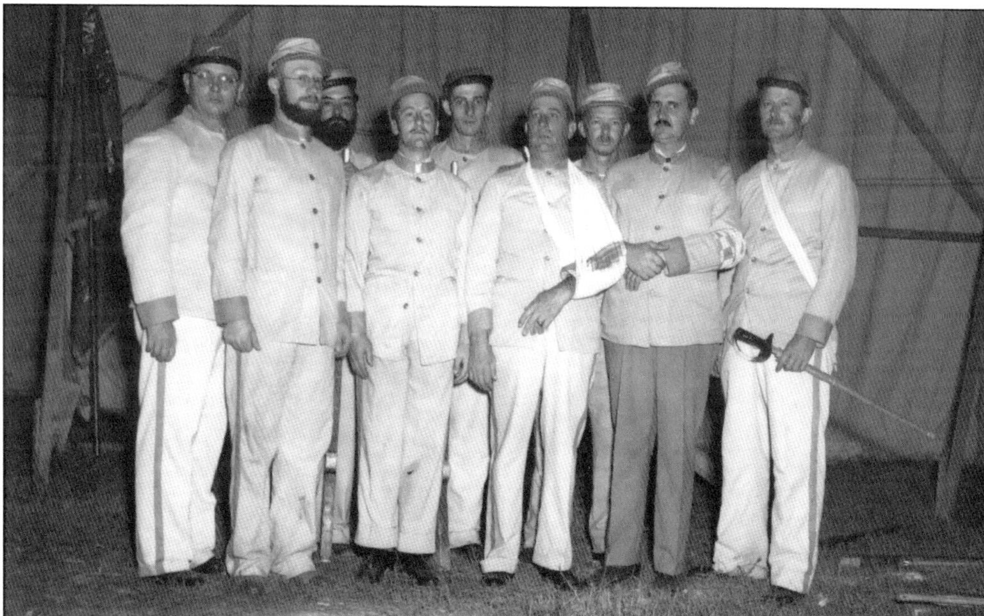

Some of the Boonville men portraying Confederate soldiers in the pageant were Gene Crissman, Harvey Gentry, and Frank Hobson. (SO)

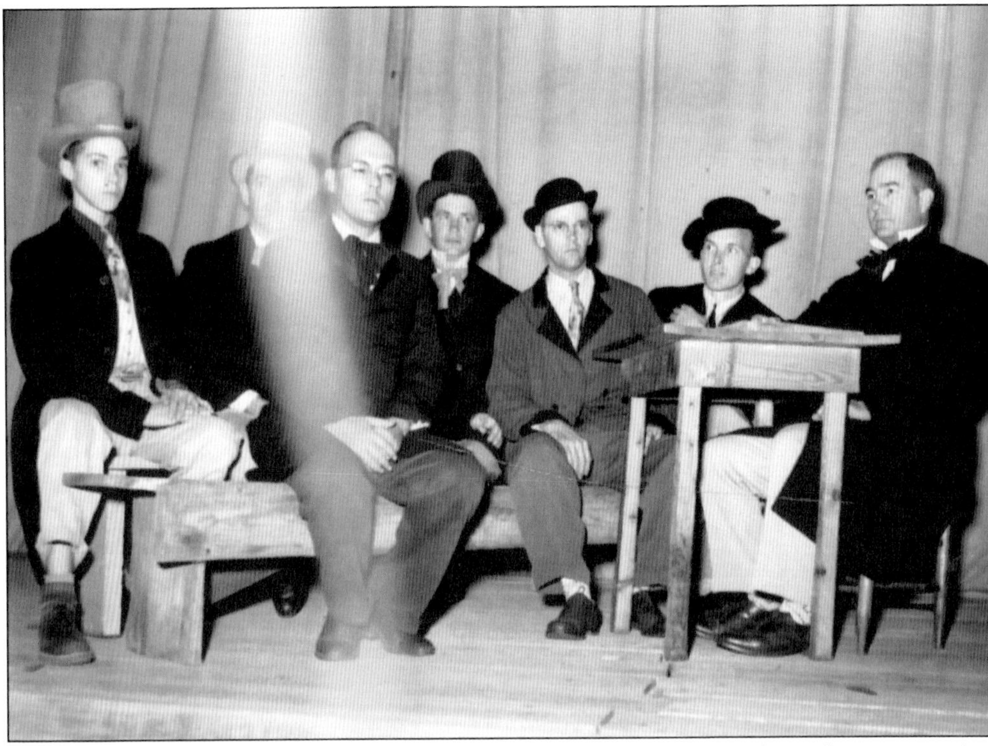

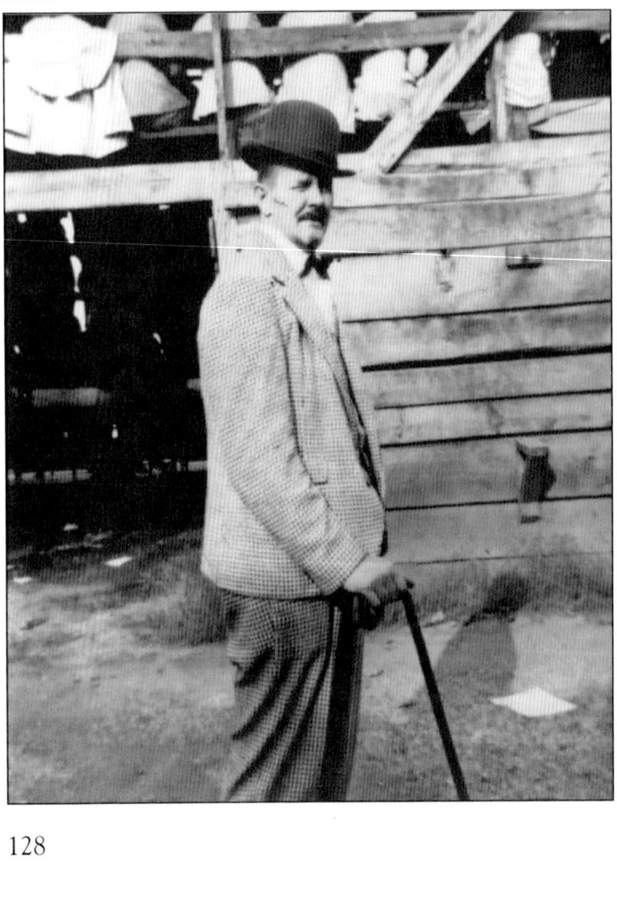

The men shown here, some of them actually lawyers, were in the pageant scene about Judge Pearson and the Richmond Hill Law School. They are, from left to right: Johnny Reece (who later became a lawyer), Woodrow Todd, Attorney Walter Zachary, Jack Mackie, Walter Reynolds, Garvey Burchette, and Attorney Lafayette Williams. (SO)

After performing the pageant each night from Monday through Friday in the Yadkinville ballpark, this tired participant, Luke Mason, seems to ask, "Is this the end?" (EGS)